# Growing Up
# Between Stops
# on the
# A-Train

For Jesse & Leslie,
So great meeting
you, Leslie! Enjoy
the book!
Jen

# Growing Up Between Stops on the A-Train

*a memoir*

Jennifer Y. Johnson-Garcia

Moröen Hus
New York

*Growing Up Between Stops on the A-train* is a work of creative non-fiction. This true story was written to the best of the author's recollection. The timeline in Chapter 9 has been intentionally compressed for succinctness to move the story along. (The car race actually happened later in the relationship.) Dialogue is as close an approximation to actual conversations as possible within the constraints of long-term memory and reflective of how events made the author feel. Some names and identifying details have been changed to protect the privacy of people involved.

Published in the United States by Moröen Hus.
Moröen Hus is an imprint of J. Y. Johnson-Garcia.

LIBRARY OF CONGRESS CATALOGING-IN-PUBLICATION DATA

NAMES: Johnson-Garcia, Jennifer Y., author
TITLE: Growing Up Between Stops on the A-Train: A Memoir / Jennifer Y. Johnson-Garcia
DESCRIPTION: New York: J.Y. Johnson-Garcia, [2019]
IDENTIFIERS: LCCN 2019905245 | ISBN 978-1-7339560-0-0 (paperback)
ISBN 978-1-7339560-1-7 (hardcover) | ISBN 978-1-7339560-2-4 (ebook)

Printed in the United States of America

jyjohnsongarcia.com

13579108642

First Edition

New York, New York

*For all the underdogs, underrated, and underestimated:
this one's for you.*

# CONTENTS

Fort Collins, Colorado - 1980

# CHAPTER 1
# Catching Crawdads

THE ONLY WAY TO RIDE A DIRT BIKE WITH THE BOYS in Colorado's dry, summer sun is with your shirt off. My dad called me to the porch of my parents' prized two-story home on Cumberland Court to explain to me that four-year-old girls must wear shirts to cover their chests. I then explained to my dad that my chest looked exactly like Gabe and Mike Bryant's and that I was as hot as they were. Dad shrugged and let me do whatever I wanted. But my ultra-prim-and-proper mother had me back in a shirt by dusk. This pattern underscored my preschool days. Mom would dress me up in frilly, billowing dresses, fancy white socks with ornate lace details, black patent leather dress shoes, and color-coordinated ribbons tied in my thin, dirty blonde hair, and I would reliably find a mud puddle to play in or a bike chain to chew up her perfect sewing on delicate dress hems.

When my mom wasn't fussing over my filthiness, she was at work. I am a child of Baby Boomers, and as such, was a kid with two "progressive" working parents (the exception back then). My dad was a self-made executive at a local bank and my mom was one of the first female businesswomen to start her own insurance agency in town. Neither of my parents had more than a high school diploma, save a few occupation-specific college courses here or there, and neither seemed to need more than that. Before kindergarten, I was dropped off at the Sweeney's each early morning for the daycare equivalent of tag-team wrestling, where ten other kids and I played freely until someone got injured by either the roughhousing or Mrs. Sweeney's wooden spoon. When my inherent hyperactivity prevented me from taking naps on schedule with everyone else, I got paddled with the spoon every day until I finally spoke up to my mom and, from then on, earned myself a spot on the couch watching *Days of Our Lives* with Mrs. Sweeney during naptime. To this day I absolutely loathe soap operas. I would rather get the spoon.

Once I turned five and was old enough to go to kindergarten, I never had a babysitter again (unless you count Cindy, my ten-year-old sister and only sibling, as a babysitter). I got up and dressed by myself; ate cereal by myself; walked to school by myself (sis became too cool to walk with me); walked back home by myself; watched *Different Strokes* and *Three's Company* TV shows by myself; rode my bike to a ditch a couple miles away and caught crawdads and guppies and snakes and turtles by myself; got beat up by the neighbor boys by myself; learned how to start fires by myself; nearly got molested by the bully of a teenage boy from the next cul-de-sac by myself (but fought hard enough, I guess, for him to change his mind once he forced down my tight Levi jeans and panties); "quit" my family and moved under our porch with a blanket and Smurf piggy bank by myself (albeit for a grand total of maybe five or ten minutes); and cracked my head open and bled for a few hours, not completely by myself, but with kids instead of adults until my dad's secretary came to take me to get stitches when my parents were unreachable. Sheltered, I was not. My childhood was as free as it could have possibly been without removing my parents completely. These modern-day "free range parents" have nothing on my mom and dad. My parents were the real, carefree, deal.

During the summer before I entered first grade, my mom and dad stepped their parenting game up a bit. Mom enrolled Cindy and me in Parks and Recreation classes. We dabbled in pottery making, ballet, painting, and often swam at the pool at City Park. My parents also enrolled me in gymnastics, where I quickly tumbled my way to Pre-team. But most significantly, the movie *Annie* came out in theaters a few days before my sixth birthday that summer. Shortly after the movie came out, cassette tapes of the soundtrack came out, too. And once I got my hands on the *Annie* soundtrack, my life changed. Instead of choke-holding

Mike Bryant until his older brother punched me in the face to get me off (I was only trying to avoid getting choked myself); instead of jaywalking the neighborhood; instead of riding my bike too far away, getting too dirty, or bringing home too many animals; instead of spilling boiling hot soup down the front of my body and agonizing in pain for two weeks; instead of throwing jelly shoes at my sister and narrowly escaping retaliatory death; I started singing.

It didn't take long for me to memorize every lyric of every song on the *Annie* soundtrack. Once I memorized the lyrics and melodies, I started working on my technique. I would play around with my throat to try to emulate Annie's vibrato. I would practice singing like I was really an orphan missing her long-lost parents or really ecstatic to have just been adopted by a billionaire. I would sing the "Dumb Dog" song to our family mutt, Pepper. I would get in trouble for singing at the dinner table and my sister would scream at me night and day to stop singing because my voice was the annoying little sister equivalent of fingernails on chalkboards. This infatuation with singing prompted my parents to explore an outlet for me. They found a group called Our Gang Singers, a non-profit performing troupe run by two accomplished musician moms, both of whom happened to be Mormon. Putting me in the group was a no-brainer for my parents, save two obstacles: first, I had to choose between singing and gymnastics—they couldn't afford both; and second, I had to audition and be accepted into Our Gang Singers.

Gay Slade and Karen Lesser animatedly greeted my mom and me when we arrived at Gay's basement (where we were directed to go by one of Gay's five kids, a number that eventually grew to seven). Gay and Karen sat together on a piano bench and fired a few questions at me before asking me to sing. When I finished singing "Maybe" (from *Annie*, of course), the pair exploded into applause, cheers, and giggles. They made me feel like I was the most talented kid they had ever come across in their entire lives. And I was feeling pretty impressed with myself until I eventually met their children, who ran gifted circles around me. Nonetheless, I had perfect pitch, a good ear for harmony, a good memory for lyrics and dance moves, and a genuine desire to perform. I started to practice with them that same week and unhesitantly kissed my potential as a promising gymnast goodbye.

My life through seven years old was rather unspectacular, albeit it privileged. I had free run of the neighborhood. Cindy and I had a fearless father who took us on motorcycle rides; built a go-kart for us; took us camping to sleep under the stars with the Boy Scout troop he led; took us on weekly excursions with Fabian (an underprivileged Mexican teenager who was paired with our family in a "Big Brother" type program); took us on family trips in one of the vans he gutted and rebuilt into a tiny, mobile apartment, one time letting us return home with tadpoles and building a homemade habitat so we could observe firsthand their metamorphosis into frogs before they hopped away; and more. We went to Peace with Christ Lutheran Church on Swallow Road with my mom every Sunday (and every Sunday, I crawled under the pews and received whispered threats that Dad would spank me when I got home, which he did). We ate "supper" (as Grandma Cooper called it, so Mom called it) as a family and said the same exact prayer every single night: "Come Lord Jesus, be our guest, let these gifts to us be blessed. Amen." I had the world's best friend, Jenny Leetham, a little Mormon girl I met in first grade and was inseparable from. We had the sweetest poodle mix mutt that Dad spanked every time she had an accident on the brown shaggy carpet, sending me into inconsolable tears each and every time (only for me to be instantly hushed because hitting animals and kids was normal back then). Our family regularly visited our grandparents in Denver, where both sets of grandparents lived ten houses away from each other on the same street. There, Cindy and I built Barbie furniture out of thread spools and wood scraps, sewed tiny clothes, recorded fake radio shows on Grandma Cooper's cassette recorder, picked fruit and veggies from both grandparents' respective gardens, watched birds bathe in the

Johnson bird bath, ate fried eggs and Sizzlean for breakfast and chicken fried steak and mashed potatoes for dinner, went fishing in tiny creeks in the nearby Rocky Mountains, ease-dropped on Grandma Johnson for the couple of hours it took for her to rise from her knees each morning after her prayers, and went to sleep each Christmas Eve in the Cooper basement and waited for the life-size portrait of Santa that Grandma Cooper hand painted onto white felt, come to life and hand-deliver our hearts' desires upstairs under the Christmas tree. We were the epitome of the four-unit family. From my perspective as a little kid, life was grand. I can't imagine a childhood much better. Then things changed.

# CHAPTER 2
# Jenny

TWO MEMORIES UNDERSCORE MY TRANSITION into an eight-year-old. First: sleepovers with Jenny Leetham (many, many sleepovers). Second: inexplicably wetting the bed. Every. Single. Night.

When I was four, I knew that bedwetting was not normal. By the time I was eight, it was the curse of my existence that kept me feeling like an absolute piece of nothing. Any time I gained even the slightest confidence—for example, being given the first full song solo at Our Gang Singers—sleep would bring with it the humiliating reality check that I was a disgusting freak of a child. Oddly, my parents didn't address it with me. They didn't sit me down and say, "This is a health problem that isn't your fault and here is how we are going to try and fix it." They just cleaned the sheets. Every. Single. Day. And I woke up and felt disgusting. Every. Single. Day.

I don't know if, before the first sleepover with Jenny Leetham, my parents gave Jenny's parents the heads up that I would, with one hundred percent reliability, wet anything I slept on. I just remember feeling absolutely humiliated, shameful, sorry, and devastated the first time it happened. The second time it happened. The hundredth time it happened. My parents sent me over with an adult diaper one time. When Jenny's little brother and sister noticed the bulky plastic under my nightgown (diapers weren't fabric-like back then), they innocently asked why I was wearing a diaper and Jenny, in her incredibly fierce and endearingly protective way, started crying and screamed at them before marching straight up to her parents' room to tattle-tell. I don't know what John and Lynda said, but Mindy and David came down bawling and each said sorry to me through red eyes, gushing tears, and snot running down each of their noses before heading straight to bed. That did make me feel a little better. The only problem was, I unknowingly put the diaper on inside out, so the bed still got wet that night despite the first recallable attempt by my parents to help me out. And yet, the Leethams still accepted me. Still loved me. Still treated me with the same respect that all of their own four children received. The Leethams' house was my safe place. The Leethams' house would eventually become the only example in my life of a functional home.

Other than being a disgusting bedwetter, I was a pretty normal kid with humble aspirations. For example, at eight, all I wanted out of life was a real Cabbage Patch Kid (versus the bootleg doll I bought at a flea market with thirteen dollars of my allowance money). So when my parents' spontaneous late-night screaming matches began, I wasn't prepared. I hadn't had a dysfunctional family life that eased me into meeting the monsters that roared behind the master bedroom door. I was thrown in the deep end without a swim lesson. When their screaming didn't wake me up, the fights infiltrated my vivid dreams, which I am known for. Every night I dream, remember every dream, and sometimes long-term remember every dream. That particular week, I dreamed that my mom, dad, sister, and I went roller skating at Roller Land. All was well until we took a break to drink soda and lick Jolly Rancher sticks. My dad opted to buy for himself a slice of cake with strawberries and whipped icing on top but, before his first bite, my mom reached over and dipped her finger in the frosting, uninvited. Dad then took a silver butter knife and cut her finger off. The dream was a telling sign of how I was internalizing all of the nighttime fighting. It ended with the real-life alarm of my parents screaming through dawn before disappearing to work and leaving my sister and me to get ourselves ready, fed, and to school with zero acknowledgement of the warzone in our home.

This cycle repeated itself until, one morning, Mom herded Cindy into my room and the pair sat on the edge of my wet bed so Mom could break some news to us: she was leaving and we weren't coming with her. Part of all of that fighting was Dad refusing to allow us to go with her. So out of desperation she made a deal with the devil and agreed, for her own salvation, to leave us with him so long as she had unrestricted visitation. Dad obliged and she never stepped foot in our childhood home again. The only problem was, Dad lied. From that point on, my time with my mom was manipulated by a good father but vindictive ex-husband who was dead set on making her suffer.

Second only to my mom's departure announcement, my introduction to separated parents began with an eight-year-old me along with my thirteen-year-old sister having to suddenly adapt to our dad's twenty-something secretary popping up out of nowhere and into our home; and later, our mom on the arm of a large-statured Italian man who hated little kids (namely, me). With the new love interests came new jealousy between my parents, and I somehow took on a new role as resident message-passer between them.

"Tell your mother that she can't see you unless I have twenty-four hours notice *and* she picks you up at a time and place as determined by me."

*Sure, Dad. I'll reiterate that verbatim.*

"Tell your dad that I will see you whenever I want as per our agreement and, by the way, how dare he drive his little girlfriend around in the Corvette I bought."

*You got it, mom. This is going to get me whipped with a belt.*

My parents didn't know this at the time, but after a few rounds of that message-passing game, subsequent messages never made it past me. I stopped telling either parent anything because I was the only one who got to absorb the furious rants that followed each message delivery. It was much easier to tell them that the other parent accepted their message without contest. They never caught on that I stopped delivering messages because, once my mom left, they almost never spoke again (except one random evening when my mom rang the doorbell to say something clever and throw a twenty-dollar bill at my dad for reasons still unknown to me, and perhaps a couple of times years apart). One thing was clear: at eight years old, I knew with utter definitiveness how much my parents hated each other. Their rage pumped through my heart, filtered through my veins, and ate away at my innocence day after day.

My few escapes from the stress of home every week were: Tuesday afternoon Our Gang Singers practice with Jenny, a Wednesday afternoon *Triangle Review* paper route with Jenny, Parks and Recreation soccer practice or games every Saturday morning with Jenny, and spending the night nearly every Saturday night (which required me, by default, to go to the Mormon church every Sunday morning) with Jenny. Jenny and her family were the dependable roadside assistance to my habitually flat tires.

Without Jenny, life was tough. I know this because we were spending so much time together, we started fighting and "broke up" one day on a bicycle trip to Our Gang Singers practice. Jenny thought it would be fun to tape flashlights to our handle bars and make the three-mile ride to and from practice, partly in the dark. I started lagging a half mile in and called it quits. Jenny screamed at me with her signature hot temper and ended whatever she said with, "I hate you!" The next day when it was paper route time, Jenny's dad delivered to me a sack of papers he had intended to surprise Jenny and me with by folding and rubber-banding everything so we didn't have to. He did this act of kindness not knowing we weren't speaking. So instead of staging an intervention, he drove up to my house, got out of his truck (the truck Jenny and I used to ride on the tailgate of, jumping on and off and racing each other to see who could deliver newspapers to each side of the street the fastest), and without a single word dropped a bag of one hundred and fifty papers in the middle of my driveway and walked away.

The fatigue I felt the previous day on Our Gang Singers Tuesday seemed worse that *Triangle Review* Wednesday. Imagining how I would deliver all of those papers by myself, by bike, was more than I could wrap my head around. I knew I couldn't break the unwritten papergirl code of honor and ditch the load. So I called an up-to-no-good acquaintance, Heather, and her older brother, Steve, and made them a deal they couldn't refuse: I would give them my entire month's earnings if they would deliver my papers for just that day. Now, perhaps this seems unusually cunning for an eight-year-old-honorary-Mormon-nothing-of-a-kid, but I had a secret dark side. With the absence of my mom came the absence of my dad. It wasn't uncommon for Cindy and me to stay home nearly full nights alone. One night, Dad came home unbelievably drunk, stumbled to and sprawled out on his bed, passed out and appeared dead for eight hours before we were finally able to see any signs of life. Another night, he was tipsy and talking to his secretary toy in the middle of the summer night while my bedroom window was getting pelted with rocks thrown by Heather and Steve. I easily snuck past Dad's room, and out the downstairs sliding glass door, and proceeded to jaywalk to our elementary school to swing in the moonlight with my bad influences. I returned home before dawn to find Dad still on the same phone call, and I crawled on top of a single sheet to sleep with no blanket because the laundry was never up to date anymore, but my bedwetting was still on schedule. As predicted, Heather and Steve accepted the lopsided newspaper delivery deal and showed up to my doorstep rather quickly.

At that Saturday's soccer game, John Leetham told my dad he received a call from the *Triangle Review*. They had never received so many complaints as they did that Wednesday, and they were terminating my employment. To make matters worse, I was having a bad day on the soccer field. My mouth was so dry it felt like it was stuffed with cotton balls. When I ran, my legs felt like they had half of my weight added to them. At halftime, the water couldn't come fast enough and the orange slices one of the moms was assigned to bring as a halftime snack, were making me nauseous. Dad pushed from the sideline, "C'mon, Jenn!" but I had zero steam left in a painfully slowing engine. When we got home and Dad asked what went wrong on the soccer field, I was not so pleasant in responding and he gave me a spank on the butt for "being obstinate." In all actuality, I kind of felt like I was dying but that was a silly idea since people don't die until they're the age of my great-grandpa Cooper, the only dead person I knew.

While I wasn't feeling much better over the next several days, a special treat was in store. Dad had arranged for Cindy and me to hitch a ride on a one-way flight to California with his coworker's family so we could meet him for a weekend at Disney Land (to where he drove with a U-Haul filled with a bunch of state-of-the-art solar panels he was in the business of selling) after a sales pitch he was scheduled to give that Friday. After that, we would drive back home with him in his Honda with the "unbelievable gas mileage" of most foreign stick shifts. *Viola!* A perfect trip to be had. But on the car ride from Fort Collins to the airport in Denver, Dad's coworker had to stop three times to allow me to puke on the side of the road. We still caught our flight but the nausea didn't stop. At the request of the adults with me, the flight attendants feverishly delivered crackers and Ginger Ale to my seat, hoping to tide my stomach over for the three-and-a-half-hour flight and, with quite an effort on my part, I was able to keep most of it down. Probably just food poisoning, they all thought. Little did anyone know, something much worse—in fact, absolutely life-threatening—was the culprit.

# CHAPTER 3
# Kissing Boys

WE TOUCHED DOWN IN CALIFORNIA AND DROVE to the cheapest motel within walking distance of Disney Land to meet up with my dad and his secretary-toy-turned-girlfriend, the latter who "magically appeared" despite Cindy and me knowing she drove with our dad because her windsurfer was jimmy-rigged to the top of his car. The adults we flew with told Dad about my nausea but he quickly shrugged it off as motion sickness and tried to change the worrisome mood by cheerleading my sister and me into excitement about going three places: Toys R Us, which I considered to be the most spectacular toy store in the world because we didn't have one in Colorado; Disney Land, every kid's dream come true; and a final stop at the beach, a nice upgrade from catching crawdads in ditches.

Cindy ended up passing on the Toys R Us visit and stayed back with Dad's girlfriend, who had a name, Amy, which I would have felt more inclined to use if I hadn't casually known her as "Dad's secretary" before she became a staple at home. Oddly, Amy wasn't the Marilyn-Monroe-Happy-Birthday-Mr.-President home wrecker one might imagine. She was short and stocky despite being an athlete of many varieties (a far cry from the five-foot, ten-inch, one hundred and twenty pound runway model type my mom was). Amy had a violently curly brown mullet with purposeful blonde highlights (my mom had naturally straight, dark brown hair), and half of Amy's face was covered with a bright red birthmark (my mom's face was simple and pretty and complimented by a couple of slightly crooked teeth). But Amy had that X-factor that wives slowly lose over time. She was blindly and wildly in love with a man whose laundry she did not have to do, kids she did not have to raise, house she did not have to clean, and bad habits she did not have to put up with. Mistresses always get the fun, half-truth of a man who should be at home trying to be a better husband. That said, Dad was an invested, good father, and his love-life was none of our business. We kids were expected to adapt without discussion.

I soon discovered that Amy had one winning quality that always made me excited to see her: a dog. A *really cool* dog. Jazz was a playful Black Labrador that could do the most impressive tricks. Don't get me wrong, our mutt Pepper was my soul mate. But Pepper's tricks began and ended with sitting, speaking, rolling over, and climbing our chain-link fence to escape (only to get repeatedly caught and spanked by Dad). Jazz was a perfectly obedient dog with an impressive bag of agility tricks. She caught frisbees, jumped through hoops, did flips on our trampoline, and even windsurfed with Amy. She was the type of dog you only see on TV and she was temporarily mine according to Amy. So other than me knowing that Amy wasn't supposed to be riding around with my dad in my mom's hard-earned Corvette while my parents were still married, I thought Amy was pretty OK. And even though I suspected in my own, innocent way, that Amy was part of the reason I didn't have a mom at home anymore, I accepted her as only an eight-year-old little girl could: with open arms. She was nice to me and let me play with her dog, so she was my friend. The math at that age was truly that simple.

Leaving everyone back at the motel, Dad and I ventured off to fulfill my singular dream of finally "adopting" a *real* Cabbage Patch Kid, at the greatest toy store of all, no less. And even though, by the time that day arrived, it was no longer cool to have a Cabbage Patch Kid, I didn't care. I might as well have been the first kid on earth to ever get one I was so excited. I had no interest in browsing the store like one does when they don't exactly know what they want. I made a decisive beeline for the doll section. There, I found the most unbelievable wall of Cabbage Patch Kids that even I, with my overactive imagination and hyper-dream-generator of a brain, could not have imagined. After seeing a few familiar faces of Cabbage Patch Kids my friends already had, I spotted him: an all-brown boy doll. With stars in my eyes, I pulled the box off of the shelf and delighted in knowing that my dream was about to come true. I was going to be a Cabbage Patch Kid mom and sign adoption papers, and change diapers, and smell the sweet baby powder scent that was permanently stamped on all of the dolls' butts. Five minutes in the store of my dreams and I was already ready to go. "You want *that* doll?" Dad asked.

"Yep! I want this one!" I said, somewhat realizing my dad had reservations but too naïve to understand or care why. All I knew was that I was about to adopt the most extraordinary Cabbage Patch Kid I had ever seen and I could barely contain my excitement, even if it was slightly muted by nausea. My little brown boy was "the one" and Dad forked over the forty-dollar small fortune without contest.

"Don't ask," my Dad would say to the adults whom questioned with their eyes my doll choice.

When we got back to the motel, the small group consisting of my dad, Cindy, me, Amy, and Dad's coworkers, all of whom were spread across three motel rooms, complained of being hungry. My dad sent my sister and me to a 7-11 next door to grab junk food for everyone, specifically telling us we could treat ourselves to candy bars if we wanted. Sweets were something we rarely enjoyed at home since Dad was always following the newest fad diet and feeding us the same health food he ate. My best chance at eating something with sugar was at the Leethams' house, where Jenny and I would have competitions to see who could eat a Twinkie fastest. Other than that, I was accustomed to granola and nuts and carrot sticks and plain iced tea.

Normally, I would have gone straight for the Charleston Chews and Whatchamacallits during such a once-in-a-lifetime opportunity, but all I wanted was water. Ice. Cold. Water. Back then, water wasn't sold in bottles yet and the tap water in Anaheim was a lukewarm, weird out-of-town flavor. So I settled for a cherry Slurpee instead, which had the exact opposite effect on quenching my thirst than what water would have accomplished. I only felt thirstier, less hungry, and more desperate for anything even remotely resembling the cool, crisp, Fort Collins tap water I was used to.

I went to bed that night without dinner because I wasn't hungry (and had a strange sort of acid reflux thing happening). The puking had subsided but I was still feeling awful. I woke up the next morning with the wettest bed of my life. I'm pretty sure my dad had to dodge the motel manager when we left after that tidal wave. And for the rest of our time in California, the thing that dominated my vacation experience was being desperately thirsty and then having to pee or puke. I didn't know what was happening to me. "It's the heat," Dad confidently assured.

Entering the gates of Disney Land for the first time I could remember (we went once before when I was one) would have been as magical as it was supposed to be had I not felt like I was stranded on a deserted island with no drinking water. Dad gave us the figurative free pass that virtually every little kid gets from their parents at theme parks, which allowed us to drink or eat anything we wanted. However, even with unlimited options, I was only torn between wanting to take my first ever bite of a greasy, sugar and cinnamon covered *churro* I had heard so much about, or continuing to search for water. I made the poor decision of getting a *churro* and instantly felt like I might as well have eaten a cup of sand and washed it down with a cup of nothing. I told Dad how thirsty I was and that I needed water. After a quick look around, he let me know there wasn't any water to be found so instead found the closest drink cart and bought me a large Coke with ice. Out of desperation I drank as many sips as I could but continued to feel extremely sick.

The sun seemed to have a permanent spotlight on me and Dad's best effort to find shade for my face by buying me a large-billed Mickey Mouse cap, which I normally would have been incredibly excited about, was lost on the fact that the park was swelteringly hot and my body was literally dying of thirst. Dad told me to smile and snapped a half-grinning-as-convincingly-as-possible portrait of me (ironically, with Coke in hand). I don't remember anything more of that trip to Disney Land. In my mind, the whole of the trip consisted of me sitting on the curb of the infamous circular round in front of Sleeping Beauty Castle in the boiling sun with a Coke and *churro*, waiting with Dad for everyone to finish having fun so we could drive home and get some drinkable ice water. I imagined myself parking my mouth under the kitchen sink and blasting the cold water, gulping as many gallons as I could until I was so full that water squirted from every pore of my body. *I'm so thirsty.*

Our final destination, the trip to the beach for Cindy's patiently awaited pre-teen tan and Amy's windsurfing binge, is a blur. I don't know what happened after Disney Land. I don't know how we got to the beach or with whom. I don't know how long we were there. I just know that I was sitting on a towel that was draped over a furnace of blazing sand, trying to hide my whole body under my Mickey Mouse cap, drinking sips from a can of soda and alternately licking sand-covered, freezer-burn-flavored ice from a styrofoam cooler. Amy snapped a photo of Cindy and me and realized something. I was pained. I was trying my best to be a good sport but I looked like death. Amy took the initiative to pull her windsurfer out of the water and tell my Dad that I really didn't look well; that maybe I should see a doctor as soon as possible (what my sister had been telling my Dad unsuccessfully all along). When my dad stopped and took a good look at my skeletal frame, blood shot eyes, bone dry mouth and stark white tongue, he finally called it quits on the vacation. Amy magically disappeared to who knows where, and Dad, Cindy, and I commenced the long drive home through death traps of deserts and the rockiest of mountains in the gas efficient Honda with no air conditioning.

Around dinner time after many hours of driving, Dad found a McDonald's to stop at to eat. I kept thinking how unfair it was that when, one of the only times Dad was allowing us to eat junk food, I wanted nothing to do with it.

"Chicken nuggets, Jenn?"

"No."

"Cheeseburger?"

"No."

"You have to eat something."

"Do they have ice water?"

They did not, in fact, sell ice water but Dad made a deal to buy a large soda with ice to the rim, minus the soda, so I could go and fill it up with water at the first drinking fountain we had seen on our trip. Even though I knew it was going to be out-of-town flavored, anything was better than nothing and the coldness of the ice masked some of the gross taste. I downed the thirty-two-ounce cup of water on the spot and then, as soon as we were seat-belted and on our way, promptly threw it all up. My sister kept urging my dad to take me to the doctor but he told her we needed to make it home first. We didn't have health insurance and an out-of-town doctor visit would be more than we could afford.

If there's any question about how obsessed my Dad was with gas mileage (or being thrifty in general), then perhaps what happened next will serve as a clue. Despite having a horribly sick kid in the back seat, Dad was still playing a subconscious game of "let's see how far we can drive on empty" to somehow prove that, even when his car was on empty, we could still go for many miles because of its superior gas mileage (and by virtue of that, his superior intelligence). It was around midnight when the gas tank dropped below the red line and Dad began to estimate how many miles we would be able to drive before seeing a sign that said the next gas station was over eighty miles away. This was the first and only time I saw my Dad panic. (I had seen him explode with anger many times, but never panic.) It was then that I had my first lesson on how to save gas with a stick shift. On downhills, dad would pop the car into neutral and ride out the hill without pressing the gas until the car dragged to below the speed limit on the straightaway. Miraculously, we eventually made it to the gas station. Had we not, a breakdown in the desert may have killed me.

Morning came and the drive was becoming more and more arduous. The clear glass of the two-door Honda was magnifying the sun and burning my boney body. Cindy kept telling Dad she didn't know how much longer I could take boiling in the back seat. I started acting strange, incoherent, laying across the backseat and tossing my head from side to side, mumbling unintelligible pleas for help. Cindy started crying and begged Dad to drive to a hospital. Dad finally said he would stop at the first hospital he could find.

I woke up to Dad laying me on a cold steel examination table in an emergency clinic in the mountains near Colorado Springs. A nurse looked me over quickly and casually theorized that I might have mononucleosis.

"Jennifer! Have you been kissing boys!?" Dad blurted.

I opened my eyes dutifully to weakly defend myself, "No, Dad." But once my vitals were checked, the team went into this-kid-is-about-to-die mode. I was immediately carted to an on-site ambulance to be rushed, with my sister riding shotgun and my Dad following behind in the Honda, to Denver's Children's hospital. From my stretcher, I looked out the rear of the ambulance and saw white puffy clouds against Colorado's breathtakingly beautiful blue sky and thought to myself, "Maybe kids *can* die. Maybe I am dying."

I awoke to the bustle and panic of an emergency room, a blinding spotlight on my face, multiple needles piercing me in both arms, and an annoying nurse firing off questions to me.

"Jennifer? Do you know where you are?"

"Hospital?"

"Do you know what day it is?"

"No."

"Can you tell me how many fingers I'm holding?"

"No."

"You have to open your eyes. Can you tell me how many fingers I'm holding?"

The light seared my eyeballs and I squeezed them closed again.

"Owweee. No."

This is the last thing I remember before falling into a coma. According to my dad, a doctor came in to examine me and ordered blood glucose tests because my breath was "sweet."

Sure enough, my blood sugar was too high to register. The Dr. explained in layperson's terms to my dad that there was no question my pancreas stopped working and that, since I didn't have insulin to process food and transport sugar to blood cells to burn as energy, sugar was spilling into my urine while my body burned fat instead of sugar for energy. That process produced a poison called ketones, and an extremely life-threatening state, called ketoacidosis.

I was sent to the Intensive Care Unit and my dad was forced to speak to my mother when he called her to break the news of my diagnosis: juvenile, type 1 diabetes.

# CHAPTER 4
## Type 1

I OPENED MY EYES TO WAKE UP TO A DIM HOSPITAL room in the Intensive Care Unit and my mom standing against the wall at the end of my bed, staring at me blankly with tears running down her face, obviously not sure if I would ever wake up. My brain told me to run and give her a big hug but my body was stiff and unmovable. My torso was connected to a heart monitor and both of my arms were stabbed with what seemed like one hundred IV lines to feed my body whatever it lost when my veins filled with poison. I was still in critical condition and, given no one in my family on either side had ever had any form of diabetes (not even dating back to the 1600's, which we know because my paternal grandmother took over the work of a long line of dedicated family historians), everyone was clueless about what to expect for my long-term prognosis.

It was the middle of the night and apparently my mom stole the opportunity to visit then instead of daylight hours because, when she came the first time, the Johnsons bullied her out of my hospital room. After my parents' divorce, one might have guessed the Johnsons (my father's side) and the Coopers (my mother's side) had always been archenemies. But that wasn't the case at all. In fact, the families had more things in common than not. According to Grandma Johnson (who was an avid family historian), the Coopers first arrived to America on the Mayflower from England in 1620, the Hyde/Bass families (Grandma Johnson's side) arrived from England in 1647, and the Johnsons (who changed their last name from Moröen) came from Norway in 1880 when my great-grandfather was five years old. Both families consisted of hardworking men and women who started from scratch working as farmers and developing other skills (such as blacksmithing, carpentry, and woodworking) in addition to serving the United States in World Wars I and II, respectively, the latter in which my great-uncle, William Marion Cooper, lost his life in 1945. My parents were what eleven generations had been working their bodies to the bone for—the torch bearers who would help cement our heritage into worldly time. They came from families who stuck together no matter what. So my parents' divorce was a shocking disappointment and slap in the face to Grandma Johnson, who endured many hellish things herself over the years, sucking it up like she was supposed to. And it seemed to me like she needed someone to blame.

In my hospital room, Grandma Johnson unapologetically accused my mom of feeding me "sugar cereal" and causing my diabetes.

When my Grandma Johnson told me this theory personally, I questioned, "Then why don't the Leethams have diabetes?" since my best friend's family had at least a year supply of "sugar cereal" (defined by Grandma as anything that wasn't plain puffed rice) per the food storage savvy Mormons are known for.

When my dad asked Dr. McGuiness about my grandmother's theory, Dr. McGuiness bluntly told my dad something to the tune of "That's not how type 1 diabetes works. Type 1 diabetes tends to be genetic. But in my opinion, this was stress-induced."

The rest of my time in the ICU consisted of: my parents marveling while I plugged my nose and chugged down disgusting fizzy "orange-flavored" (death-flavored) potassium drinks so that my fingers would resume their correct anatomical position instead of bending up towards the sky; me milking for all it was worth Dad hand-feeding me hospital food like a baby; getting a visit from Dad's friends, including his secretary toy, who brought me a teddy bear and a coffee cup filled with Hershey's Kisses that I reached for before a nurse broke the news that I "can't eat sugar anymore" (*Life. Over.*); seeing my parents coexist in the same room without fighting (perhaps partly because they didn't speak); family diabetes training sessions where we practiced giving shots by injecting oranges with saline solution; learning how to eat according to diabetic food exchanges (for example: one fruit exchange, one protein exchange, one starch exchange, and a free-food exchange for lunch); learning about the problematic nature of attempting to have children one day (which was way over my 8-year-old head); hearing of the child next door with terrifyingly severe burns over her entire body and being (rightly) reminded of how fortunate I was; and finally going home after five days in the ICU and another week in the main hospital.

Once I was back home, fully hydrated, not throwing up, and generally feeling good (albeit a little shaky from the low blood sugar that punctuated my early years as a diabetic while we got used to the unpredictable nature of slow-acting insulin shots), the hardest parts about getting used to diabetes were: kids thought I was contagious; almost none of the adults around me knew anything about the disease; when you're bone thin without an ounce of fat on your body, shots in muscles hurt like heck; and we suddenly became poor after both parents were forced to file for bankruptcy after my hospital stay because we didn't have health insurance. Despite these things, I was raised to suck things up. As long as we had a roof overhead, food, and medicine, even if it meant that Dad and I had to routinely cut my blood test strips into slivers to stretch fifty strips into one hundred and fifty, we were better than fine.

Life went on. The only thing different about my first day of fourth grade was that there was a bit of attention drawn to me when I pulled out my mandatory morning snack, a peach, which promptly yielded whining from all of the kids in my class.

"Where's my snack!?" the voices whined. I once tried to give out bites before Mrs. Brown intervened and told my classmates that I needed the full peach. It was also a new experience to almost pass out during reading time.

I told the substitute teacher who kept calling me out for appearing to nod off, "I'm diabetic and I think my blood sugar is very low."

I was on the verge of fainting. My body shook and my tongue went numb. But the uninformed teacher only offered me a sugar-free mint when what I really needed was a sugar-*filled* fix, like juice. I barely made it to lunchtime with my life.

Even though I assured my friends that my diabetes wasn't contagious, most kids started keeping their distance from me. At one point, I resigned to the idea that I simply wouldn't have friends anymore. Then, Lynda Leetham called. She wanted to talk to me, personally. I picked up the phone and both Lynda *and* Jenny were on the line (a strategy Lynda used at least a few times during our friendship to help Jenny and me have polite conversations following fights). I hadn't spoken to Jenny in what felt like forever and Lynda asked in the fearless way she was known for if I would like to spend the night that weekend. I instantly told her that I can't sleepover anymore because I have shots and blood tests and a special diet. Lynda asked me to put my dad on the phone. When he hung up, he told me I was going for a sleepover. Lynda's father was an insulin-dependent diabetic and she had many years of experience giving shots, checking blood sugar, and counting food exchanges. Even though I was a little nervous about what my new body might do, I accepted the offer and Jenny's family started making my life easier again.

By the end of fourth grade, my grades plummeted. When Mrs. Brown sat me down and I mentally prepared to confess my terrible procrastination problem, she did all the talking for me. She offered anecdotes about how hard it must be to have divorced parents. Then, she gave me a second chance to complete my final report. I bit my tongue, delivered a scrapped together report, and got a consolatory A marked down to a D for being three days late. With that, I passed fourth grade and that deal of a century marked my very first perk of being a kid with divorced parents. Oddly, I got no credit for the diabetes. Mental note made.

On the home front, despite everyone struggling to make ends meet, Mom personally ensured that I made it to singing practice every week. I almost never missed. And despite sometimes not having money to eat, she forwent her own needs to make sure I had the opportunity to grow my talent. On what I thought was another regular practice day, Mom surprised me with a pricey purple jumpsuit before French-braiding my hair up-side-down so that the braid started at the back of my neck and ended at the side of my head, where she tied a ponytail, covered my face in grown woman makeup, and told me to practice the hardest song I knew how to sing while she drove. That day after practice, The Colorado Academy of the Arts (what Our Gang Singers was eventually renamed) held auditions for The Pros: an elite group of girls who got paid to sing. To make it into the group required a lot of talent and, preferably, an attentive stage mom. I auditioned and I made it in. But after six months of hitting and missing marks, I was released from the group on my tenth birthday with the single explanation from my director (who created a kid-version of the speech she gave my mother): "You're too nice for this group." In plain English that meant, "Happy Birthday, but we have girls in here who sing laying down with a stack of telephone books on their stomach every night. Your Mom can't get you here with curled hair and makeup?" But the honest truth was, when I arrived at performances without my hair curled, makeup on, or wearing tap shoes instead of ballet slippers, it was because I had a hard time remembering on my own everything the other girls' mothers at home naturally put in order for them. While my mom did her best, not living together and not speaking to my father made it more difficult to keep up with the many demands of a professional singing career.

To add injury to insult, after that last practice as a pro, Mom surprised me with a home-made sugar-free Jell-O cake that was rapidly melting into mush, alongside a regular cake for everyone else. *I'd rather eat worms.* (Fast-forward five years, I finally had to sit my family down and tell them to stop trying to make sugar-free versions of my favorites like pumpkin pie and cookies and cake. I knew they had the best intentions but being their human guinea pig for disgusting concoctions they wouldn't eat themselves, and then blaming my rude obnoxious attitude on my diabetes, was getting on my last nerve.) So after that fatal tenth birthday's "firing" and pitiful birthday cake finale, I joined the academy's "Just Say No" show, a troupe that ended up being far more relevant than The Pros ever were anyway and where I sang a good majority of the solos, traveled constantly, and even wrote a song that was broadcast live on the most popular radio station at the time.

Jenny had long since dropped out of Our Gang Singers because she was an impressive athlete and only sang to be with me. Seeing her again fulltime pretty much saved what was left of my childhood. Her parents took me in like one of their own and I got to do everything their kids did—Water World, Elitch Gardens amusement park, sporting events, hiking, camping, church—everything. Most memorably, Jenny and I would pack sack lunches and jump in John Leetham's truck for a long day at "the fields," where John checked crops for pests. You would think this would be boring for us but it was anything but. We would catch giant grasshoppers, chase bunnies, stare down bull snakes, and everyone's favorite, take home a box turtle if we were lucky enough to find one. Since there was no way my dad would let me have a turtle, the Leethams let me keep the one I found, which I named Twinkie, at their house. When the sun started to go down, we would hop back in John's truck again and, if it was well past dinnertime, almost fall asleep before John would get our attention by treating us to Wendy's hamburgers.

Once my mom was no longer living in her car, I went with her for sporadic overnight visits that began at a dark, ugly studio apartment in the "hood" of Fort Collins, then eventually graduated to a one-bedroom apartment with a ladder leading to a carpeted loft that Cindy and I fought over near Colorado State University, before a move to a two-bedroom apartment, complete with a new Golden Retriever puppy near the CSU football stadium, and a final stop at the duplex at Horsetooth Reservoir that Mom and Dad co-owned with my mom's parents before Dad bailed and stuck them with a bad deal from what I could tell. When I wasn't visiting Mom, I was either at Jenny's house or on some sort of adventure with Dad.

Trips with Dad were usually as fun as they were arduous. We almost always went to a destination at least a few hours away. The drive to Dad's favorite place, Lake McConaughy (which we pronounced, Mc-con-uh-hey) in Ogallala, Nebraska, was always long and hot. Dad was so frugal that, even in his later years in life when he was well off and bought his first, spanking-new vehicle, he still got roll-me-up windows. So you can imagine the used cars we drove to and from the lake in: bare boned, stick-shifted, manual everything, air-condition-less, bumpy ride, sweat shops. If Dad would have told us to stick our legs through the floor and run or tilt a solar panel out of the side of the window to activate a homemade second engine, I wouldn't have been the least bit surprised. But no-frills cars or not, we always made it in one piece and always found an adventure waiting at the other end.

Lake McConaughy had beach-like white sand and little "horny toads" (Horned lizards) everywhere you looked. The adults used to dig little holes in the sand to fill with beer before placing toads in the middle to laugh at how they absorbed the alcohol through the thin layer of skin on their underbellies and hopped away drunk as skunks. Despite hating the long drives and some of the ways Dad made us really rough it (for example, foregoing sleeping bags and tents), I loved the lake. Dad had so many friends that we all shared a huge artillery of lake toys—

windsurfers, catamarans, speedboats, jet skis, water skis, inner tubes—plus food and drinks. Dad kept a cooler filled with sugar-free soda just for me, which gave me belly aches because it was sweetened with saccharine back then. But his effort was not lost on me. I was thankful to have something sweet and cold to drink. And with every imaginable way to have fun within reach, I not only tried but was successful in every water sport available to me. Since Dad always told everyone I was fearless I typically did my best to live up to his advertisements. Water skiing—up on the second go. Windsurfing—pulled the adult-sized sail up with my pint-sized body. Inner tubing—ate white water like a champ. Jet skiing—held on for dear life while an adult went way too fast and turned way too sharply. And at night, when I froze between two blankets under the stars in my swimsuit, the white sand below absorbed and hid my darkest secret. No wet bed. No public shame. No humiliation. No self-loathing. Just the same start to the beautiful day everyone else got: a bath in the lake with a bar of soap (plus an insulin shot and blood test afterward.)

In autumn I still got to go trick-or-treating like all of the other kids. Dr. McGuinness said I could have two snack-sized candy bars that day. The rest of my Halloween candy was deposited into Dad's big Tupperware bowl to redistribute to the kids who rang our bell. During the school year, singing practice at the academy was held twice per week and my calendar was continuously peppered with performances ranging from modest recitals at Foothills Fashion Mall to opening a concert for country singer, George Straight. The singing me was the outer-body superstar of the nothing me.

In the winter, when Dad got lost driving to his secretary toy's cabin in a late-night snowstorm, I cross-country skied like everyone else for five miles in shin-high snow with nothing more than the moon to light our path, with no questions asked and no excuses despite chronically low blood sugar from following a hyperactive, thrill-seeker of a father. And it seemed like every time I was near-death, I'd catch a break. For example, when we were within a quarter mile of the cabin and I thought I would surely pass out, "Uncle Mark" (a younger, more handsome version of my dad in unrelated, coworker form) came to scoop us up with a snowmobile. *Still alive. Still standing.*

Notwithstanding having divorced parents who refused to speak to one another, newly diagnosed type 1 diabetes, an old bed-wetting problem, and a failed career as a professional singer,

I was really quite privileged. While my life wasn't very easy, it also wasn't very dull. And after Dad's solar panel company bombed and his love affair with Amy fizzled out, things got even more interesting.

# CHAPTER 5
# Ladies' Man

MY DAD WAS A SELFLESS FATHER, WHO DID everything in his power to give us a great life. Even in our poorest days, when my wardrobe consisted of ill-fitting hand-me-downs and holey second-hand sneakers, we never went without anything. In fact, we had many luxuries. We had Pepper, a poodle-mix mutt that was my dad's nemesis but who the rest of us adored so he put up with her. We had a giant trampoline that followed us between three houses, three elementary schools, and three junior high schools every time my dad would rent or sell or foreclose until the trampoline mat ripped to irreparable shreds and the springs fell off. We had a homemade go-kart, traded and followed by a homemade mini-bike, both of which started as steel frames and ended up as lawn-mower-engine-powered speed machines. Dad took an electric hand saw to the toy hotdog stand I got from a very generous Santa Claus, cutting out circles where fake burners were painted and inserting real burners so I could boil water and sell hotdogs to awestruck garage sale shoppers in the summertime. He hand-made a Ghostbuster "Slimer" Halloween costume out of chicken wire, papier-mâché, green food coloring, and a baseball helmet, winning me a prize at the school costume contest. For my sixth-grade science project, Dad made a four-chamber, beating heart out of pink balloons and an electric board and wiring kit while I sloppily pasted photocopies of encyclopedia excerpts on folded presentation boards instead of writing an original report by hand. Had I done my part, we would have received a prize for that project, too. There truly wasn't an idea my dad couldn't pull off. He was *the* Jack-of-all-trades. He used his talents to provide us with the ultimate adventure of a childhood. The best childhood I can imagine given all of the loopholes. And he just happened to be a ladies' man.

Dad was an attractive, outgoing, and funny Leo of a woman-magnet. After his fling with Amy crashed and burned, entered Lana and her twelve-year-old son, Calvin, who was way cooler than I could have ever hoped to be. I remember three things about Lana and her son: first, risking my life (and street credit) attempting every skateboard trick that Calvin did; second, my new "brother" inviting a group of six of my up-to-no-good classmates to sneak over to my house in the middle of the night and talk about forbidden things like sex, which another boy demonstrated on me by dry-humping my bony nine-year-old frame on the same couch my pre-divorced family used to sit on to watch *The Muppets* every Friday night; and third, Lana being the first person to convince Dad to make me eat fish. (Does shark count as fish?) I sat until one o'clock in the morning in front of that shark steak with sandpaper-like skin that felt like it was grinding my taste buds off every time I attempted a bite. My dad swore he would sit up all night until I ate it. He sat behind me on a couch in the living room, where he secretly (more like obviously) watched my mirror image from sliding glass doors. I somehow pulverized the steak into a big, cold, inedible fish ball thinking my dad wouldn't really make me eat it. But as it grew later and later I realized he wasn't budging. Finally, I devised a plan to act like I was eating by cutting the shark ball into smaller sections, stabbing each piece with my fork, raising the fork to my chin, opening the neck of the homemade puffy paint T-shirt I wore religiously, and letting the cold, rough fish bombs-away down the bare skin of my belly to accumulate near my waistline. I added fake chewing for good measure. Finally, I showed my dad the finished plate.

"See? That wasn't so bad," he said victoriously. He excused me from the table and I ran to the bathroom and dumped the fish that was sitting inside the bottom of my shirt into the toilet. I think he thought I threw up because he asked, "Are you OK?"

*Well, other than having fish slop running down my stomach, yeah, Dad.* "No, Dad. I feel sick," I replied out loud in an Oscar-winning whine.

Dad never made me eat shark, or any type of fish, again. Whether he knew about my shirt trick and let me execute it through completion for his own entertainment, or not, we will never know.

After Lana there was Geanie, her daughter Victoria and son John Henry, both of whom were a couple of years younger than me. It was around a month before the end of fifth grade when Dad sold our childhood home, moved us across town, and enrolled me in my new school where I didn't know anyone in my grade and where I spent most recesses trying to blend in with brick walls and hide behind tetherball poles. Classwork was super confusing and my new teacher flat out told me she didn't know what to do with me. But since we only had a month left of school, she passed me on, assuming I learned at least the basics at my previous school. That summer, Geanie gave me the job of de-snaking her backyard, paying me two dollars for every Garter snake I caught and relocated to a ditch several blocks away. (My record was twelve dollars—six snakes—in one day.) And despite the plentitude of serpents, I only put a snake in a shoebox one time to ding-dong-ditch a random family across the street. Later that summer, we all drove to Pennsylvania to Geanie's family's house somewhere in Amish country. I marveled at how green everything was and how dreadfully humid the air felt, and I delighted in seeing my first firefly and catching softball-sized toads. When we got there, my dad suddenly took on a Texas accent and said "Howdy!" before asking directions from a local farmer on a tractor at an intersection (which fake accent I teased him about for the rest of the trip). Later that trip, I hopped on a motorcycle and burned the heck out of my calf on the tailpipe, which dad solved with butter and crutches made out of tree limbs to make me feel fixed, I guess. It didn't stop the pain though.

With the end of the summer came the end of Geanie and, by the time the first day of sixth grade rolled around, we were in full swing at our new house, with a new neighbor girl who was annoyingly thrilled to have a playmate next door, and yet another new school. I readied myself to have a year like my last-month-of-fifth-grade-nothingness before lucking out and instantly being adopted by Angie, the most popular girl at Dunn Elementary. At Dunn, there were two categories of popular: the well-off kids with sharp clothes, good looks, and good grades; and the not-so-well-off kids with low income, low test scores, and high personality. While my second-hand clothes landed me in category two, I found that both categories intermingled seamlessly.

My sixth-grade teacher, Mrs. Reader, took a very special interest in me that year. I guess she noticed I could use someone in my corner. She was so invested in me, one day she left our classroom in the hands of the school nurse to personally drive me home shortly after school began because I realized I forgot to take my insulin shot and my parents were MIA. And despite missing school rather frequently to perform with The Colorado Academy of the Arts, with Mrs. Reader's help I made the honor roll and spelling bee. And as an unplanned graduation gift to me, Mrs. Reader canceled her lesson and instead spent half of my last day of sixth grade painstakingly removing tons of sequins from the only dress I could find to wear to graduation: a bright pink satin "puffy dress" my mom made two years prior for sole use at a Stars of Tomorrow audition that only materialized in a letter inviting me to try again next time. Mrs. Reader's kindness didn't spare me entirely from the humiliation of wearing a terribly-too-small performance dress. But at least my embarrassment wasn't exacerbated by the sequins equivalent of jazz-hands. Mrs. Reader was the type of teacher whose greatest influence had little to do with textbook contents. Whatever I didn't learn about compassion and charity from the Leethams, I learned in sixth grade.

After Geanie, Dad started bringing around "Barb the Cop," a single police officer with no kids and no personality. She walked around with distrust chiseled on her tan and weathered face. She didn't say much to me and I didn't say much to her. To this day, all I really remember about Barb the Cop is that she taught my dad how to use mud from Boyd Lake to paint over the expired license plate on Dad's catamaran trailer (purchased in the Secretary Toy era) after we went boating one day, which I found odd since she was supposed to enforce the law, not break it. I guess Dad was as unimpressed as I was because she disappeared rather quickly.

After Barb the Cop, my sixteen-year-old sister had a terrible fight with my dad that reminded me of the terrible marital fights he had with my mother. To preface this fight story, it's important to note how many times my sister took a belt on my behalf (figuratively and literally). So many times, that by the time I was eleven, I felt indebted to her. So when I heard my dad lose his mind and go straight for her jugular, I mustered up the courage to go into her bedroom to break it all up. There, I found my sister hunkered down in the corner of her bedroom with her hands to her ears and the fear of death in her crying eyes while my dad screamed at the top of his lungs a millimeter away from her nose like a drill sergeant. I looked around the room and instinctively grabbed a large, ceramic vase we bought in Tijuana during that trip to California that almost killed me. I walked up behind my dad with the plan of crashing the vase over his head and saving the day but completely chickened out and, instead, stood there watching my broken sister get verbally battered until the screaming finally stopped. Before I knew it, I was the last person standing in my father's household when my sister went to live with my mom, stepdad, and two older stepsisters (a mistake that taught her—and me—that stepsiblings get treated like royalty and we get treated like our abused mother who could barely demand respect for herself, much less us). No longer having my sister's watchful eye or the leftover chicken she brought home most nights from her part-time job at KFC, Raisin Bran and skim milk after nighttime insulin shots became critical to my survival when Dad didn't come home from his job in Denver until late each night.

Barb the Cop has an identifier after her name because after her was "Barb the Nurse" and her fourteen-year-old daughter Amy, who had all of the idiosyncrasies of a fatherless child: wild in a you-want-this-party-animal-as-your-friend kind of way, but disrespectful, spoiled, and promiscuous in the you-want-to-knock-some-sense-into-this-kid kind of way. Amy was so excited to have me as a "sister" that she treated me like a celebrity every time she visited (before she and her mother quickly moved in and Amy took over my real sister's old room). Highlights of the Barb-the-Nurse-and-her-daughter-Amy era included: Amy giving me a new hairdo (a softly feathered—instead of dead straight—mullet), "new" (oversized hand-me-down) brand name clothes, and an honorary spot in a clique of teenaged cool kids. Most memorably, Amy brought me along to sneak out one night when our parents were gone in exchange for me teaching her how to start and drive my dad's VW Rabbit, which was a stick shift.

"Put it neutral. Press the clutch down all the way. Start it. Keep the clutch down. Put it in first gear. Let go of the clutch slowly and start to press the gas," I explained the way Dad had showed me when I reliably wanted to know how it—and everything—worked. The car ride with Amy was about as smooth as an execution in an electric chair as the gears grinded and vibrated our bones until we reached Amy's boyfriend's house, where a capable driver took over.

Amy taught me how to French kiss pillows and how to measure a boy's penis with fingers "when you feel them out." I sat quietly confused and appalled during her presentation of sign language and an imaginary penis. *Why on earth would anyone ever want to touch a penis?*

My dad proposed to Barb the Nurse and her penis-touching daughter, only for Dad to end it and my new "sister" to permanently disappear. But the French pillow-kissing lesson eventually came in handy with my first crush, Sam, who introduced himself to me by passing a message down the lunch table asking if I would "go steady" with him. Wanting to fit in (and instantly noticing how cute he was), I naturally said yes. Later, when everyone from sixth grade gathered in Maggie de lo Santos' aunt and uncle's empty new house, Sam and I went into a closet with two other "couples," counted to three, and essentially head-butted each other with open mouths and tongues out for a total of two seconds.

"You're a good kisser," Sam said.

*Thank goodness.* I breathed a sigh of relief. *I thought that was horrible.*

I grew up overnight the summer after sixth grade graduation thanks to Angie, my bestie from Mrs. Reader's class. While Angie was around my same age, her body was about three years ahead of our time. She was tall, had adult-sized breasts despite her thin build, and had already started her period—something I was relatively clueless about since I was being raised by a man. She could easily pass for a fourteen-year-old and usually did. When my dad let me take Angie to Lake McConaughy with us for vacation, she instantly attracted the attention of nearby teenage campers and I spent all night in a tent watching a seventeen-year-old boy play a French kissing game of "guess-what-salt-water-taffy-I-just-ate" with Angie. At the time, I wished I was her. Despite my literal two seconds of kissing experience, I was intrigued by the whole kissing thing. It seemed so thrilling. But deep down I knew it was the furthest thing from what any eleven-year-old should be doing. Honestly, I was relieved when the vacation was over so I could have some good 'ole, G-rated fun with my friend who I liked better when we were in her messy bedroom listening to Guns N Roses and using a curling iron, hairspray, and hair dryer to make our bangs stand up as high as they were long.

My first three days at Blevins Junior High School were a whirlwind. I was still hanging out with the popular kids from Dunn Elementary and for some reason I was an older boy magnet. I couldn't walk down the hall without boys looking at me, whispering, and then pushing a spokesman up to me to ask if I would "go out" with (call on the phone every night) one of their friends.

Dad always told me "pretty girls have all the problems—you don't want to be a pretty girl." So I figured that meant I wasn't. But the eighth-grade boys at Blevins seemed to think otherwise. The popularity I gained among boys was offset by my popular best friend, and the girls who followed her, dumping me out of the blue. Maybe it was because I didn't want to smoke cigarettes they stole from their single mothers to smoke at the big oak tree. I don't know. All I know is that befriending the unequivocally biggest loser in school was better than standing completely alone during breaks. So my new (and only) friend, a rather obese girl who had the prettiest face and ugliest attitude, would have to do. The relationship with my new friend didn't get much further than her saving me from a planned beat-down by my popular ex-friends and one sleepover. That night was capped off by her giving me a hair and clothing makeover before my dad picked me up for a planned photo shoot. As a result, our family photo turned out to be the most uncoordinated, embarrassing portrait a single dad could ever order copies of to distribute to the family as proof of our "happy," motherless family.

To my complete benefit, my dad foreclosed on his house and we moved again; meaning I was transferred to a new junior high school where my beloved childhood best friend, Jenny Leetham, attended. Finally, a drastic and abrupt life change that I was thrilled about.

After Barb the Nurse was Jillian and her dog, Bear. Jillian was a quiet, tofu and bird seed eating, sweetheart of a woman whose gentility was almost frightening to a kid like me who had probably lived more in my eleven years than she had in her whole entire life. Jillian was just what an underdog like me needed—a soft voice in a shrill world. But Jillian's soothing effect in my life was short-lived because that breakup happened as soon as the serious dating began.

After Jillian, Dad stopped bringing women home and I got to live a preteen-with-single-father-do-whatever-I-want-whenever-I-want dream. Then, Dad fell head-over-heels in love with "the one."

# CHAPTER 6
# Step "Momster"

WHEN I MET THE SICKENINGLY HAPPY, BLONDE haired, blued eyed, hundred and fifteen pound soaking wet, googly-eyed-in-love-with-my-dad new girlfriend along with her two kids, I didn't think much more of the trio than any of the other women and "siblings" whom had twirled in and out of my life. I had long since stopped calling these temporary companions family and learned my lesson not to use the term "brother" or "sister" too loosely. Even so, I was intrigued by her cheery attitude, southern twang, lighthearted spirit, and the compliments about me that she delivered to my dad.

"Jennifer is an angel compared to my kids," Betty Lou told Dad in front of me.

Betty Lou scored additional points with me by taking me on a shopping spree for new clothes and by the fact that she didn't get very mad the first time I forgot to take my insulin shot (forcing us to drive back home right after we had arrived where we were going in the first place). And I couldn't help but notice my dad's happy countenance when he was with her. She made him happy in a way that I hadn't seen before.

After what seemed like only a couple of weeks, Betty Lou, her eight-year-old daughter, and fifteen-year-old teenage son moved into our house. Soon after that, I found myself wearing a homemade, peach-colored, family-of-the-bride dress, singing "I Can't Help Falling in Love with You" (the absolutely most ridiculous song a twelve-year-old girl could ever be asked to sing) during a small ceremony at a church I had never seen or attended before. My dad actually did it. He committed to staying with only one woman for the rest of his life and, as nice as his new wife seemed, I felt a little robbed when my dad didn't ask for input like he sometimes did before. I mean, I also didn't have any say when my mom married the big Italian guy rather quickly after my parents' divorce. Mom eloped with her groom and from then on I typically didn't see much of the new stepdad. (He wasn't into little kids, so when I visited I kept a safe distance away from the living room where he reliably laid on the floor eating pizza, watching Miami Vice or WWF wrestling, and having full conversations with their two Golden Retrievers.) Dad's marriage, on the other hand, was different. Since my sister moved out on her own into a rundown apartment on the bad side of town and supported herself—starved herself—through her final year of high school, I was trapped as the only stepchild and resident second-class citizen in the stepmother takeover of my home.

In a blink of an eye, I went from being left completely alone in a house and having almost no supervision while my dad commuted to and from Denver for work every day, to having a stranger of a woman come in and start making rules and putting her hands in my discipline. I went from grabbing laundry out of the dryer whenever I needed it, to folding towels at the kitchen table, only for my dad to unfold them, throw them back at me, and tell me to do it Betty Lou's way. In other words, the dad who used to think so highly of me that he let me fend for myself most of the time, began nitpicking me for folding towels the wrong way. My life was under attack and my dad was sleeping with the enemy.

Ultimately, no matter what this lady did to convince me she was as sweet and innocent as her Texas accent made her seem, there was no selling me. Life as I knew it was completely altered in the blink of an eye. Now I had rules. Now I had a strict routine. Now I had to have my time organized for me, my room decorated for me, a bedtime that was earlier than when I was five years old, a one-bath-towel-per-week rule, a homework before TV or videogames rule, a wake up an hour early and wash and dry your sheets first thing every morning rule, a don't enter the master bedroom rule, a don't touch the garage rule, a don't do anything without asking first rule. And that was just the beginning.

I really tried my best to coexist, fit in, and make things work with a family that, my experience showed, probably wouldn't last. But the divide between Betty Lou and me progressively widened. I noticed everything that made me an "other" in our household. Betty Lou's kids got name brand everything. I got generic Cheerios, which wouldn't have even occurred to me in my past life of eating whatever I could find in the cupboards as a matter of survival. But the difference became glaringly amplified against the contrast of spoiled step siblings. Betty Lou's kids got a playful nudge to clean their rooms or do their homework. I got Dad breathing down my neck the second Betty Lou complained. Betty Lou's kids could talk back to their mom in the most disrespectful way that would have gotten me whipped with my dad's belt. I got reprimanded for saying the word "fart." Betty Lou's kids got sack lunches with Cheetos and Little Debbie cakes. I got stuck on the school's hot lunch line. Betty Lou's son got a round of chuckles when he told a racist joke where the punchline involved saying the n-word three times. I got snapped at and sent to my room when I said with a purposeful attitude, "I don't think that's funny at all." Betty Lou bought her daughter an expensive show dog for her ninth birthday. On that same year on my thirteen birthday, when I came home thrilled about a brand new mountain bike my mom bought me from Walmart, I was told to put the bike in the garage and sit at the kitchen table so I could get yelled at by a furious stepmother for "stealing" her Paul Mitchell hairspray when, in fact, I did not.

You name it, I got blamed for it. For example, almost killing plants I was supposed to (and did) spray with water several times per day while the parents were away.

"You didn't water them on purpose!" she said.

*Listen, lady. I've killed a cactus before. I did what you said to do. I told you I had a grim reaper of a green thumb.* "Sorry," I said while Dad's eyes threatened me with punishment.

Betty Lou's mood swings, menstrual cramps, and migraines, which often forced her to stay in bed for full days at a time, were also my fault (because of whatever it was that week that was my fault). But probably the worst of all, one morning as I dutifully ate my bowl of generic Cheerios before school, she yelled at me for allegedly peeing on a pillow my little stepsister put inside of her puppy's kennel.

"Jennifer. You are NOT to use Heather's pillows," she snarled.

*What are you talking about!?* I couldn't speak out loud.

"Sorry," Betty Lou finally mumbled in a snotty voice when her daughter swore on her life the show dog did it.

*Flip off, you mean horrible person. How could you even say that? You terrible horrible awful person.* I exploded inside in the only way a raging teenager who was absolutely prohibited by my dad from swearing could while staying completely silent on the outside with tears in my eyes.

"She said sorry, Jennifer. What do you say?" Dad warned me.

*Flip off you flipping witch.* "OK," I forced myself to say, fuming that now my nine-year-old stepsister might find out that the reason her mom thought I peed on the pillow is because, at thirteen years old, I still had a bedwetting problem that my parents still hadn't attempted to fix and that made my life an absolute living hell; no less, with a new stepmother who had zero compassion and was now going as far as to rub it in my face in front of everyone during breakfast. *I hate her.*

Maybe it was a horoscope thing, a low blood sugar thing, a teenage hormone thing, or just a consistently crappy stepmom thing, but once Betty Lou betrayed me in all of those ways, there was no winning me back. My memory was long and my grudges were permanent. By the time I was fourteen, that woman became my number one enemy, besting even my mother's kid-hating husband, and I promised myself I would never get caught slipping with a tear in my eye or a quiet mouth again.

Now, you would think that a girl who was under constant scrutiny wouldn't dare do anything certifiably wrong, but at one point I felt like I had absolutely nothing to lose. I couldn't count the number of times my phone privileges had been taken away, how many times I was grounded from friends, how many times I was lectured, yelled at, shamed, or how many times I was given the silent treatment or outright screamed at for relative nonissues. Even when I got a paper route delivering *The Coloradoan* with my Walmart mountain bike every morning before junior high school so I could buy my own things instead of burdening the family budget, there was no praise to be had. So when a week before my fifteenth birthday, Dad and Betty Lou decided I was old enough to stay home by myself for the weekend while everyone else went away, I instantly put into motion a sleepover with three of my closest girlfriends.

My friends' parents had no reason to believe that their daughters would be unsupervised that night since all of them heard about how penitentiary-like my household was. As the girls got dropped off one by one, and as the sun started to set, we started doing what fourteen-year-olds do best: call boys. Within the hour, we had two cars-full of boys at our house, including one who promised to bring beer but showed up empty handed. It wasn't long before that beer-less boy found Betty Lou's liquor cabinet, pulled out a near-full bottle of vodka, and made a deal with me to replace it by morning. In the meantime, a popular football player was putting the moves on me in my bedroom, which was purposely spotless for company. Before I knew it, I was losing my virginity on my day bed while my drunk friends popped in and out of my bedroom door laughing.

I wasn't prepared for sex. All I knew was that I was one of a few girls, out of all of our friends, who had yet to have it. I set out to "do it" that night because I thought, at nearly fifteen, I was way behind. I hadn't even started my period yet I was so behind. So if it was sex this football player wanted, it was sex he would get. The absolutely most painful, awkward, slow, half-drunken (on his part), anticlimactic (on my part), pitiful, waste of virginity. A one-night stand that had zero significance to me other than the fact that I was no longer Miss Goody Two Shoes.

My parents never told me about sex. Never told me to save myself for my husband. Never told me what a sin was, how I go about committing one, or how I go about recovering from one. Never told me about love or commitment or following the steps of finishing school, going to college, getting a good job, and starting a family with the most sensational person I could find. At one point in my life, I had the good example of my parents. I also had the example of my best friend's family, the Leethams. But examples, without some sort of discussion about the difference between a committed and faithful family, and multiple girlfriends coming in and out of one's life (read: my dad's life), are somewhat useless. It was only after I lost my virginity (thankfully, with the use of a condom because I was a mega-fan of the R&B group, TLC, who promoted safe sex), that I realized I had done something that should have been way more meaningful. I figured out on my own that the feeling I had after that night was not happy or excited, but regretful. I told myself I would never make that mistake again.

After everyone went home, I was left with a disaster of a house to get back to perfect cleanliness by the time my dad and stepmother arrived. I worked tirelessly for hours until everything was cleaned to my satisfaction before realizing one, major, problem. That boy who said he would replace Betty Lou's vodka bottle, lied. There it was on the kitchen counter, nearly empty. I called the boy only for him to tell me there was no way he could get alcohol of any kind and sorry that he lied. Out of desperation, I filled the rest of the bottle up with cold water, gingerly placed it in the liquor cabinet facing the same direction as the rest of the bottles, and prayed that tactic would buy me enough time to figure out how to find someone old enough to buy a bottle to replace it.

The family came home and the usual routine ensued until a few days later when my dad came up to my room.

"Jennifer? Did you have a party with boys while we were gone?" Dad questioned calmly.

*Take everything to your grave, Jenn.* "No."

"Are you sure about that?"

"Yes."

"I'm only going to ask one more time. Did you have a party with boys?"

"I had a sleepover with Jenny, Jessica, and Nicole."

"And that's it?"

"Yes."

"Are you sure about that?"

"Yes."

"Betty Lou found a condom in your little sister's wastebasket."

*Son of a biscuit! Fast on your feet, Jenn.* "It was a joke. We were playing jokes on each other, like freezing each other's bra. That was a joke. I'm sorry, Dad, that I had my friends spend the night."

*Prepare for hell fire.*

"I'm disappointed in you but I'm just glad you didn't have boys over. I'll talk to Betty Lou."

I couldn't believe it. Did I just get away with murder? And who had sex in my stepsister's bedroom? Who would I kill when I got to school on Monday? But more importantly, did I just escape certain death? No yelling. No humiliation. No chasing me down the street. Just a calm, collected, dad. Was I dreaming? Was something going to blow up in a few days instead? Maybe Betty Lou was so satisfied with proving to my father what a bad kid I was that I didn't even get punished. I didn't know but I stayed on my very best behavior for at least two weeks, completely forgetting about the Vodka I had yet to replace.

Dad and Betty Lou invited Jack and Jill (yes, the gentle Jillian who didn't make Dad's cut and her new, perfectly named husband) over to visit. Jillian was such an angel, I abandoned my teenage attitude and came down to say, "Hello." Betty Lou escorted everyone to the patio and then returned to the kitchen to prepare drinks. As I walked up the stairs, I heard the liquor cabinet rattle and I stopped in my tracks. I saw Betty Lou pull out the vodka bottle filled with water, take a look at it with satisfaction, and walk over to the kitchen. I spied while she combined cranberry juice, water from the vodka bottle, and ice into four glasses, which she served the guests. I panicked and locked myself in my room. I waited. And waited. And waited. I was sure my dad would boom through my door with a belt with my name on it. Instead, there was silence. Not one peep. Not one hint of anger from anyone. Maybe the universe thought I deserved a break. Maybe there was just enough vodka left to make all of that water kind of taste like vodka, too. To this day, I don't know the science, or the luck, or the merciful parents behind it. All I know is that I never heard a peep about the vodka. And getting away with a party that would have gotten any one of my other friends grounded for a year, gave me confidence. From then on, when the adults spoke sideways to me, I talked back.

# CHAPTER 7
# Quartet

NOW THAT I WAS TALKING BACK, FIGHTS escalated from one-way parent-to-child rants, to me throwing a punch at Betty Lou after she and my dad burst into my room while I was sleeping to yell at me about something. During that process, she accidentally hurt Pepper, who was sleeping with me and gave out a big yelp. And in my half-asleep stupor, I accidentally almost knocked Betty Lou's front teeth out, except that my punch completely missed her face and only caught air. That fun wakeup alarm was followed by me feverishly trying to call my mom, my dad ripping the phone cord out of the wall, me racing down the stairs and out the back door to the snow-covered yard, hiding under a bush in my Bart Simpson nightgown, panties, and bare feet, and watching while Dad scanned the snow for me. He gave up rather quickly and, instead of going back inside for certain punishment, I found his van unlocked and crawled into the back seat, where I slept with one eye open under a blanket Dad used as a seat cover. Once I started to see daylight, I tried to sneak back into the house before everyone's alarms went off, only for my dad to catch me and tell me to get dressed and he would drive me to school. I was blown away when he used the drive to apologize for Betty Lou's behavior. Even so, he let me know I would still be grounded because he was stuck in the middle and had no choice in the matter. That day, I went to school without so much as running a brush through my hair. It was the type of arrival at school that you have nightmares about.

After what would have been the knock-out of my life, which I would have held close to my heart until I could tell my grandbabies how I put that wicked stepmom to sleep with a single punch, something happened that I had been waiting years for: I started my period. Waiting longer than all of my friends to finally unlock the mystery of becoming a certifiable woman was a mindboggling challenge. So when I went to the bathroom one day and saw pink spots on my white underwear, I was ecstatic. I was proud. I was finally not so different from all of my friends. I was . . . without feminine products.

Without a mom at home to celebrate with, I went downstairs and swallowed my pride in the way only children can, announced to Betty Lou that I started my period, and asked if she had a pad I could have. I thought she would be excited, or give me a talk, or walk me through my different product options, or give me a secret handshake, or buy me a cake or something. But what I got was a single pad followed by a lecture and a ride to Walmart when my dad got home.

"Don't ask Betty Lou for anything ever again," Dad scolded. "If you need something personal, it is your responsibility to get it or tell me and I will get it for you."

So much for a period party.

Thanks to my mom's diligence over the years in taking me to The Colorado Academy of the Arts like clockwork every week, I had something in life that made me feel normal—even good— about myself. There, I was treated just like everyone else. I easily earned solos, reaped constant praise, was generally liked by the rest of the girls (notwithstanding normal spats between hormonal preteens), and was not required to sleep over at anyone's home so I could pretend I was as normal as everyone else. So when the academy, my safe place, became dysfunctional, I felt it tenfold.

I don't know exactly what happened but I could feel conflict in the air. The academy changed hands to the tune of my beloved director, Gay, leaving and being replaced by a woman named Elaine. Elaine's daughter, Shey, was a mega-talented performer with a singing voice at eleven years old that could already compete with adults on Broadway. I felt that, if I could refine myself to sing and perform as well as Shey did, I might have a shot at becoming a star one day. In fact, that's exactly what Shey did. She joined a girl group called Pretty in Pink with Chaka Khan's daughter and landed herself on the Arsenio Hall Show at the height of its popularity. She was living the life I imagined in my head for myself. Shey's success became a subconscious benchmark I measured myself by.

Following Gay's departure from The Colorado Academy of the Arts, she called my mom and asked if I was interested in leaving the academy to join a quartet with her daughter and two other girls who didn't have the coveted academy credential. Leaving the group I had been singing with for nearly a decade was incredibly frightening to me. The company had already churned out one star and I was dead-set on becoming the next. Leaving would mean immediately losing the prestige that I thought being an "Academy Kid" earned me. I figured I could forget about ever doing anything as big as singing at a Governor's Ball, or appearing on the local kids' morning TV show with Blinky the Clown, or on KS104 radio station, or at the Special Olympics in Colorado Springs, or touring schools telling kids to "Just say no to drugs!" like I did with the academy.

Staying with the academy was my inclination. Singing was my safe place. Singing earned me praise from adults and peers and a smidgen of self-esteem. Singing was my connection with my mom. She picked me up for practice at least once, twice, thrice, or in my professional days, five or six times per week, stayed up whole nights sewing costumes, carpooled myself and classmates to practice, attended shows and auditions, and showboated me in front of the ladies at the nail salon, where I dutifully sang and danced. By leaving the academy, I would waste everything my mom and I had invested together—time, money, practice, and a few tears on my part—just to start over at what I considered to be square one. But because I was the ultimate "other;" because I hated bullies; because I had a sneaky suspicion that my favorite director was booted by a big shot; and because I thought Elaine, a cutthroat stage mom and person I liked about as much as Betty Lou, would be my new "boss," I chose to go with the underdogs.

Singing was a liberating escape from real life but always short-lived. Home life was seriously stressing me out. Any time I heard the slightest noise on the staircase leading to my room, my body stiffened and adrenaline rushed because I expected to be yelled at and punished for some wrongdoing. At one point, I thought I was getting stomach ulcers because of the way Dad's house made my organs turn. I laid in bed at night imagining black holes widening inside of my pink stomach until my guts spilled out of my belly onto the floor. And when I wasn't stressed out about Dad and Betty Lou, I was stressed out about my social life.

I kept a small circle of girlfriends who stuck by me despite my sporadic bedwetting problem, which they mercifully refrained from exposing to the world. And even though sleepover invitations made me dreadfully anxious, the certain adventure of an overnight with my group of besties was worth the internal torment I experienced silently. The only problem was, by fifteen, we began to get ourselves into constant trouble. From stuffing ourselves into a tiny hatchback with boys who veered recklessly off of the road and down a snow-blanketed ditch to avoid a head-on collision, to getting sprayed with glass shards when a liquor bottle shattered the back window of Jenny's mom's car when a fight broke out between boys in Steph's front yard, to me starting my first committed relationship with a local boy named Kurt, I was up to no good.

Naturally, every time Dad caught wind of my various misdeeds, I was punished. And every time Mom inquired why I was punished "this time," I swayed her to my side. Eventually, after talking to my mom like a best friend every time she picked me up for singing practice, she heard enough and drew a line. Alas, around sixteen years old, I finally got what I had wanted deep down in my heart since my parents' divorce: to live with my mom.

# CHAPTER 8

# Firefighters in My Bedroom

WHEN I MOVED IN WITH MOM, MY STEPDAD, Ricco, still kept his distance but didn't show obvious signs of actually hating me. In fact, Mom's house was a breath of fresh air. I was the only child since all of the older girls were long gone. It was quiet. I didn't have formal chores. I didn't have my homework checked every night. I didn't have a formal bedtime. I didn't get sick to my stomach when I heard adults come or go. I got to bring my lifelong companion, Pepper the poodle, with me. Moreover, Ricco had a senior Golden Retriever named Whiskey, and Mom had a puppy Golden Retriever named Sunny and a rescued cat named Felix. This small pack of animals ended up serving as highly therapeutic family members who were always happy to see me.

I stayed out of trouble at Mom's house because we were nestled at the top of Horsetooth mountain and I was completely reliant on her providing for me in every way. On weekday mornings, I would ride shotgun in Mom's black Monte Carlo with tinted windows and rich, burgundy interior, for the thirty-minute decent to Rocky Mountain High School. On the way to school, Mom would listen to cassette tapes of Zig Ziglar (a motivational speaker) and I developed the habit of making fun of Zig until Mom could barely drive she was laughing so hard.

"You can do it, Carol! You can do anything you set your mind to!" I mocked in my best Zig voice.

When we weren't listening to Zig, we were listening to Whitney Houston or Mariah Carey on the radio and singing along.

"I love hearing you sing," Mom would say, which was awkward and made me immediately *stop* singing.

Often times, Mom would talk about her adult problems and I would do everything in my power to try to come up with solutions. Even though I was still an ornery, world-hating sixteen-year-old, living at Mom's house went rather smoothly until I got more serious with my boyfriend.

At sixteen, Kurt was trying to fast-forward our relationship to adult level. We spent every spare minute together—lunch breaks at school, hours of phone calls at night, and eventually round-trip drives from Mom's mountain home to our high school in place of my mom driving me. When Ricco, a former police officer from Rochester, New York, noticed how immersed I was in a teenage relationship, he got curious and he got sneaky. He tapped the phones at our house and started recording my conversations with Kurt, which were laden with sex talk. Ricco then turned the tapes over to my mom, who was stunned that her sixteen-year-old was sexually active. Soon, I was addressed by an angry mom who was both furious at her husband for recording my calls and extremely disappointed and concerned about my extremely serious relationship. Like a mob boss, my mom gave me the directive to end it with Kurt.

Without a boyfriend, I refocused on friends, singing, and my job as goalie on the junior varsity soccer team at Rocky Mountain High School. One Friday game night, I was playing for the first time in six weeks after splitting my finger in half like firewood in a previous game. This night, we had a game with a team from Cherry Creek, a well-to-do town in Denver where the girls were as tall as their parents' bank accounts. All eyes were on me when I took the risk of coming all of the way out of the goal to go one-on-one with a giant forward who was about to score on us, the way Coach taught me. I fell to the ground to grab the ball from my opponent's capable shoe tips and she was forced to jump over me instead of making a perfect shot on goal. The team screamed with delight and swarmed around me as if I had just saved a penalty shot in the World Cup. That moment gave me the greatest high but, in my excitement, I missed one, two, three, four subsequent shots on goal that ended in an embarrassing loss for our team. After the game, Mom treated me to Taco Bell and drove us home. I took my routine evening insulin shot and went straight to bed because I had a babysitting job I had to wake up for at four o'clock in the morning. Dad, who I got on good terms with when I didn't have to live with him, arranged for me to babysit for a friend-of-a-friend who was down on her luck and I agreed to the good deed.

The next morning, when Mom heard my alarm go off but no sluggish footsteps to the shower, she got up and hollered down the stairs for me to wake up, not unlike what she normally did on school days. When she got no response, she came down to my room. Still, no response. She turned on my light and came to shake me to wake me up when she realized I was stone cold and wet with perspiration. She panicked and started yelling to get me up. She opened my eyelids only to find my eyes rolled to the back of my head. She thought I was dead and started screaming. Ricco woke up as my mom called 9-1-1, screaming and crying, trying to wake me up to no avail. The dispatcher on the line told my mom she needed to calm down or she could risk making me go into cardiac arrest. As the clock ticked, volunteer firefighters assembled from their respective mountain homes and inched their way up the steep and narrow dirt road that led to my mom's house on the mountaintop. However, there was nothing they could do until the ambulance from the city arrived. I was in full-blown insulin shock. My blood sugar was as low as it could go before a heart attack was my body's natural reaction. The only thing that could save me was a Glucagon shot, which would force my body to release sugar stored in my liver to rapidly raise my blood sugar.

The ambulance finally arrived, a tech quickly assessed me and injected me with Glucagon. I woke up sweaty and shivering to a blurred vision of firefighters surrounding my waterbed and a lady in a dark blue uniform telling my mom I was coming to. I laid quietly with a numb tongue and confused brain, thinking for a moment that I was having the best dream of firefighters coming to surprise me and tell me what an awesome goalie I was or something. Instead, when I was finally fully awake, they wagged a finger at me after examining my make-shift Tupperware box of scattered needles and insulin vials with no test strips to be found. My diabetes kit was the equivalent of a teenager's messy room.

My mom and stepdad thanked the first responders for their efforts and, with tears in her eyes, Mom told me to never scare her like that again. That event, the closest I had come to death since my diabetes diagnosis, scared me straight. Going forward, I started checking my blood sugar at night without fail.

After that scary bout with low blood sugar, an unrelated miracle happened: my dad bought me a truck. I had carried a learner's permit for quite some time but didn't get my license at sixteen like most kids in town did because Ricco didn't think I was responsible enough for the privilege. But Dad had the final say. Before I knew it, I was driving a rather beautiful 1984 Ford Ranger with white and green two-tone paint, two sets of top-of-the-line rims, and a stick shift that I picked up seamlessly given all of the training Dad gave me as a little kid. Soon, I got my license and way more freedom without having to rely on others to get me off of the mountain.

When home life was the best it had been for as long as I could remember, school became the problem. My group of girlfriends developed a tiff with another group of girls and a fistfight became imminent. One day after school, our enemies caught Steph alone in the light blue, antique Karmann Ghia that was passed down from her mom. Steph, our clique's resident responsible kid and salt of the earth (save the one day when she came to school hilariously drunk for kicks, yet still aced a test), attempted to avoid any fighting. But one of the girls opened Steph's car door while she was in reverse, reached in, and sucker-punched Steph in the face.

Since I rarely mentioned my diabetes to anyone, most acquaintances would have never known that under my tough exterior was a rather medically fragile kid. But diabetes or not, no one was going to get away with hurting one of my loyal friends. I felt like it was my duty to retaliate. Accordingly, I orchestrated a roadblock at Taco Bell—the local hangout on Friday nights. I waited with twenty other girls to catch the sucker-puncher. And when a truckload of the sucker-puncher's friends showed up without the girl responsible for my bestie's black eye, I quickly selected one of our enemies to make an example out of. I rushed up to a girl within reach who sat like a duck in the bed of our enemies' truck. Without warning, I punched the girl so hard in the face, her head ricocheted off of the back window of the truck's cab and my hand broke on the spot.

When I explained to my mom the next day that I hurt myself and probably needed to see a doctor, she fumed. It was one thing to provide necessary health care for me. It was another thing to spend a fortune on a frivolously fighting kid. Mom took me for x-rays, which were sent away for review by a radiologist, and grounded me for the rest of the weekend, which meant I would miss out on going out with friends on Saturday night. But I went out anyway knowing there would be hell to pay. And once that bad decision was already made and I realized the magnitude of what I had done, I got scared and I decided to run away from home.

# CHAPTER 9
# Drag Race

KRISTINA MARTINEZ WAS A STRAIGHT SHOOTER with confidence, clear opinions, and no problem telling them to you. She was the type of girl I wanted to be more like. So if she wanted to be my friend, I wanted to be hers, too. This particular night, I needed an accomplice to pull off my reckless decision of running away from a decent home just because I didn't get my way. So I partied with Kristina the rest of the weekend and ditched school on Monday until word got to me through my friends' parents that my x-ray results were in and my hand was, in fact, broken. I needed a cast and I needed to come home.

Unlike Dad's house where Betty Lou called the shots, Mom dealt with me without Ricco in tow. She took me to get a cast placed on my arm and I got grounded for a few weeks. But after that, I continued to get myself into trouble to the tune of drinking a wine cooler for the first time, getting into another fight and beating a girl up with my cast, and getting stopped by police and receiving a citation. When I reported yet another poor decision back to Mom, she was livid and at a loss for what to do with me. She gave me a stern talking to and instructed me to keep the classes and fine the judge slapped me with to ourselves, save she had to face a husband who would certainly kick me out. And after causing Mom so much heartache and cash, I was going to have to pay her back. She directed me to get a job and get back on the straight and narrow.

I landed a job at Dunkin' Donuts in town but got fired a month or so after. After that, I straightened up enough to be hired for Steph's old filing job at a car dealership when Step got a better job for herself at the local bowling alley. There, I felt the pressure of following in the footsteps of a really good kid with a stellar work ethic. I made sure I didn't give Steph a bad name. I worked diligently, painstakingly filing masses of car service invoices until I was promoted to a receptionist position.

The summer of eleventh grade came and went and it was time to prepare for my senior year of high school. Dad spoiled me with two hundred dollars for school clothes and I arranged for my mom to drive Steph and me to Denver to buy the baggy jeans and skintight bodysuits that were popular in 1993. Hip-hop and R&B filled the radio airwaves in our town and it was through music where most of us gained our first exposure to African Americans. Our town was so white, one would probably have a better chance of seeing a ghost than seeing an African American in-person. But that didn't stop the majority of the kids in town from appropriating African American culture in the form of music, dance, clothes, and street vernacular. We swarmed to everything from hardcore rappers like NWA and Eazy-E, to commercial rappers like MC Hammer, and R&B groups like Boyz II Men and the plethora of African American artists who consistently dominated Top 40 radio charts.

When Mom refused to go shopping with Steph and me (so long as I insisted on dressing in jean shorts paired with black boots) I decided to drive the hour and a half to Denver myself. Steph and I reached Denver all right but after exiting a drive-through after grabbing lunch, a car t-boned my truck when another driver signaled for me to go ahead as if the coast was clear. Wrecked, my truck was towed away and Steph and I, uninjured, received a consolatory ride home from her dad, who lived in Denver and met us at the accident scene.

When I got back to Mom's house, I explained what happened and before I could elaborate, Ricco said, "Don't you dare blame this on anyone but you."

And while I knew he was right, I still resented him for saying it. Having just turned seventeen, I was certain I knew better than everyone else.

After the wreck, my dad bent over backwards to fix everything. He rented a dolly twice to retrieve my truck. (The first time a chop shop had the truck taken apart because they wanted to buy it from us without so much as consulting anyone.) He interacted with the insurance company to get the money to fix it. He even agreed to my idea of buying a temporary car with the insurance money while my truck got fixed, and then selling the temporary car and paying for the work on the truck. My dad was so helpful and understanding, I half wondered why I ever left his house in the first place. And since it was looking like I would be grounded for life at Mom's house after proving Ricco right about being too irresponsible to drive, I asked Dad if I could move back in and he said yes.

The first few weeks back at Dad's were fine. Betty Lou and I had such a long breather that we almost forgot how much we hated each other. More than that, I had the distraction of a new boyfriend whom I was head-over-heels in love with.

Cruising College one night, my girlfriends and I met a group of Airmen from the Air Force base an hour away in Cheyenne, Wyoming. The group of nineteen-year-old young men consisted of a short, thin brown boy named Felipe; a tall, stalky African American boy named Mickey; and a short white boy named Justin. The boys were perched against a glossy black 1988 Mustang 5.0 that boomed the bassline of the hottest song out at the time: Tag Team's "Whoomp (There it is)." My best friends and I drove by once, checking the boys out. Then twice, hooting and hollering at them. Then, on the third time, we worked up enough nerve to stop and flirt in-person. We were so used to seeing the same old faces in our town, this new and exotic group of young men was highly interesting to us. We convinced the boys to follow us to Steph's house to hang out. Once there, the short, thin one looked antsy.

"You OK? I asked.

"Me? Yeah, I'm good," Felipe assured.

"You look terrified," I replied.

"You could say that," He paused. "Hey, anyone hungry? I'm hungry," Felipe announced to the room. No one replied but, intrigued by the boy's nervousness, I volunteered to go with him to grab some food. Once in the car, he spilled the beans.

"Thanks for saving me," Felipe said as if we were old fishing buddies.

"Saving you?" I was confused.

"One of your friends in there was eyeing me. Not for nothing, but she's not my type," he confessed.

"Not for *anything*, but you're not *her* type," I laughed. "Let's see. For one, you're short. Second, you don't have blue eyes. You do have perfect teeth, though. Did you wear braces?"

"No," Felipe grew increasingly uncomfortable.

"Anyway, she likes white boys. And you're from...India... right?" I took a wild guess.

"India?" he laughed. "I'm Puerto Rican. Born and raised in New York City."

"What's Puerto Rican?" I was clueless.

"Puerto Rico? The U.S. territory in the Caribbean?" he sang as if trying to jog my memory.

"Never heard of it," I admitted. "So you're Caribbean?"

"No. I'm Spanish," he looked at me, shocked.

"So, what *is* your type?" curiosity killed me.

"Open that glove box there," Felipe instructed.

I opened the glove box on the passenger side of Felipe's immaculately kept Mustang to find a single photo of a beautiful Spanish girl with caramel skin, a tight white dress, and a short black hairstyle a la Halle Berry, posing in someone's living room.

"That's my type," he reconfirmed.

"Ah! You have a girlfriend! No wonder you're so nervous," I solved the mystery.

"*Had* a girlfriend," he corrected me. "I followed her to Florida and then she dumped me. After that, I joined the Air Force," he cut to the chase.

We sat in awkward silence for a moment as I returned the photo to the glove compartment and we arrived at a drive-through where Felipe ordered. As we sat in his idling Mustang, I became fixated on the running engine.

"Your timing's slightly off," I blurted.

"Timing? Uh, look, Jenn. It's Jenn, right? You seem like a nice girl but I'm not looking for a relationship," he apologized.

"I'm talking about your car engine," I laughed at him.

"What do you know about cars?" Felipe challenged me.

"I know I could show you a thing or two about what this car can do," I replied without blinking.

"Oh, really?" he raised his eyebrows.

"Really," I said flatly.

After Felipe collected his fast food, he pulled out of the drive-through, parked the Mustang, and told me to switch seats. He was calling my bluff, fully believing I would sooner stall the car before getting it to move. I hopped in the driver's seat, carefully pulled onto College Avenue while I got used to the car's stick shift, and headed downtown to find someone to race with. But someone found us first. A kid I recognized from the previous year's senior class pulled up next to us at a stoplight in his dad's beefed up Chevelle and revved his engine, signaling a drag race. I nodded and revved Felipe's Mustang to the redline with the clutch pressed down like my mom used to do when she drag-raced her Corvette at Colorado National Speedway. I knew that, if I let off the clutch too quickly at the green light without enough gas, I'd either stall the car or take too much time getting up to speed.

The stoplight turned green, the tires of both cars screeched, and a race ensued. I bobbled slightly on my launch but quickly corrected, quick-shifting and overtaking the Chevelle by several car lengths, easily winning before pulling over and handing the driver's seat back over to Felipe.

"Well, alrighty then," Felipe joked before we both burst out laughing.

Felipe and I drove back to Steph's house and all he could talk about was the race. He had never seen a girl drive a car like that. And before the group of boys left for the night, Felipe made it a point to ask if he could see me again.

# CHAPTER 10
# Middle Fingers Up

THE NEXT WEEKEND, THE GIRLS AND I MET UP WITH Felipe and friends again, ate dinner at IHOP, and then split up into couples and drove up to a lookout area at Horsetooth mountain not too far from my mom's house. In contrast to the confrontational boy from the week before, Felipe wanted to know everything possible about me. We spent hours chatting and I told him a sugar-coated version of my childhood and how I planned on becoming a famous singer one day. As I finished reciting my impromptu autobiography, he started looking at me with a love-drunk gaze that warned he was going to go in for a kiss, which he did.

Felipe kissed me passionately like nothing I had experienced before, framing my face softly with his hands and whimpering as if we were making love. The heated car cabin had the soft scent of leather seats accented by men's cologne, while a mixtape of reggae songs I had never heard before played quietly in the background. The windows began to fog and Felipe's foot pressed down on the gas pedal, making the engine roar and jolting us out of a kiss from fear we would accidentally drive off the cliff. Once Felipe double-checked that the car was in neutral and the emergency brake was on, he pulled me back in and we kissed passionately again as if time and the world around us were obsolete.

It grew late and the friends in the cars next to us honked and laughed at us, signaling it was time to go home. Felipe and I ripped ourselves apart and bid each other farewell until the following weekend, promising to call each other during the week.

Long-distance phone calls weren't included with home phone plans in those days and ran anywhere from ten to twenty-five cents per minute. Felipe, who was operating on a fresh-out-of-boot-camp airman budget, had to be mindful of minutes when he called me. I, on the other hand, spoke freely when I called Felipe from Dad's home phone, not considering the cost. After a month of phone calls, Dad brought a several hundred dollar phone bill up to my bedroom to show me what I had done. However, instead of punishing me, he simply instructed, "No more long-distance phone calls."

Some days later, I heard Betty Lou yelling downstairs. She reached her breaking point and Dad beckoned me to a sit-down in the living room. After several years of going through a cycle of constant wrongdoing or accusations of such on my part, hell-raising on Betty Lou's part, and punishment on my father's part, we were all drained. I, too, had reached my limit.

Adrenaline flooded my veins the moment my foot touched the staircase for the decent to certain destruction. As soon as Betty Lou started speaking to me in a condescending voice I already knew I was going to send her to hell. She started yelling at me for wearing her beautiful angora sweater, ruining it by balling it up and throwing it in my hamper. Before she could say any more, I stood up and told her to shove her sweater straight up her ass. Stunned, my dad slapped me across the face with a knee-jerk reflex and I flew out the door and started to run.

Without stopping to grab the keys to my truck, which would reliably be held for ransom, I ran a mile to a gas station and used a payphone to call my mom collect to ask for help. However, since I had already burned my bridges at her house, she had no choice but to put her foot down: I wasn't allowed back. I talked her into driving down from the mountain to at least take me to the police department so I could report my dad for slapping me.

After an hour or so, my mom's sleek Monte Carlo pulled up and rescued me for a moment in time. Mom drove me back to my dad's house so I could retrieve my messy Tupperware box full of needles and insulin. Inside, my dad sat calmly at a desk he built inside of a closet in the kitchen and allowed me to have the last word without contest.

"You're never gonna see me again!" I promised.

When I returned to Mom's car and we started driving away, we encountered Betty Lou who was apparently out taking a brisk walk to calm herself down. Without a peep out of my mouth, Mom instinctively rolled down her window and started yelling at Betty Lou. With that, Betty Lou turned around and gave my mom the finger.

When Betty Lou's middle finger went up, it might as well have been in slow motion with accompanying fireworks, a marching band, and a choir singing "F. YOU." Mom reciprocated with her towering middle finger, crowned with a fiery red acrylic nail, and continued to talk smack out of her window as she drove away. We made the forty-minute trip from deep South College Avenue to the far north end, where Mom delivered me to the doorstep of the police station in the darkness. And with the toughest love she had ever exercised, she reluctantly drove away.

I rang the bell of the station door and a police officer arrived and took me inside. I explained how I got slapped across the face and the officer called my Dad for his side of the story. When the officer hung up, he explained to me that, if his child talked to him the way I talked to my dad, he would have done the exact same thing—I deserved it. I was then led to the front door without further comment. The adults were all on the same page: let the girl learn the hard way.

I walked to City Park and found a bench to lay on like homeless people do in the movies before telling myself how ridiculous and pathetic I was and getting up to start walking again. I found a payphone and made a collect call to my sweetheart at the Air Force base, begging him to come rescue me and smuggle me on the base overnight while I figured out what to do. Once on base, I laid awake until the sun rose and called my sister. I told her I was going to leave home for good like she did, except that I intended on dropping out of high school so I could work fulltime at the car dealership. Cindy stopped me in my tracks and told me she didn't care what I did except one thing:

"Do NOT drop out of high school. Whatever it takes, graduate. It's the best thing you can do for yourself," she said.

Felipe had to report to duty that afternoon so drove me back to Fort Collins before his shift. Since I was too proud and stubborn to beg for more mercy from either of my parents ever again, I got my hands on a newspaper and looked through classified listings for a place I could afford with my part-time car dealership job. I quickly found a room in an old house with two other girls near the Colorado State University campus for two hundred and ten dollars per month. The girl who was subletting the room needed to move out as badly as I needed to move in so agreed to prorate the rent and only charge me two hundred and fifty dollars—most of which served as a deposit—to move in a week before rent would be due again. The only people I knew with two hundred and fifty dollars cash at their disposal were Grandma and Grandpa Cooper. I knew their phone number by heart and gave them a call. They were disappointed, skeptical, and not happy about my decision to become homeless. But after consulting with my mom, they decided to drive down to Fort Collins and put their money on me to stay in school, keep working, and graduate at the end of the year. I signed the sublet contract, conveniently failing to mention I was only seventeen years old. But the deal went through and, with the stroke of a pen, I was free.

# CHAPTER 11

# Rent

O N MY FIRST NIGHT ALONE IN MY RICKETY OLD box of a bedroom with dingy, stained carpet and the same smell that gags you when you walk into a Good Will store, I was struck like a baby after birth when I realized I was completely on my own. No truck, no bed, or blankets, or clothes, or stereo, or computer, or food in the fridge, or plates to eat off of, or any conveniences of any kind. All I had was my backpack full of homework, my Tupperware box of needles and a vial of insulin, and the clothes on my back. A more logical way to approach one's first move-out would be to prepare and plan. My life from the day I stepped foot in the same room that was probably met with excitement and liberation by the college junior who grew up and out of it, was a big slice of humble pie. I thought I had it all figured out. I thought I was smarter than everyone. Then that room showed me that anything I needed or wanted from then forward I would have to provide myself.

I didn't cry. I refused to cry. It was my personal mantra to never cry. So I took out my homework and sat on the filthy carpet floor and completed my assignments. The scare from nearly dying from low blood sugar at Mom's house the year before wore off the same way going to a doctor who tells you to lose weight before you have a heart attack does. Test strips were expensive and I didn't even have fifty-nine cents for a bean burrito from Taco Bell the next day, much less thirty or forty dollars per week for test strips. I learned to start detecting my blood sugar by how dry my mouth was (or wasn't), how hot or cold I felt, if I was shaky or stable, if there was perspiration on my forehead or not, and if I had eaten a meal with the shot I took. When in doubt,

I skipped shots at night. I knew that, when it came to surviving overnight, it's better for blood sugar to be too high, than too low.

I stayed afloat that first week on my own through a combination of eating my roommates' food; using my roommates' shampoo, conditioner, and deodorant; calling my boyfriend in another state on the house phone when the roommates weren't home; and wearing loaner clothes and hitching rides to school from besties. Then, I successfully plotted and executed a break-in to Dad's house during a school day when the adults were at work to steal my truck and fill a black garbage bag full of my clothes. Later that week, I was brave enough to break in again to take the stereo and tower speakers from my room, which I never asked for but which Dad bought me for Christmas, and which Betty Lou despised.

Not long after stealing my stuff from Dad's, I talked the manager at the car dealership into doubling my time on the clock, paying me one more dollar per hour, and giving me an extra shift in the Service department on Saturdays. Moreover, I was able to enroll in an employment program that counted my after-school work hours as elective credit, so I could go to school while working fulltime and still graduate on schedule.

I handled living by myself as well as a stack of cards handles a cyclone. I nearly starved all week and took insulin shots with used needles only to blow my paychecks like a high roller on the weekends. I wore the same clothes so much that you would have thought they were uniforms. I ditched the exact number of classes one could miss and still pass. I stopped fighting altogether because I had way bigger problems than name-calling between cliques. I skipped prom. I skipped buying the senior yearbook. I mastered the art of the check bounce. But three things I DID NOT DO were: show up late to work, miss a day of work, or pay my rent late. If I knew nothing at all, I at least knew that a job and a roof overhead were of paramount importance.

None of my teachers knew I was on my own. They would give the class lectures about none of us having any excuse to be late, to be unalert, to be tired, to be moody, to be anything but one hundred percent focused on schoolwork. I kept my mouth shut. One day, the director of the work-for-credit program sat me down after bumping into me in the girl's locker room after gym class. She said she had just gotten off of the phone with my employer to let them know I was close to failing two courses. She then proceeded to tell me how unfair it was of me to fail in school when there were people like her, who suffer from chronic conditions. In her case the chronic condition was pain in her leg. I had a decision to make at that moment. I could send her to hell the same way I sent Betty Lou and probably lose my job and the chance to graduate; or I could keep my mouth shut tight enough to not spill the beans about living on my own, working late nights, managing type one diabetes with used syringes, and barely managing anything for that matter. I nodded yes when she asked me to commit to raising my grades and sign a paper stating I knew I was on probation in her program.

When I arrived at work, I got a mouthful from my manager.

"What are you doing, Jenn? I thought you were a straight-A student," she scolded. I tried my best to be respectful, professional, and obedient to my boss in the way a child would ideally be to her parent—the way I was terrible at being in real life. I tried a little harder in class. I woke up a little earlier. I worked diligently at the car dealership. And I graduated. I graduated with as low a cumulative grade point average one could earn and still graduate, but I graduated.

After my graduation, my mom, maternal grandparents, boyfriend, and a few friends gathered in the backyard of my little old college girl house and sat in a circle talking, drinking soda, and eating hot dogs, chips with dip, and cake. This lasted a few hours before everyone said their goodbyes; except Felipe, who stuck around to explain to me that that was the most frightening party he had ever attended. At Puerto Rican parties in New York City, there was music and booze and *salsa* and *merengue* and *Titi* Ali making a mean pot of *arroz con gandules* and *pernil* and potato salad and *pasteles* while the rest of the family screamed with laughter, roasting people with jokes behind their backs. By contrast, at my party, Felipe legitimately thought one of us was going to tip over and die of boredom. I honestly couldn't understand what he was talking about.

Several weeks after graduation I turned eighteen. Finally, I was an official adult. I didn't have to hide my age from my teachers or my landlord or generally lay low anymore. I could do whatever I wanted and no one could say a single thing. And as soon as I realized this, I simultaneously realized that I should probably call my dad so that I didn't end up going years without talking to him like my sister did. So I picked up my roommates' phone, dialed his work number, and got his voicemail.

"Dad? It's me, Jenn. If you ever want to talk to me again then you have to call me back within thirty minutes. Bye."

That was the most ridiculously demanding voice message I ever left anyone in my entire life. I don't know if I was experimenting with my new adultness or trying to be tough or if it was just a good intention gone seriously bad, but it worked. Dad called right back and I was so afraid to hear his voice, I let the answering machine get it.

"Jenn? It's your dad. I called right back just like you asked. Please call me back. I look forward to speaking with you soon," I heard Dad's voice say.

I could tell that Dad was nervous and guarded because he switched from sounding sincere and slightly worried to a more professional vernacular at the end of his message. I took a deep breath, closed my eyes, and dialed him back.

We met for lunch at Perkins restaurant near the center of town the next day. We greeted each other without hugs, which was normal for us because Dad was never a big displayer of affection. We exchanged small talk as if I never had that explosive departure from his house. He took his wallet out and gave me all of the money in it—around one hundred and thirty-three dollars—and congratulated me for graduating. Since I didn't invite him, he found out by seeing my name amongst the graduates listed in the newspaper.

I felt a few feelings in that moment. First, shame for not inviting him out of spite. Second, shame for being such a bad kid who couldn't just get along with everyone and keep him a part of my life fulltime. And lastly, tickled to the point of holding back tears that he was so eager to be there for me, to congratulate me, to display his pride or encouragement or love that he emptied his wallet including all of the singles. At that moment, I was so grateful we were speaking again and that all seemed to be well. Dad mentioned that, at some point, we would need to sit down and reconcile with Betty Lou but it never happened. We all just moved on. And for that, I will always be thankful. Rehashing everyone's grudges was the last thing I wanted to do as a new adult with a pocket full of promise and everyone back on the same team.

On our car rides between Wyoming and Colorado, Felipe and I would get lost in conversations about anything and everything. At some point, he was struck to ask me what I planned to do with my life and where I planned to go now that I graduated. My parents never sat me down and talked about college. It was nowhere remotely on my radar. In my mind, I was born to sing. Period. End of story. End of discussion. That's it. Nothing more. Nothing less. Just sing. So I told Felipe, "I'm going to go where the wind takes me." But what I finally admitted at the risk of making him feel like my dream of being a singer was more important than him, is that I fully intended on moving to New York City as soon as possible. Felipe started laughing at me, which he did often and which was endearing because, with his beautiful smile and perfect teeth, one could watch him laugh all day irrespective of who was at the butt of his jokes.

"Why would you want to move to New York City? Everyone there is trying to get out of the place!" he said knowingly.

"Because I want to sing. I *need* to sing!" I replied like the naïve teenager I was.

I didn't know how in the world I would do it. I just knew I wouldn't do it staying in Colorado.

After my sublet ended, I squatted briefly in a property my dad owned before asking Grandma and Grandpa Cooper if I could stay with them temporarily, fully intending on moving to New York City and, as such, quitting my dealership job. However, without enough money for a plane ticket on my first day visiting my grandparents, Grandpa Cooper was quick to point out I needed to get another job. He didn't think I'd *really* move to New York City and he refused to provide for a perfectly able-bodied teenager. With that, he sat me down for a talk about how the early bird gets the worm:

*Grandpa Cooper once was a young husband and father with a wife and three children to feed. But before that, he was a young man who would eventually have to make it on his own in the world. Back before there were employment agencies and alarm clocks, there were newspapers and roosters. Grandpa recounted how he landed one of his first jobs. He methodically prepared his work clothes at night for the following morning; he slept with one eye open until the black sky hinted blue (even before the cocks crowed); he got up and walked to the front steps of the newspaper press to be first in line to get a newspaper before daybreak so he could be the first in line to get a job; and, sure as the sunrise, he was the first strapping young man to show up at a farm that needed a workhand and he was hired. After that job, he did the same at the next and the next until an accident at work resulted in a permanently collapsed lung and he was forced to retire. He worked his body until his body didn't work anymore. And Grandma's resume was just as impressive. Before Grandma became a mom, she worked at the cash register at the counter of S. H. Kress & Co. in Grand Junction for thirty-five cents per hour and, after her three children were born, she continued to work both in and outside of their home.*

With that, Grandpa instructed me to take the classified section of the Sunday newspaper when it arrived and be the first person in line on Monday for a job. I followed Grandpa's instructions to the letter and landed myself a job at a fancy department store on Monday morning. When I came home and shared the news, Grandma asked why I wasn't already at work and Grandpa grinned and chuckled, pleased that his advice was fruitful.

"I don't care what they say about you. You're alright with me," he teased, which gave me a complex.

*What are 'they' saying about me?*

Had sheer will not been enough to get me to New York City, the untimely death of my truck's transmission and an offer from Felipe to drive back home with him and a fellow airman did the trick. I sold my transmission-less truck for one thousand dollars, I quit my job, I packed my clothes and my insulin, and I kissed Colorado goodbye.

New York, New York - 1995

# CHAPTER 12

# Welcome to New York City

W E REACHED THE CITY THAT NEVER SLEEPS IN the middle of the night and Felipe zoomed through his childhood stomping grounds to a pizza place in the West Village. The streets were dark and only dimly lit by orange fog that fell from street lamps a block apart—nothing like the blindingly bright billboards of Broadway, glowing strip of Vegas, or kaleidoscopic jubilee of New Orleans I had rolled around in my mind for so long. It was garbage day on West 4th Street and the storefront we parallel parked in front of was barricaded by a mountain of slick black garbage bags stacked so high they practically reached the fire escapes of the residences overhead, and stuffed so full, some oozed rotting goo onto the sidewalk and down the gutter where rats the size of prairie dogs scurried among shadows below a starless sky. From there, Felipe sped so fast to 113th Street in Richmond Hill, Queens, I didn't have time to absorb the snippets of barely lit scenery or notice the Lefferts Boulevard A-train whining overhead while Felipe narrowly squeezed his muscle car between two bumpers. Once parked, Felipe swiftly herded Mickey and me into a two-family house and up a steep, narrow stairway to a two-bedroom railroad apartment overhead.

Despite the odd hour, Felipe's mom, Carmela, welcomed us in as if we had arrived at a reasonable hour on a Saturday morning. She greeted Mickey and me with the same enthusiasm she smothered Felipe with, as if she was as happy to see all of us as she was her only son. She spoke Spanglish, weaving together pleasantries in accented English with Mickey and me, and rapidly firing Spanish at Felipe in sentences that lacked pauses or periods. Back in Colorado, it would have been rude to accept an offer of a hot-cooked meal in the middle of the night because it would place such an inconvenience on one's host. But because Felipe's mom only spoke Spanish to him, Mickey and I didn't see it coming. Within an hour, Felipe, Mickey, and I had a hot plate of *arroz con gandules y salchicas* slid under our noses and marching orders to "*comes—eat!*" When Felipe saw the uncertain look on my face, he explained quietly to me that I needed to eat it all or else I would be considered extremely rude and offend his mom. So, with a giant slice of pizza still lining the bottom of my belly, I stuffed down an overloaded plate of rice and beans with Vienna sausages and a tall glass of sweetened lemon iced tea—a meal I didn't love when forced down on a full stomach but that I would eventually crave more than anything.

After our midnight feast, Felipe and I were directed to share the twin bed of Felipe's eight-year-old sister, Ana, who slept in her mom's room, while Mickey took the couch. Back in Colorado, my family would gasp at the idea of openly sharing a bed with a boyfriend (even though they knew full well what teenagers do when unchaperoned), but Felipe's mom treated us as if we were grown adults and the act was commonplace—a courtesy I was instantly appreciative of. Any chance at being treated like an adult by an adult was alright with me.

After only a couple of uncomfortable hours of shut-eye we woke to bright sunrays blasting through the window and projecting a shadow of a black fire escape on Ana's light pink walls. We got up and showered before walking a block to grab fresh-made bagels from a shop where a pretty young Italian girl manned the register with a face so serious and accent so thick, she seemed angry when she said, "Have a nice day." After adding the best bagel I had ever eaten in my whole entire life to the pizza and rice and beans still sitting in my stomach, we headed back to Felipe's car for a trip into the city to see his dad for what I would call a "money run." (Only son asks for money. Hard-working dad forks it over.)

Felipe deactivated his car alarm as usual but stopped in his tracks when he realized his car's fancy tinted headlight covers were stolen and a beat-up jalopy was jammed against his back bumper, sanding through the perfect black paint of his showroom quality car. After assessing the damage, Felipe popped his trunk, reached around for a couple of tools, and proceeded to calmly slice the tires of the offending vehicle behind him before moving his car, inch by inch, out of the impossibly small space.

Unlike our barely visible arrival to the city the night before, driving to New York City from Queens in broad daylight was beyond my wildest imaginations. Sparks from the clash of steel wheels ill-fitted to ancient subway tracks from the train overhead showered down upon drivers and pedestrians who carried on without flinching. One-legged pigeons hobbled shamelessly up to native New Yorkers for food crumbs and, if kicked away, broke masterfully into flight with concourses of friends that flew in harmonious figure-eights until settling on rooftops. Women young and old pushed foldable aluminum shopping carts, filled with groceries or laundry or small children or small pets or any combination of them all, along uneven sidewalks where tree roots cracked through the concrete like snakes hatching through eggs. Homeless people peppered parks collecting cans for change in between begging or scavenging for meals. When possible, some emptied whole garbage bins to steal thick government garbage bags to wear over their dirty clothes to trap body heat in before unforgiving winter nights in case they got kicked out of a heated train or station. Super-sized buses with accordion centers turned on dimes and beeped loudly at stops, sighing with swooshes of hot exhaust each time they dropped below the curb like low-riders to pick up passengers.

Past Northern Boulevard and just over a long, gradual hill before the Brooklyn Queens Expressway meets the Long Island Expressway, I got my first glance at Manhattan Island before my view was swallowed up by public housing projects. My eyes widened as I beheld the magnificence of New York City's shaded silhouette resting quietly against a candy corn colored sky before realizing such beauty was boldly underlined by an unexpected bird's-eye view of three hundred and sixty-five acres of tightly packed headstones, tombs, and monuments so tall, they competed with the Empire State Building from my vantage point.

"New York City has cemeteries?" I asked Felipe.

Laughing at me at the obviousness of a stupid question, he confirmed I was indeed looking at the largest graveyard I had ever laid eyes on. But instead of continuing to stare at the breathtaking skyline, I used the fleeting seconds to examine the thousands of crooked, moss-covered limestone and acid rain-stained marble headstones, inordinate statues that begged for attention over modest grave markers, and large, concrete tombs at the top of the tallest hill, setting apart the wealthiest dead people from the poorest as if their predicament wasn't the same. Death was not something I contemplated much despite coming close to it a couple of times, so I naively thought little more than pity for the dead souls below, forgetting in that moment that no one is immune from such fate.

Once in the underbelly of the Williamsburg Bridge, I looked right and left to see just a few inches between the rail guard on one side and a car driving next to us on the other, both of which Felipe flew between without flinching. When I looked down to find little separating us from a death-drop to the East River, I felt concerned for a split-second before deciding driving above the Little Thompson River through Colorado canyons on the way to Estes Park was scarier. I again heard the rumbling, clanking, and screeching of subway cars that played constantly in the background in Queens, this time finding a graffitied Q-train flying past us through the middle of the bridge. Once we were poured out on Delancey Street in the Lower East Side, Felipe whipped his car around a bunch of side streets until we parked illegally under an overpass at South Street Seaport.

Felipe's dad, also named Felipe but not a senior, met us in front of the Peking—a colossal early twentieth century exploration ship that had been traded between many hands before being docked at Pier 16 and used as a museum. Big Felipe looked nothing like Little Felipe, the latter who, besides missing his mother's gene for blue eyes, was Carmela's spitting image in male form. Big Felipe scared me from the get-go. He smiled to see his son and said, "Hello" to Mickey and me but got straight to business. His face turned from a forced smile to a grimace that said a million things, the most important of which was: he didn't like his son's new friends. Mickey suggested we go take a walk around the Seaport, which reeked of fish guts from the daily morning fish market that came and went with the sunrise, while the two Felipes caught up. Mickey was a Senior Airman but little more confident than I was at navigating the cobblestoned streets that served as our official welcome mat to New York City. Cautiously, we only ventured two buildings away to a storefront with an engaging sign that led to a food court (that was an underwhelming, empty warehouse) until throwing in the tourist towel and heading back to safety. We shook Big Felipe's hand again and made sure to reiterate what a pleasure it was to meet him before he rattled something off in Spanish to Little Felipe while I continued to try and match the textbook Spanish I learned in high school with the Puerto Rican accent of Felipe's parents. (I finally figured out that "*yo*" in my textbook dialect was pronounced more like "jo" in a Puerto Rican dialect and that that informal dialect transcended all "ya" sounds. "Be-ja" means *bella* [gorgeous], "toaja" means *toalla* [towel], "jamada" means *llamada* [call] and so on.) By the time Big Felipe was done talking, I was able to figure out just enough Spanish to confirm they weren't talking about me. (Yet.)

I blinked and the week was over and my cash was severely depleted from takeout food, a splurge on a hat that I felt transformed me into a New Yorker when I placed it on my head, and a ferry ride around the city. Felipe and Mickey were due back at the Air Force base in Wyoming and there was no way I could even dream of supporting myself from scratch without money in my pocket and a job, much more a signed lease on an apartment and bare minimum necessities to fill it with. Felipe asked his mom if I could live with her until I got my feet on the ground and she obliged. Mentally, I felt confident I could do the same thing I managed to do in Colorado: get a job within days; save quickly; and find my own place. But the realization that I had no family or friends to lean on, if only emotionally, mocked my confidence. To add injury to insult, I had barely left the comfort of Colorado and had no idea how to get around Carmela's neighborhood on my own, much less all of New York City.

I decided I should venture outside by myself while Felipe was still around to call in case I got lost or in case I completely chickened out and wanted a ride back home. I was confident I could navigate the A-train forty-five minutes to Fulton Street in Manhattan and back like Felipe had when we went to visit his mom during the week at her banking job. I headed outside, walked three blocks, climbed the steel stairs to the elevated train station, and bought a token from an agent who spoke *at* me through a microphone to tell me to pay first since I didn't push my cash under the window reflexively like everyone else. I boarded the A-train to 207th Street and stood holding a pole despite the plentitude of vacant seats on the train during the day. But after around thirty minutes I panicked. Did I miss my stop? Was I going the right way? Was I even on the right train? The train stopped at High St. and I got off and found a pay phone. I dialed Felipe's mom's house and within a couple of rings was relieved to hear Felipe's voice. I told him I was lost and he started laughing at me.

"The train only goes two ways, Jenn. Up and down. If you want to go to Fulton St., stay on until Fulton St. If you want to come back home, get on the train going the opposite direction— you know, the sign that says "downtown"—and take it all the way to Lefferts Boulevard. But don't forget to transfer at Ozone Park if the train says it's going to Far Rockaway."

The directions seemed simple. Go up for the city. Go down for home. The signs were all written in English but I froze with fear. I ditched common sense, mustered up the nerve to ask a stranger to tell me which side of the platform I needed to stand on to go to Lefferts Boulevard, ended my experiment, and took the train back to Queens being certain to take the train that said "Lefferts Boulevard."

My complete flop as a straphanger filled me with a combination of embarrassment, fear, and a flight response that would dwell within my troubled soul for years to come. Deep down in my heart I felt I was smart, capable, strong, and independent. But that first attempt at riding the subway by myself put me back in my place. I thought about how I rode Fort Collin's bus system by myself the summer before sixth grade, muscling a me-sized case of bells to percussion class since my procrastinating dad didn't sign me up for an instrument on time and all of the appropriate bell sets were rented out. I thought of how I drove along unpaved edges of sky-high roads that bordered deep Colorado canyons and cross-country skied in blackness with low blood sugar. But I couldn't successful go up and down on the subway? Maybe New York City was my nemesis. Maybe I finally met my match.

With Felipe's departure nearing and a forced decision impending, I kind of just wanted to turn straight around and head back home. But I knew as certainly as anyone can know that Colorado had absolutely nothing to offer a misfit girl with little more going for her than a beautiful singing voice. I also knew that I had not tended to back down from any challenge and that, if the huge spectrum of varyingly capable people I saw riding the subway—

a single mom with three kids and one stroller, a blind man with nothing more than a stick guiding his way, a homeless man who claimed the corner seat as his home, or a business professional in a dress suit and high heels—could do it, I could do it. So I took the lump of Felipe laughing at my pathetic navigation skills, I swallowed the gigantic pill of depending on mere (albeit wonderful) strangers for as long as it took to get my own place, I devised a clear plan of exactly what needed to be done to "make it," and I decided to stay.

Felipe and Mickey left Queens on a Wednesday morning after Carmela, Carmela's boyfriend, Enzo, and Ana headed to the city where Carmela dropped Ana off at a private Catholic school before meeting Enzo at the bank were they both worked. Felipe spent a few minutes with me for hugs goodbye and was cool as a cat when it was time to officially hit the road. Thanks to Felipe, the soundtrack to the Bruce Lee movie that came out the year before was playing in Carmela's living room when I walked Felipe down to his car and gave a final, hesitant wave goodbye. As I took the dreaded walk back up the staircase that I already associated with defeat, an orchestra played The Dragon's demise, which seemed like my own, depressing soundtrack of demise. Uncharacteristically, my eyes filled with tears and I cried quietly knowing there was no way to change my mind. What was done was done. Although it had only been a matter of minutes, it felt like Felipe was already a lifetime away and there was no yellow brick road or shiny sequenced red shoes to click to get me back home. It was do or die time. I needed to learn how to ride the subway. I needed to find a newspaper and start looking for a job I could apply for at the crack of dawn the next day. I needed to carefully stretch my remaining money for a bottle of insulin, pack of syringes, and PBJs. I needed to do my share at Carmela's apartment until I could get a place of my own. I needed to pray that I wouldn't utterly mortify myself with a good-for-nothing nighttime bladder. And if I could accomplish all of those things, I needed to sing.

# CHAPTER 13

# Beepers

I DIDN'T GO FURTHER THAN THE BAGEL SHOP outside of Carmela's house my first few days without Felipe in Queens. Google Maps and cell phones (much less, smartphones) didn't exist back then so you didn't just search for an address and go. You had to ask strangers and hope like heck their directions were right. Then, once you figured out how to get to where you were going, you had to figure out how to get back to where you came from. Not rocket science, but not a piece of cake, either. Extremely conscious of my place as a houseguest who was expected (if only by my grandparents) to get straight to work, I woke when Carmela's family did and, after Carmela, her boyfriend Enzo, and her daughter Ana, left for work and all-girl Catholic school in the city, I would venture a few blocks out to buy a newspaper and a fresh bagel that was still warm from the oven with a heavy hand of whipped cream from the grumpy Italian girl, and spend my day scouring classifieds for jobs. When the local papers failed to produce any entry-level leads before the weekend came, Carmela encouraged me to commute with her into the city on Monday morning and see if I could find a job in-person. I did just that and before I knew it I was in an interview at the building next to the bank Carmela worked at with a woman who stated bluntly that my resume was too good to be true for a receptionist and filing clerk position so insisted on giving me a spelling test to ensure that the candidate in front of her was the candidate on paper.

I missed a couple of easy words on the test but because I spelled the word "prerogative" correctly, she felt I "must be intelligent," in her words. I restrained myself from telling her that the only reason I knew how to spell that word is because Bobby Brown's "It's My Prerogative" was one of my favorite songs back in the day. I figured liking R&B music, much less aspiring to sing it, would quickly disqualify me from any form of employment. In the end, I faked it enough to get hired and the lady-boss handed me over to a chubby gay guy—the first openly gay person I had ever met in-person—who could not wait to pawn off on me the job he hated. After he showed me filing duties that I was supposed to complete during my lunch break, he showed me the tiniest reception area consisting of nothing more than a desk and a fake plant just a few feet from the elevator bank that dawned the company's name on a shiny silver sign that was way too fancy to match the rickety office. As a receptionist, I would be paid eight dollars per hour to sit for eight hours per day with thirty minutes for lunch and thirty minutes for filing. After two hours of sitting, staring at the opposing wall with few calls, no visitors, and no breaks, I knocked on the boss' door and found a highly irritated woman about to chew me out for leaving my post when I quickly interrupted her impending tirade and told her that the position was not a fit for me and I was leaving right then and there. Furious, she rattled off as many reasons why I was a horrible person as she could fit in between the seconds it took me to jam the doors of the elevator shut and I ran from that company like I ran from everything in Colorado. I didn't feel the least bit guilty until I arrived at Carmela's job and she asked, "What happened?" in a way that bled disappointment. I explained I couldn't sit all day for made-up reasons I thought would make sense to her. But the real reason I couldn't sit in that box was because I didn't risk everything to sit in front of a phone the rest of my life the way I had at the car dealership in my small town. I risked everything to sing. And by hook or crook, I was going to find a way to support myself until my voice could skyrocket me to stardom, fame, and enough money to never worry about disappointing anyone ever again.

As the days ticked by, my grandfather's tough talk about working every day that I'm blessed to be able to, hovered over my thoughts like a parent monitoring homework. Living with acquaintances rent-and-board-free was not something I was aspiring for. In fact, it was the opposite of the independence I prided myself on. I was going to have to dig deep and take anything I could get and make it work.

I found an ad for an "opportunity to make up to one thousand dollars per week" and figured out on my own how to take the A-train to Fulton Street and show up at a gutted office next to the South Street Seaport before seven o'clock in the morning the following day. Despite the sketchy building, being within steps of Felipe's dad's house and ten blocks from Carmela's job, made me feel like I knew where I was and gave me enough piece of mind to decide I was going to do whatever it took to get this mystery job. I checked in and was quickly greeted by an extremely excited twenty-something girl who wore a black turtleneck and dress pants (an outfit unfit for business even by my small-town standards) for a ten-minute crash-course about the opportunity at hand. In short, the mission (should I choose to accept it), was to sell ten products per day, all the while recruiting other people to sell ten products per day under my direction until I reached a management position like her. After that, I could sit back and rake in the dough. However, there were catches. First, the product was a beeper (also known as a pager—a wireless box that clips to your belt and alerts you with a phone number when someone wants you to call them). It was the only way to get in touch wirelessly back then. One person would call the other person's house. If no one answered the house phone, and said person was savvy, cool, or well-off enough to afford a beeper, the caller would then call a different number and type in a callback number at the beep. The callback number would then be sent via satellite to the beeper and buzz or beep letting the person know that someone was trying to get in touch. In short, a beeper was a discretionary consumer product that wasn't on anyone's "must have to survive" list—it wasn't an easy sell. The second catch was, I had to walk the streets of New York City aimlessly every day until I convinced ten complete strangers to fork over thirty-five dollars in cash in exchange for a piece of paper saying a Skytel Skypager would be mailed to them in three weeks. In other words, getting the job didn't seem to be the problem. The job *was* the problem.

Desperate to do anything but waste my life at a desk with a wall for a view, I told the overly-enthusiastic interviewer that I was on board, figuring that walking the streets of New York City would give me a better chance of meeting someone in the music business than any office job could. With that, she asked me to sit on a steel folding chair in the middle of her "office" while she consulted with the big boss. She reappeared with a balding thirty-something guy who was thin and looked like what I imagined a serial killer would look like. His remaining hair was as black as his beady eyes and he wore a grey and black sweater that was the male equivalent of the unprofessional turtleneck his subordinate dawned. He fired a bunch of questions at me with the clear aim to determine how ruthlessly willing I was to make him money. I provided all the answers I knew he wanted to hear and I was congratulated on being the newest member of the team. I was quickly ushered into the next warehouse-like room where thirty people formed a circle and followed the chants of a single ringleader.

"Everybody!" the boss-man yelled. "This is Jennifer. Who wants to put Jennifer to the test?"

A Filipino girl who was around my age stepped forward and the room started cheering and chanting, "Who's gonna ring the bell today? Stacia's gonna ring the bell today!"

I didn't know ringing bells was involved in selling beepers but it was too late to run from the thirty people who also banked their livelihoods on beepers, so I followed Stacia's every move until we were released from the cheesy, pep rally of a morning meeting, to go sell beepers.

Stacia got straight to business, telling me that I would shadow her and, at the end of the day, she alone would decide if I would be hired or not. We walked the outline of the Seaport towards the Brooklyn Bridge and Stacia rattled off her quick sales pitch to anyone who would listen. She did this until noon without a single sale and then asked if I liked Indian food. I lied and said yes despite having never really eaten Indian food, save the pan-fried bread my Native American classmate's mom cooked for our class during a show-and-tell in kindergarten. But when we entered the restaurant, I realized that what she called "Indian," we called "Arab" back home.

I didn't know if I should bow, or wait for a signal, or just grab a plate and dive in, so I decided to follow Stacia, who grabbed a plate and started serving herself. I loaded my plate with the same things she did, save the seafood and fish, and headed over to a table where I mirrored her every sentiment.

"The chicken tikka masala is soooo good."

"Right? Best I've ever had!"

"I love curry!"

"I would bathe in curry if I could."

"I'm so full already."

(Starving) "Me too—so full!"

I guess lying through my teeth to agree with everything Stacia said softened her up to the point she confided in me.

"Truth be told, I want to be a singer," she said as if I expected that selling beepers was some prestigious job she would ride into retirement.

"A singer?" It took everything I had to downplay the fact that, not only did I also sing, the whole reason I was vying for a pyramid scheme of a job selling beepers was to become a superstar.

"I sing exactly like Toni Braxton," she bragged before giving me an impromptu performance.

Indeed, she was an exact replica of what I heard on the radio. I felt a mixture of "wow, she's really talented" and "but she's not going to be famous like I am." If there was one thing I never doubted about myself, it was that I was an exceptional singer. So despite loathing myself, my straggly permed hair, my chubby freckled cheeks, my crooked teeth with silver metal braces, my disproportionately large calf muscles, my thick, Johnsonesque carpenter hands, my good-for-nothing bladder, and an additional curse of type 1 diabetes, I was unapologetic about my utter narcissism when it came to my singing voice. Even so, I played it down because I needed the job.

"Wow, Stacia!" I cheered. "You're going to be a star!" I assured her.

Stacia agreed with me and we spent the second half of our day epically failing to sell even a single beeper but she still gave me the job that night and I showed up the next morning and headed out on my own, armed with only a pen, a stack of papers, and a memorized sales pitch.

Some of the salespeople traveled together but I grabbed a subway map and decided to sell along the subway lines by myself. Over many months, I traveled through the Lower East Side, Coney Island, Staten Island, Brooklyn, Queens, Hell's Kitchen, Midtown, the Bronx, and even took the PATH train beneath the Hudson River to Jersey City. But the neighborhood that opened my eyes the most was Harlem.

I emerged from the A-train stop at 116th Street and Frederick Douglas Boulevard and followed the wind west until I hit a literal brick wall (that enclosed a park up above) before rerouting uptown, which direction I had finally mastered by simply following the street numbers up. My first stop to sell beepers was at a random hair salon buried in between brownstones. A pair of bells tied to the handle of the glass door chimed as I pushed my way in. I expected to introduce myself and pitch my product as usual but all of the patrons and hairdressers carried on talking and laughing and having what looked like the best time as if I wasn't there.

I spoke up and said "Excuse me?" as if to say, "Do you see me standing here?" and a spunky, young-looking but old-acting African American hairdresser told me to sit tight and she'd be right with me.

I quickly let her know that I was not there for hair, but to offer her an incredible deal on the newest beeper out. She quickly declined but allowed me to pitch all of her clients, none of whom were interested in buying. I accepted the loss but something about being around African Americans whose R&B and Hip Hop music I adored, made me work up enough nerve to ask if I could sing for them (the way I used to sing for strangers at the nail salon my mom patronized in Colorado). The same woman who tended to me first told her colleague to shut the radio off and gave me the floor. With nothing to lose, I immediately started singing Mary J. Blige's "Real Love" up to the first chorus, when the entire salon joined in and then started hooting and hollering and clapping so loud, I broke every performer's rule and stopped singing on the spot. These ladies had more star power, showmanship, confidence, and uninhibitedness in their little pinkies than I did in my whole entire body.

"Somebody get me that girl's autograph! She sound just like Mary!" the spunky one said with her fists still full of hair. "You need to go to the Apollo, girl!" she encouraged me.

I signed a random paper with my fanciest initials—JJ—and thanked them for their time with my little-kid chuckle and steel-colored smile. They didn't know it but they made my day. The African American people in that salon *actually liked* my singing. In my unexposed mind, an African American person liking my singing was the equivalent of a superstar liking my singing.

I made my way up to 125th street and headed east. I went store-to-store with my sales pitch but got shut down every time. Mid-block, I ended up at an outdoor shop that sold blue denim in every form: pants, vests, jackets, button-downs, baseball caps, bows, ties, you name it. A dark-skinned man with long dreadlocks and a Jamaican accent greeted me and asked what I'd like to buy. I quickly told him I was there to sell, not buy, and pitched my beeper. He passed on the beeper but stopped to tell me I would look nice with braids in my long hair.

"Oh yeah?" I asked.

"Yeah. Here, let me show you," he replied as if we were longtime friends. He braided the front pieces of my hair and handed me a mirror. "See? Much better," he smiled.

I delighted in, not only being accepted by yet another person in Harlem, but having some snazzy new braids to show off for the rest of the day. But I didn't make it out of his store without being sold a pair of jeans. (Zero, Jenn; One, Jamaican guy.) Despite failing to sell anything and spending my precious cash on jeans I didn't need, I stepped out of the store satisfied and looked up to find I was standing across the street from the famous Apollo Theater where an amateur talent show was filmed every week (which I had seen on TV at Carmela's house a couple of times by then). I walked up to the door to see if there was information on how to audition, to no avail. And with beepers left to sell, I knew I didn't have time to investigate further.

When I reached the end of the block, I walked another without attempting to pitch anyone before making a right turn and heading back downtown on Malcom X Boulevard. The sun was shining but the street felt barren and empty, with a mix of residences, purposely demolished buildings, and everyday people carting their groceries or laundry or walking furiously to who knows where. Desperate for a sale, I approached a huge, bodybuilder of a man who was sitting on a stoop next to a stack of t-shirts and went for a sale. But the only sale that was made was from him to me when I paid my last ten dollars of cash for a knockoff Mike Tyson t-shirt I didn't really want or need. Resigned, I found my way to a train going downtown and took a walk of shame down Fulton Street and into the warehouse of beeper-selling colleagues to report zero sales. But despite disappointing the bosses that day, I felt inspired. I felt accepted. I felt talented. I felt like I was the crappiest salesperson but, more important than anything, the *best* singer. And I decided then and there that while I was in New York, I would not again let a day go by without singing to every person I met.

see the promoter again until the night of the
after I sold every ticket to Carmela, Enzo, and
their friends. I had only dropped about five pounds
promoter saw me in my sparkly dress, stockings, and
boots, his jaw dropped as if I had lost one-hundred.
your money," I told him as I handed over the dough. He
and told me to hop up onto the stage for a microphone
re the show started an hour later. I was the only white
the building but my fellow artists cheered me on as
mily. A group of four teenage boys who were already
still unknown, assured me I was going to be next to hit
ey pulled me to the side to tell me I was the best female
of the night. But when it came time for me to sing for
ng the show, I didn't get the hyped up introduction that
other acts got. And I didn't get applause or cheers when
oter sloppily announced my name "Jennifer? JJ?"
J," I corrected him.
ies and gentlemen, I present to you, JJ," he said rather
edly.
intro of my Mary J. Blige song came on and the audience
clapping to the familiar track. I put the microphone to
and sang the first line and the audience started clapping
wling as if they expected an utter disaster but got Mary J.
erself. Then, at the climax of the song when I pulled off a
cal trick that Mary J. did, which wasn't all that difficult for
e crowd lost its mind and I ended my few minutes of fame
cheers and applause. The promoter acknowledged I did
well but still didn't appear impressed so I grabbed Carmela
nzo and left with the satisfaction that my friends, and my
ds' friends, thought I was amazing.
s Enzo sped away from the Harlem nightclub half-drunk, he
owingly side-swiped a yellow cab.
Um, Enzo? You just hit a car," I said kind of cynically.
No I didn't!" he refused to believe me.

# CHAPTER 14

# Singing on the Subway

I HAD NOT YET RUNG THE BELL FOR SELLING TEN
beepers in a day but I consistently sold around six, which
made me enough money to buy insulin over the counter and
keep my stomach full, but still not enough to help Carmela out
with rent. Felipe and I spoke often and at some point he put me in
contact with an old high school friend, Jake, who Felipe thought
might be able to help me further my singing career despite the
pair being more rivals than friends. I met with Jake for lunch and
was abnormally nervous the entire time for two reasons. First,
my hair was a huge, embarrassing mess of frizz after a humid,
rainy day. Second, I didn't have enough cash to buy lunch so I
was hoping beyond hope that the stranger in front of me would
cover the bill. Jake interrogated me for an hour, asking how I met
Felipe, how long we had dated, what school I went to, what I did
for a living, and the like. I cut to the chase and told him I came
to New York City to sing. To my surprise, Jake stopped asking
questions and started providing answers. He pondered quietly to
himself for a moment before telling me that one of his coworkers
was searching for talent to manage and that he would love to put
me in contact with her. We spoke about the prospect before it
was time for Jake to get back to work. I thanked him profusely
and motioned for the bill, acting like I intended to pay but he
intervened the way I had hoped he would and paid for the lunch
himself.

I was scheduled to meet with my potential new manager
the following week and feeling a combination of anxiousness
and home-sickness so decided to treat myself to a night out the
following payday. I set my sights on heading to The Village to get
a tattoo. From childhood, my dad always vehemently petitioned

me to never get a tattoo. But as a newly minted adult in New York City, getting at tattoo was my way of exercising my adulthood. So I disregarded my dad's sound, hard-fought advice, and I committed to going against the grain. I walked aimlessly down St. James Place before stumbling upon a random tattoo parlor. I brought a sketch of a cryptic lizard-looking dragon wrapped around a yin-and-yang sign, which I thought was the best drawing I had ever done. But when I showed it to the tattoo artist at the shop, he handed me a book and recommended I choose a better design. Stubborn and absolutely convinced my drawing was the best, I refused to get anything other than what I came for: my drawing on my arm. So the guy shrugged, asked for seventy-five bucks, and went to town. I only got a split-second glimpse of the final work before he smothered Vaseline on my arm and bandaged the work up. But on the A-train back to Lefferts Boulevard, I peeked under the bandage and was struck with panic. The tattoo was horrible. The lines were shaky, the fire coming from the dragon's mouth looked more like a block of bacon than a flowing flame. The yang was missing an eyeball. I wanted to cry. Making adult decisions wasn't as liberating as I thought. Maybe moving to New York City was a great idea, but getting a tattoo was not.

Some days later, I met with Jake's co-worker, a forty-year-old secretary named Natasha, and talked about what I needed to do to become a star. For starters, I needed a headshot. Then, I needed a demo. After that, I needed a lucky break. She would help me with everything in exchange for a piece of the pie. Why wouldn't I say yes? I knew no one. I had no money. I had nothing to lose. Natasha became my new manager on a handshake and sealed the deal by putting up the money for my first headshots (which somehow included a glimpse of the world's worse arm tattoo). The only downside was, Natasha didn't really know a thing about music. That was going to have to be completely my department.

I continued selling beepers and singing every day with no advancement in any direction. I knew I had to do more if I was ever going to make it anywhere. I noticed a newspaper

called *The Village Voice* a
see if the classified ads wei
ads I routinely kept my eye
grabbed *The Village Voice* th
Its classified ads were bursti
for singers. A band needed a
background vocals, a promotei
a producer needed a star to w
a songwriter, a songwriter nee
needed a studio, a studio need
Other than recording one take
to her friend at a radio station,
of sing-along songs I recorded a
studio. And other than a handful c
considered myself a songwriter. I w
I should find a way to get out there

I met with a promoter in a tiny
to perform in a talent show he was
from the Apollo but he promised thei
there who could take me "places" if
hearing me sing, he acknowledged I h
impressed. Then he got to business.

"You're going to need to lose some v

I wondered how he could tell that s
on. I guessed my chubby cheeks and ave
star-quality. Slightly embarrassed, I nodc
he gave me a second set of instructions.

"You're also going to need to sell twe
qualify to perform."

I hesitated, remembering my mom q
who said that any real opportunity in the n
never come with a price tag attached. Des
was desperate for an opportunity to perform
grabbed a fistful of tickets and left.

The cab driver next to us rolled down his passenger window and started yelling at Enzo to pull over, which Enzo finally did. But instead of calling the police and figuring out insurance and tickets, and who would pay for what, Enzo insisted to the cab driver that he did nothing wrong, told the cab driver to shove it, got back in his beat up old grey Ford Taurus, and merrily drove us home to Queens. Carmela and I laughed until we cried at the fact that Enzo just legitimately (and drunkenly) told that poor cab driver that he was imagining the accident when Enzo had, in fact, hit the cab driver's car. I felt bad for the cab driver but was still completely entertained by Enzo's antics. And I might not have gotten any further with my singing career that night but I did get something: two new fans. Carmela and Enzo were completely on board with my dream to become a singer and now had the proof of a performance to swear by me.

I figured out how to present my beeper sales pitch in Spanish and my sales went up slightly to the point I actually sold ten one day. I hesitantly rang the bell (because I felt like such a weirdo doing it) and Shawn, a six-foot-five African American kid with a raspy voice and expert salesmanship, came over and congratulated me with a high-five.

"I've been noticing you for a while," he confessed.

"Oh, thanks," I replied not realizing he was hitting on me.

"A bunch of us are going to the movies tonight. You wanna come?" he asked.

I didn't see why not, so I accepted. We watched the movie (which I struggled to enjoy because I always had the attention span of a toddler) and I felt an arm go around me. It was Shawn. He tried to go in for a kiss but I gave him a cheek. Even though I wasn't physically with Felipe, we were still in a monogamous relationship. Being there with a guy who was looking to hook up made me feel like a cheater. But I was so insecure in so many ways, I didn't have the guts to just flat out tell him I had a boyfriend. So I pushed him off the rest of the night and found my way to the A-train around two o'clock in the morning. I called

Carmela's house from a pay phone on the subway platform and she answered, sounding exhausted.

"Hi, Carmela? I'm sorry I'm calling now. I went to the movies. I just didn't want you to worry," I explained without taking a breath.

"It's a little late!" Carmela reprimanded. "You should have called *before* you went."

"I'm sorry," I said disappointed in myself. "I'll be home soon."

I tried to duck and dodge Shawn at the job but he always managed to find me. Each time he made an advance, I found a way to justify how it wasn't really that big of deal. But after weeks of a cat-and-mouse game, with my ego constantly boosted and the love of my life completely out of sight in Cheyenne, Wyoming, I got sidetracked. Shawn and I kissed one day after work, which I passed off as nothing. We went back to his mom's condo in Harlem another day after work, which I passed off as nothing. We proceeded to tempt sex, half-naked in an empty condo. And then we began to have sex, a few minutes of which jolted me into the admission that I was decisively, at that very moment, cheating on the love of my life with a kid I didn't even like. What was I doing?

I stopped, got up, got dressed, and shut the whole show down, saying goodbye to Shawn for good without explanation. I was livid at myself—hugely disappointed for succumbing to temptation that wasn't even that tempting. From anger, I moved to denial. Since it was only sex for a minute, it wasn't really sex. Since no one knew I was ever with that boy, it never really happened. Since Felipe was thousands of miles away, it wasn't really cheating. I ran these things through my mind over and over until I believed them. Lying to myself felt way better than facing the fact that I was a lowdown, dirty, rotten, good-for-nothing, lying, ungrateful, two-faced, girlfriend.

With Shawn out of the picture, I resumed complete focus on singing. I sang every chance I got and I still got nowhere. After a long day on the A-train back home, I sat with a couple of fellow beeper-sellers and complained about making the same money singing on the street than selling beepers that day. They didn't respond but a stranger reached across the aisle to get my attention. A bald African American man with nerdy glasses and a gold tooth pulled a pair of giant headphones off of his head and asked, "You sing?"

"Yeah, I do," I said with the ever-so-slight New York accent I was beginning to acquire from all of the fast-talking I had been doing with native New Yorkers.

"I'm Christopher Buttons," he said as if I was supposed to instantly know who he was.

"Oh yeah?" I replied not knowing what else to say.

"I'm a producer," he said.

"Oh, nice!" I replied not expecting anything further.

"Take my card. Let's link up. Maybe we can work together," he said before grabbing his briefcase in a hurry and barely making it out of the closing doors at the Clinton Avenue stop in Brooklyn.

I studied the fancy black card with a bright red piano and musical notes flowing off to the side, with Christopher's name and phone number printed in fancy gold lettering, and my stomach filled with butterflies. Of all places and times, my big break came on the subway during the one time I wasn't even singing.

I called Christopher the minute I got to Carmela's house and by that Saturday, I was in his tiny railroad apartment in Brooklyn auditioning.

"You can definitely blow. Damn!" he praised approvingly. "Do you write?" he asked

"Yes, of course," I lied through my teeth.

"Do you have anything I can hear?" he pressed.

"Not anything worthy of your talent," I schmoozed having just heard his respectable chord progressions on the synthesizer next to his couch.

Chris conceded to start working together and see how it went from there. Within minutes, he came up with an extremely catchy chord progression he borrowed from The Gap Band's

"Outstanding"—one of the old school greats he used to listen to—and I, for the first time, spot-wrote a song. First verse, done. Chorus, done. Second verse, done. Chorus, repeat. It was as if God Himself sent a song through my pen to the paper. It was catchy. It was with the times. Inspired by the one-hit-wonder Adina Howard's "Freak" song at the time, it was sexy, descriptive, provocative, over-the-top, and despite not being anything like the actual tom boy I was, it was the perfect key and sound for my singing voice.

"Your hook is slamming but you're missing a bridge," Chris coached.

"A what?" I said, forgetting to hide the fact I didn't know what I was doing.

"A bridge. You know, the climax of the song. Like this," he switched chords.

I quickly scribbled down words and followed his chords until we had a full song. When I went home to Carmela's house I was on top of the world. I couldn't get my own song out of my head and I couldn't believe I had an actual producer. Me, a no one, was *someone* to someone. I excitedly told Carmela about everything but she couldn't truly understand what it all meant. Producing, writing, sessions—those words weren't in her banking vocabulary. So I called home to friends and gushed instead. The only problem was, my friends weren't as excited. They had bad news—or some small-town gossip—to break to me. The long of the short was, they said Felipe was cheating on me with Mickey's girlfriend's best friend. In fact, they said he had an orgy with all of them. Fire filled my veins until I suddenly realized that Felipe and I were now even and I no longer had to keep lying to myself like I wasn't a filthy cheater. I told my friends to keep an eye on him. In the meantime, I had bigger fish to fry.

I called my manager, Natasha, and raved about my new producer, who she arranged a meeting with immediately. At the meeting, Chris and I performed a live version of our new song and pressured Natasha to get me into the studio immediately (which required her money since I didn't have any). Natasha agreed that, if Chris could get her a good deal on studio time, she would move forward with my project. Chris called a fellow producer and recording studio owner, Arcenius Curtis Bryant, for the favor and recording my first demo tape at Noise in the Attic recording studio ensued.

In the dark, soundproof recording booth that was outfitted with a window that allowed me to see everyone in the production room without them seeing me, I went between being a complete natural and an awkward newbie who wanted her earphone volumes adjusted one hundred times before every take. But after each completed song recording, I came out of the cozy capsule to high praise—mad props—from the only people who counted: Chris and Arcenius. Natasha was over-the-moon with my voice but not as impressed with my price tag. She complimented my singing but nagged about the accumulating expenses; especially since we didn't have a contract in writing.

Weeks of writing and recording and mixing and listening and remixing and selling pagers flew by until June arrived, which meant one very important thing: Carmela and family were moving and I wasn't invited to come along. I either needed to buckle down and secure my own place or go home to Colorado where being homeless was a lot easier. I went against the independence I so desperately wanted back and asked Natasha if I could live with her. She refused without even a second of contemplation because she had a bad experience with a previous artist, which was ultimately a relief since I didn't want anyone else to find out I had a sporadic bed-wetting problem. I preferred to be viewed as a star in at least one person's eyes. So I was left with two options: sell enough beepers to secure an apartment (which was unlikely since I was barely keeping myself alive) or sell enough beepers to buy a ticket back home—what seemed like my only real option.

Carmela told me her move-out date and I bought my one-way ticket back to Colorado a month in advance. I used my remaining days in New York City to finish my demo and try to restore any shred of self-respect I once had by being a somewhat decent person before my flight home to Felipe's arms. But one thing I had not yet learned during my time in the city was how to say no. Chris was starting to heavily flirt with me despite being sixteen years older than me. He was the furthest thing from what I found attractive even if I had been single. I didn't intend on flirting back but I also didn't want to offend the only person who was actually getting me somewhere with my music. So I walked the fine line of going with the flow. The only problem was, the "flow" entailed unexpected things. For example: Chris telling me to get naked for a "completely professional" birthday massage, during which ordeal he scared me to death when he whispered in my ear, "You have a pretty pussy," as if he was about to rape me; or after escaping that event unharmed, in our next session Chris insisting I get naked to cuddle all night instead of working on music, which I did somewhat robotically without the act leading to anything more than a naked bear hug for several hours (which I hoped would be pathetic enough that he never wanted to do anything like that again); and lastly, Chris finally getting his way during our final listening party after everyone went home and demanding the worst, most unwanted sex because I owed him. Even though I felt justified doing Felipe dirty on my last slip up (since he was at home doing the same), falling in the predicament of sleeping with my producer the day I was scheduled to reunite with the young man I truly loved, made me feel as despicable as I was.

I tried to tell myself a thousand things to make the whole ordeal go away but lying wasn't working anymore because the truth had already damaged my soul. All that was left to do was grab my bag of clothes, a few cassette tapes with my freshly mastered demo, my headshot, my insulin, my plane ticket, and run.

# CHAPTER 15

# Wanderer

I TOUCHED DOWN IN DENVER AND FELIPE WAS waiting for me at the gate as handsome, well-dressed, and well-mannered as ever. As I hugged him and felt his sincere grasp, and smelled his soft cologne, my soul wept within for betraying my true love. The right thing to do would have been to confess my sins and take my consequences. But instead, I carried on like a saint and began to happily recount my time in his hometown. I started to bring up the rumors I heard before cutting myself off and leaving it entirely alone. I figured that, even if Felipe did everything they say he did, what I did was still much worse. He was forgiven for anything he did, but I would never forgive myself for my transgressions.

Now more than ever I needed to get straight to work. My dad lent me a car and I hit the pavement running, fudging up a resume that made me look like a highly capable Girl Scout and going door-to-door to apply for jobs in person. My short-term goal was to grab a room share, save money, and move back to New York City so my dream team—one member whom I absolutely never wanted to see again—could continue to aim me in the direction of stardom.

By the next day I received a call from Rocky Mountain Insurance Pool, a warehouse and lot of wrecked cars that the company bought from insurance companies and auctioned off. The owners were impressed that I was a jack-of-all-trades who could drop an exhaust manifold or tow a twelve-wheel car trailer without flinching. They hired me without hesitation.

My job as the company's "lot boy" (lot girl) was to fix what could be fixed; salvage what could be salvaged (like taking apart and cleaning up flooded vehicles); move wrecked vehicles around with a gigantic car lift; dig through crumbled vehicles past blood stains and IV lines that were left from emergency crews to find personal belongings or valuables to return to families or sell for the company; and anything else asked of me to make the business run smoothly. On several occasions, I had to escort guests to the vehicles of their lost loved ones and hold them when they couldn't hold themselves up. Most memorably, a small-statured man stood angry and crying after finding two large empty booze bottles in the car his daughter crashed, killing herself and the man's infant grandbaby instantly. These hard situations ended up being the most important work I did for the company. And having the opportunity to extend compassion in many strangers' time of need helped soothe my own soul, too.

Finding a room was just as easy. I showed up to a house, interviewed with one very awkward man, was given for free the furniture from the last roommate, and handed a key for just a couple of hundred dollars. But since I spent most of my time with Felipe on the Air Force base, the room ended up being a relative waste. Nonetheless, it was there when I needed it and the creepy guy I lived with kept me on my toes enough in terms of spying on me for me to try and keep my nose out of trouble.

Back in New York City, Natasha had her lawyer prepare a fancy management contract for me to sign. But when I read it, I knew without consulting anyone that the percentage of my income she was prepared to take if I "made it" was astronomical. Granted, she paid for my headshots and my demo—things that added up to a few thousand dollars. But I didn't think that meant she should be able to get a sizeable slice of my monetary worth in the long run. I declined to sign the contract; declined to hire an attorney to hash it out; and Natasha cut her losses and declined to manage or deal with me any further. Either way, manager or not, I knew that getting back to the city would be my sole responsibility.

At work at the insurance pool, I impressed everyone with skills completely unrelated to singing. Big, burly truck drivers came to get their trailers loaded with crashed sports cars and oohed and ahhed as I dangled in the air in the cab of the gigantic tractor of a car lift while delicately placing three-thousand-pound cars inches apart. One fellow was particularly fond of my talent and always gave me a big pat on the back. But his praise was lost on me because I was more concerned with his huge, swollen feet that were bursting out of specialized shoes and making it barely possible for him to walk, much less drive a huge rig.

"Diabetes," he explained, which scared me to death.

I hadn't seen a doctor for diabetes in at least two years and all I did to manage my blood sugar was take my shots, eat normal meals, and drink juice if I felt shaky with low blood sugar. This man's weekly visits reminded me that I was mortal.

Dad needed his car back so I took my first few paychecks and bought a Chevy S-10 long-bed truck for a thousand dollars. Meanwhile, Felipe bought a motorcycle and often showed up to my house in Fort Collins offering me a ride back home. For the most part I declined until one day I threw my hands up in the air and hopped on. Felipe then proceeded to speed one hundred miles per hour down I-25 and successfully scare a girl who had yet to be afraid of anything to the tune of me never riding a motorcycle again. Ever. And if that terrifying ride wasn't enough, receiving for my bosses a Harley Davidson bike with the rear end completely smashed in and meeting the woman who drove it and barely escaped with her life, scared me enough to never, ever aspire to ride a motorcycle. At least in this area, it was possible to scare me straight. However, in other areas I was still about as smart as a lump on a log.

When Felipe wasn't riding his crotch-rocket with his friends and when I wasn't working on cars at my job, we were being young, in love, and carefree in every way. It wasn't until I arrived at the base one night extremely sick that things got a little more serious. I was repeatedly projectile vomiting, much like the way I did when I had yet to be diagnosed with diabetes. I didn't have supplies to check my blood so I guessed that my blood sugar was very high. The only catch was, I was shaking like it was low. Confused and desperate, I asked Felipe to take me to the hospital. After a short time in the quiet triage area of the Cheyenne hospital, a nurse appeared and asked, "What do you think your blood sugar level is right now?"

"Five hundred?" I guessed.

"Try forty," she replied.

"Four-zero?"

"Four-zero. And by the way, congratulations. You're pregnant."

I was stumped and terrified all at once. *What will I tell my family? Wait, I'm an adult now. I don't have to tell anyone. But I need my family. So I'll tell them.* I went feverishly back and forth with different scenarios in my head until, after drinking a glass of orange juice, my blood sugar rose and I felt more grounded and less panicked. OK, a baby. The doctors always told me I couldn't have a baby. But the nurse said, "Oh you can and you will."

I spent the night in the hospital for monitoring and in the morning a doctor trailed by six or seven observers entered my room. He reviewed my predicament with everyone there, shaming me whether he realized it or not. And then he noticed a round scar on my left shin.

"What is that?" he asked me.

*You should know. You're a doctor.* I thought to myself.

"Is it from your diabetes?"

"Yeah. I've had it since I was ten or eleven."

"Do you remember the name."

"No, it's really long. It's a skin disorder secondary and specific to type 1 diabetes. It's not that rare but not that common for non-diabetics. They say it's ugly but that's about it. It's not contagious or anything."

"So, you're pregnant. Sorry to hear that."

"I'll be fine," I said obstinately.

"Well, good luck," he said.

Felipe wasn't thrilled about the news to say the least. But he sucked it up an accepted it. I went back to work at the junkyard the next day and informed my bosses why I missed the previous day without calling. They congratulated me as if my pregnancy was a good thing and the wife of one of the owners warned me to not lift anything. But that was impossible. Within seconds of receiving that advice, I had to swap out car batteries and carry bumpers and pull off tires and climb up to check the oil on the tractor. I needed a job to have a baby so rules were going to have to be broken. Instead of hiding the news from my family I decided to finally do something morally right for a change and tell them. Well, my mom's side, at least. I was too afraid to tell my dad. No one was happy but they appreciated the fact I told them. Then, the day after I let the cat out of the bag, I started to bleed.

I raced to Poudre Valley Hospital in Fort Collins, where my mom met me. After some tests, the staff quickly determined I was miscarrying. I panicked and kicked my mom out of the room because she was trying to be a good mother and be there for me and I just wanted to be completely left alone. Here I had reset my mind to forget about singing and focus on becoming a mom. I had accepted all there was to accept and even told my grandparents the embarrassing truth that their granddaughter was a major sinner. And not a day later I lost it all. I shouldn't have told anyone. I could have just gotten away with another huge mistake without mud on my face. But that was that. The baby was gone and the only lesson learned is that it really sucks to go without health insurance because now I was thousands of dollars in debt for something that should have been two co-pays.

I had no choice but to bounce back to Plan A. In a blink of the eye everything went back to the normal I had created when I came back home. However, while everything was going relatively well for me considering my only goal was to make money and get back to New York City, what I didn't know is that the whole time I was on the East Coast, Felipe was getting into a bit of trouble himself. His friends created a little weed-selling operation that he got pulled into and, after months of surveillance by the military, two of his friends were finally arrested. However, when one of the friends agreed to wear a wiretap to frame Felipe into admitting he was also in on it, said friend actually ended up protecting Felipe, giving him the heads up on what was about to go down. So when the wiretap went live, Felipe wisely admitted his part in the drug ring but said that his participation was a huge mistake and that he would never do it again. That recording was eventually played for jurors who let Felipe off with a dishonorable discharge while his two friends went straight to jail.

Once Felipe was kicked out of the military, he had to make a quick plan for the next Chapter in his life. And that plan ended up being to move to Melbourne, Florida with his pregnant sister, brother-in-law, and their three-year-old daughter while he put the pieces of his future together. While singing was my number one priority, working at a virtual junkyard was distracting enough for me to think accepting Felipe's invitation to Florida was a good idea. Call me young and stupid. Call me hopelessly in love. Call me anything you want. But don't call me logical because I went with my heart instead of my gut, cut ties with my hometown once again, and followed this boy to Florida (but not before selling the S-10 that broke down on me and convincing my grandparents to co-sign on a Suzuki Samurai—the aluminum can equivalent of a Jeep—because I thought I was responsible enough to manage it). My grandparents, on the other hand, regretted their decision immediately and no sooner did I drive off the lot did they pay the four-thousand-dollar loan off in cash because they were certain I would otherwise destroy their credit. And they were right—I would have.

As regretful as my grandparents were about co-signing (and outright buying) a car for me, I was equally regretful for impulse-buying a vehicle that could barely reach sixty miles per hour downhill. It was the worst decision I made since, well, the last bad decision and I was beating myself up left and right. What I didn't realize at the time was, moving to Florida with Felipe would be the crème-de-le-crème of bad decisions.

Felipe conveniently failed to mention to me that his sister didn't know I was coming. In fact, he didn't even bother to ask. Completely in the dark, I blindly followed him. Running away became my comfortable impulse. But before we left town, I decided to do something I thought was really good for a change. Something that would help and not hurt. We went to the local animal shelter and I adopted a dog (because what nineteen-year-old well-intentioned idiot wouldn't?).

Goodbye, again, Colorado. Hello road trip in a tin can of a truck, trailing Felipe's far more solid Chevy 454SS, with a bag of clothes, my insulin, a few cassette tapes, my headshot, and a Rottweiler.

# CHAPTER 16

# Bouncer

I FELT BAD THAT MY NEW DOG HAD TO RIDE SO MANY miles in a loud, breezy, vibrating truck. At a rest stop I asked Felipe to take him in his nice, air-tight truck. However, once we swapped, the dog whined the whole way so came back to ride with me when we stopped to refill our gas tanks. At the gas station when Felipe was in getting snacks, a man popped out of nowhere and tried to talk to me when my new best friend appeared at my side and barked in a way that assured the stranger that the dog would rip him apart if he stepped any closer. It felt so good to have someone who was there for me, would protect me, and couldn't care less about the stupid decisions I made in life.

We made good time. Despite it being December, the weather was gradually becoming hotter and more humid the closer we got to Florida. Having only stepped foot outside of Colorado long enough to see New York City, I didn't know what to expect when we arrived in Florida. But within minutes of parking in front of Felipe's sister's house, feeling the thick warm air and walking on grass that was more like weeds, I already hated it. I wanted to go home but there was no turning back. Moreover, when Felipe's loud, bubbly sister came out to greet him and discovered my dog and me, it was difficult for her to hide the fact I was not expected, wanted, or welcome. Nonetheless, his sister invited my huge new dog and me in and Felipe proceeded to win everyone over with the charm his sister both loved and despised him for.

Unlike how welcomed I felt at Carmela's, Marta and her husband had concern and maybe even disgust written all over their faces. And who could blame them? Here they were expecting their brother and they get some dumb girl and a dog to boot. They had no idea where I had been or where I was going. All they knew is that they went from a tidy family of three to a messy family of six (including the quadruped) in a matter of minutes. I absolutely loathed depending on others for a home and I knew it was only a matter of time before my bladder would give out some night and utterly humiliate me and the love of my life. The clock was ticking and I needed to move.

Within three days I got a job that was kind of like Florida's equivalent of New York City's beeper-selling scheme. Except this time I would be selling Hoover vacuums door-to-door. When I arrived at a cattle call of a job interview, around forty recruits were ushered into a room and seated to listen to a man brag about how rich he had become selling Hoovers. He was so rich, in fact, that he was going to give one hundred dollars away right on the spot. He pulled out a number and told all of us to look under our seats. I was the winner. I never ran so fast to snatch a bill. I needed that money more than anyone could possibly understand and I took a moment after that introductory meeting to look to the sky and thank whoever was responsible for such fate. I returned home and happily told the family I was gainfully employed, which obviously shocked them—Felipe included. Behind closed doors, I told Felipe I wanted his family to know that I wasn't a person who was looking for handouts and that he needed to get a job, too. We couldn't expect his family to support us even if they didn't have their own problems (which they did—which everyone does).

The next morning I reported for work and was assigned to a car with three young men, who would show me the ropes.

"What, are you going to a funeral?" one of the said to me, laughing.

I was wearing all black, not because I thought it was appropriate, but because it was all I had. I had been working at a junkyard for a few months and in that time replaced my beeper-selling clothes with jeans and t-shirts. I was lucky to find an all-black outfit for the day.

I shadowed one of the guys for a few hours of not selling anything before asking if I could break off on my own.

"Oh. Sure you can. Take the demo in the back," he said as if I was a complete joke.

But within the hour, I had my first sale. We were trained to approach our sales with a four-part system. First, we were supposed to make up a reason why we needed to sell Hoover vacuums so badly. My made-up reason was that I wanted to go to school to become a police officer, which was all there was to do in Melbourne (or "Mel-boring" as Marta called it) based on my search through the classified ads. Second, we had to give a complete demonstration and show our potential buyer how absolutely filthy their house was and how the Hoover would solve their disgusting problem. Third, as soon as we convinced someone to buy, we had to call back to the headquarters and literally get down on our knees and beg the boss for a discount, thereby making the buyer feel like they were getting the very best deal. Finally, we had to reassure our buyer that this was the best decision they ever made and, thanks to them, our every dream was about to come true. In other words, I thought selling beepers was hard until I sold Hoovers. But with one sale under my belt, I kept going.

One of the guys in the car was upset that I sold at a house he was "just about to go to" and made a sexist joke about how I used what I had to get the sale. When I clapped back at him, he asked me if I was on my period or something.

"No, I'm not, actually. But what's your excuse?"

The rest of the guys mocked him for getting served by a girl and I set my sights on the mobile home park we pulled into. My first house was a lady who was so old, I didn't have the heart to put her through a demonstration. I sat and shot the breeze with her instead. She clearly needed company, not a vacuum cleaner. The second house was a woman and a six-year-old child—her granddaughter. My demonstration revealed that they desperately needed a vacuum cleaner. Maybe not a thousand-dollar vacuum cleaner, but a vacuum cleaner at that. As I got on my knees to execute phase three of the sale process, the boss told me to give the woman the Hoover at the lowest price yet and also throw in a Disney vacation.

"You're not playing around with me, are you? I really don't want to con this woman." I whispered while the lady fetched me some lemonade.

The boss was resentful that I even asked and assured me that this woman would not only get a used, eight hundred dollar vacuum, but also a Disney vacation. So be it. I sold a second unit.

It was almost eight o'clock at night and our team was still out. I was ready to go home but the guys insisted we wouldn't until someone made one more sale. I approached a trailer with yet another vacuum and two gay men and a pug answered the door. The man of the house wheezed from the cigarette dangling out of his mouth as I completed my demonstration and attempted to convince him that it was his carpet—not his chain-smoking habit—that was causing his dog's allergies. Buying a Hoover would clear everything up. He bought the vacuum for his dog and we all got to go home. However, I was the only one in the vehicle with any sales. Three to be exact. And all of my colleagues swore it was because I was a girl. But by that time, I couldn't care less what they thought. I just wanted to go home.

The house phone rang early the next morning and it was for me. My aunt Cheryl—my father's sister—called to inform me of the sad and shocking news that my grandfather passed away.

"Grandpa Johnson?" I asked, expecting confirmation that the wrinkled old man who I hadn't seen in ages had passed.

"No, honey. Grandpa Cooper."

I was devastated. Grandpa Cooper, the man who gave me the most valuable pep-talk of my entire life? The man who joked and chuckled and loved his family to the moon and back? The man who just paid the price of my stupidity, literally paying thousands of dollars of his hard-earned money on a lemon of a truck for his third eldest grandchild, was suddenly gone? No warning. Just gone?

I hung up with Aunt Cheryl and dialed the Hoover people to tell them I wouldn't be at work that day.

"My grandfather passed away," I told them bluntly, not fully believing the words that were coming out of my mouth.

"Look. Don't lie. Just get into work. We'll hold the van for you."

"I'm not lying. My grandfather died." Annoyed, I hung the phone up on the guy on the other end and hung the job up while I was at it. I packed a bag of clothes, left the dog with Felipe, and flew home thanks to my stepdad, Ricco, springing for my ticket.

My mom picked me up from the airport and was strong and stoic as if she had a passport to heaven and could visit Grandpa anytime she liked—as if she didn't just lose her beloved father. I didn't dare open a can of worms, honestly just thankful to be home. She took me to a mall to buy a nice outfit for the funeral the next day and I asked her if I could sing. For the first time she broke and with tears running down her cheeks she said she'd like that. I didn't know much about my Lutheran religion so she helped me pick out a song, The Lord's Prayer, to learn and sing. By the afternoon, I was prepared to sing but my aunt—my mother's youngest brother's wife—wanted me to first "audition" with her in a car parked outside of the house (where the family wouldn't hear me). Offended but desperately wanting to pay my grandpa my respects in the only currency I had to give, I sang the song and got my aunt's approval.

Before the funeral, a viewing was arranged and I thought it would be a good idea for my sister and me to go and "see" Grandpa. We stopped by JC Penney's to buy dainty necklaces with crosses as if giving a nod to our religion, and proceeded to the funeral home. We held each other as we walked into Grandpa's viewing room and Cindy burst into tears, immediately regretting coming along and barely able to stand up. I held my emotions in until I spotted the tie I bought for Grandpa on the Christmas before I left for New York City and then I cried as if I was at Jesus' feet. I was so undeserving of that meaningful gesture (that I later found out was my grandmother's purposeful doing) and I felt utterly ashamed of myself. He didn't deserve to be in that coffin. I did. I felt like a wretch of a person and he was the most wonderful person I had ever met. Why? Why did God take him? I thought God was supposed to be fair.

The funeral service came and I sang The Lord's Prayer without so much as a bobble from the rafters of Gethsemane Lutheran Church (the church my grandparents had attended since forever—where my parents were married and I was baptized). Before I began, I gave myself a firm talking-to. I was a recording artist. Grandpa deserved my best.

*Don't you dare cry, Jennifer. I'll never forgive you if you do.* I warned myself before carefully pulling off the tear-free vocal performance.

As everyone departed the burial site, my mom stayed behind and I stayed with her. It was then that she lost it. She placed her hands on top of Grandpa's coffin, which had yet to be lowered into the ground, and she wailed, talking to Grandpa through her sobbing. I had seen my mother go to war with my dad. I had seen my mom look entirely put together after sleeping in her car. I had seen my mom be the epitome of a lady in the worst scenarios. But I had never seen my mom cry like that. My heart was broken. All I could do was stand by her and allow her to mourn.

I touched back down in Florida a changed person. I had not before taken the time to contemplate the preciousness of life or the imminence of death. There was no time to waste. I needed to make it happen. And "it" was everything. I needed a good job, my own place, food in my belly, and insulin in my fridge. And for some reason I could never explain, I needed Felipe.

When I reached Marta's house I was back at square one. I couldn't go back to selling Hoovers because I would be damned if I let someone tell me I was lying about the most real and devastating ordeal. Felipe was still unemployed and we were so desperate for money, I pawned the only thing I had left of value besides my truck—a dainty diamond necklace my mom gave me—for fifteen dollars so I could feed the dog. Then, after doing that, Felipe made me take the dog to the pound because it was snapping at his niece. The only way I could have avoided losing my dog was to move out. But I was broke and too afraid of losing Felipe.

Marta's husband felt sorry for me and tried to go back to the pound to adopt the dog back, thinking we could figure out a way to make it work, but the dog was already gone. Even though I had a million reasons to be mad at Felipe, losing my dog made me the most upset. I lit into him and told him we had to immediately find a way to secure good jobs so we could get our own place and live our own life. And I thought of a way to do it.

I called the smallest mom-and-pop shop of a security company in Melbourne and arranged for Felipe and myself to show up together for an interview. The morbidly obese woman behind the desk, along with her dusty relic of a husband, agreed that Felipe and I would both be great additions to their nearly employee-less roster. The only problem was, neither of us had a security license. But I already had a sales pitch ready. I explained that there was a three-day course in Orlando we could take for two hundred and twenty-five dollars a piece. If they would pay for our courses, we would pay them back with our first paycheck. They easily agreed and Felipe and I enrolled in security school the same day, graduating a few days later with perfect test scores (which annoyed me since I studied like crazy and Felipe didn't even bother to pick up a book). But just like that, we were gainfully employed as security guards and were quickly assigned all of the worst jobs.

I worked a school dance where I broke up a fistfight between teenage boys and then took a routine overnight shift at a power plant while Felipe worked overnights at a zoo, where he had to walk rounds to check on the animals, including walking over a wooden bridge above a tank full of crocodiles. I know this because, after I was done with my shifts, I went to keep Felipe company at his. The only problem was, I had signed on to babysit for Marta, who absolutely refused (with good reason) to let a person with zero sleep watch her child. So while I scored points for getting us jobs, I fell back on Marta's bad side for being hopelessly in love with her brother and the most irresponsible, responsible teenage girl she had laid her eyes on.

When the overnight shifts took a major toll on both Felipe and me, and when our repayment of the security school loan was better than paid, we jumped ship for twenty-five cents more per hour at another security company. With our new salary, came more interesting jobs; namely: driving golf carts around gated communities at night, providing security at a beachfront hotel, and most interestingly, becoming stand-in bouncers at the hotel's night club. I was in charge of keeping an eye on the crowd, keeping drunken females in their place, and once, walking a supermodel of a mother of six children to her car after a solo night out she stole for herself. In one incident, a drunken girl climbed the rooftop of parked cars and taunted me, yelling.

"You probably only make eight dollars per hour, rent-a-cop!"

In fact, I only made seven.

Meanwhile, back home I was in trouble. My bladder failed after working crazy hours that made it impossible to avoid deep sleep. Felipe addressed me head on about the wet bed, fuming that I embarrassed him and demanding I replace his sister's mattress. I was mortified. Logically, I had a disability that I was sometimes lucky enough to not have to deal with. But to everyone around me, I imagined I appeared to be a good-for-nothing, disgusting, horrible choice of a girlfriend for a golden child of a son and brother. I thought I had reached low points in my life. But my bedwetting problem sunk me all the way to the bottom.

I called my mom to beg for a few hundred dollars for a mattress (which she indeed sent) and during the call, Ricco asked to speak to me.

"Jenn, your mom and I are concerned. You didn't look well at the funeral. You seem depressed. You gained weight. But your voice—your voice was like an angel. I never realized how talented you are. Come home and live with us. I'm inviting you. Come here and get yourself back together so you can do what you're supposed to do. So you can sing."

My jaw was on the floor. Ricco was not only being nice and caring and compassionate, he was personally offering me a way out of the hell I had created for myself. And as hard as it was to say goodbye to the love of my life, I packed a plastic bag of clothes, hopped in my lousy truck, and said *adios* to Felipe for good. Or so I thought.

# CHAPTER 17
# Boomerang

I HAD NEVER MADE SUCH A DRASTIC, DIFFICULT, AND correct decision. My instinct was to run straight back to Felipe's arms but I knew with all of my heart that I had to move on. I started driving and I didn't stop, driving long into the night and refusing to take a break unless my gas tank was empty. Finally, after seventeen hours of driving I reached my wall. I pulled over at a random motel and handed the desk person forty dollars in cash for the twenty-nine dollar motel. He couldn't take it. I needed a credit card to stay there. I begged. I could barely keep my eyes open standing there talking to him and he could tell. He called over his female colleague and they conversed between each other, trying to figure out a way to get around the credit card. I could feel their compassion. They weren't just trying to be good business people. They seemed to actually care that a teenager was out in the middle of nowhere in an unsecured cloth-top vehicle and had no other option than to keep driving if they didn't help out. Still, after trying everything, including calling my parents for a credit card over the phone (which they provided but the motel still couldn't take), the motel staff sent me off to sleep in my truck.

The night was as dark as they come and the area was sketchy. By then, I knew what evil the world was capable of and I wasn't willing to risk the obvious ways I could put myself in major danger in that parking lot. So I chose to keep driving. I rolled down my windows, blasted the radio, sang songs, talked out loud to myself, chewed gum, and rubbed my eyes but I kept dozing off until I woke up panicked, my truck completely stopped, stalled in the middle of the highway with my headlights still on and key still in the engine. By the grace of God—or Grandpa?—I had not been in an accident. I could only conclude that I fell asleep, let my foot slip off of the gas pedal, stalled my truck, and coasted perfectly down the highway to a complete stop. If that wasn't a sign I had an angel (or concourses of them) in my corner, nothing was.

After such a scare, I couldn't fall asleep if I tried. The sun rose as I drove and I found myself in St. Louis. Being able to see beyond my headlights was a great relief and while the ideal thing to do was to pull over and nap, I just wanted to get home. I used a single map to figure out how to get to I-70 through Kansas City when the winds kicked up to a level I had never encountered before. I used a trick I saw my dad do, wedging my truck behind a semi-truck to enjoy a suction-cup-like invisible tow and my speed was automatically increased by ten miles per hour thanks to the eighteen-wheeler's draft. The trucker knew what I was doing and tried to shake me before we all became preoccupied with three funnel-cloud looking storms just off the highway. I thought that tornados were supposed to come from the sky but these funnels were originating from the ground. So I put two and two together and concluded that I wasn't in the middle of a tornado, but if three tornadoes were about to happen, they were going to happen right where I was looking. I drafted the semi-truck in front of me as long as I could hold on but he got rid of me on a steep hill that my worthless truck couldn't handle and I slowed to a pathetic forty miles per hour on a sixty-five mile per hour highway. After thirty-six hours of non-stop driving, I pulled up to my mom's house atop Horsetooth mountain, said, "Hi," and collapsed. Grateful to be home in one piece, I couldn't have cared less about Felipe or Florida or even about singing. I just wanted sleep.

The next morning Ricco had a heart-to-heart talk with me, reiterating in greater length what he already told me over the phone. He wanted to see me get a job, save my money, and get back to New York City where I belonged. He wanted me to do that because he knew I wanted to do that. He wasn't speaking down to me like I was a juvenile delinquent. It was like he was having an adult conversation with a teammate. And I wholeheartedly thanked him for his support.

I couldn't be back home without calling and visiting all of my besties. Steph was my favorite at the time and even though she was in a serious relationship with a young man who was as stiff as a martini, I made her promise to me that we would have a girls' night out as soon as I got my ducks in a row. Jobless, I knew what I had to do. So I put on the two-piece suit my mom bought me for my grandpa's funeral, stopped at my mom's insurance agency to fabricate a new resume, and hit the pavement. Instead of answering ads, I decided I wanted to be a waitress. No sitting in front of phones, no stuffy offices, and no selling stuff—I *hated* selling stuff. So I popped in what felt like thirty restaurants before landing on the northeast side of town at the Colorado Grill, where I found my childhood next-door neighbor working as an assistant manager. The childhood version of Pam was a sassy redhead who wanted nothing to do with me as a child because she had my far-cooler older sister to hang out with. The grown-up version of Pam was beautiful, polite, and willing to give my resume a look. Within two days, the main manager from the restaurant gave me a call for an interview and I was hired.

Being back home was a huge blessing. Summer was coming, the weather was warm, skies were blue, and I had a fun and easy job that earned me sixty dollars in tips every day. I had parents who were treating me more like an adult than a teenage hoodlum. I had a bestie who was going out to local clubs with me several times a week, where we danced so much, I shed twenty pounds without even trying. Ricco gave me a huge glass jug full of coins to kick off my NYC savings fund and I started filling it with my tips. I was genuinely happy. I was having fun for the first time in years. I was able to come home without my stomach instantly tying in knots. I was able to exist without having to strategize my every move. I had money in my pocket and square meals in my belly, thanks to the discounted meals at my job. In fact, I was so well off, I even squeezed in an appointment to have my braces tightened—something I had neglected the entire time I was in the city.

Life was so good, I almost forgot the clock was ticking and that I needed to get back to New York City sooner rather than later. Steph and I were having so much fun, she dumped her boyfriend and we became regulars at Tangz nightclub on the strip near Colorado State University. We knew the busy nights and we always showed up and danced like someone was paying us. With access to my mom's sewing machine and basic sewing skills I had been taught from toddlerhood, I started making skimpy outfits to wear to the club. Steph and I lived for attention and we reliably got it. While I made a firm promise to myself that I would be celibate and never again let a man just have his way with me, I still had fun flirting with zero guilt or allegiance to anyone. At some point, I caught the eye of a big linebacker of a guy named Nick, a football player from the Kansas City Chiefs who was visiting his nephew, who was a star player on the CSU Rams. Nick tugged my skirt like a toddler from below the speaker I was dancing on top of and asked for my number, handing me a napkin and a pen. I gave it to him and carried on dancing, not really caring to start a conversation in a booming nightclub and figuring if he really wanted to, he would call. And he did—the next day.

I could never figure out if Nick had a girl back home and just wanted some companionship, or if he liked me but was taking it slow, or what the deal was. He was anything but a steady boyfriend but we sometimes kissed after the club or met up for lunch during the week. Beyond that, we just played a cat and mouse game of maybe seeing each other at the club and maybe not. And that was a relationship I could definitely handle.

Since I never signed the managing contract with Natasha, my only connection to music back in the city was Chris. I plugged my nose and called him to check in and we spoke as if our whole awful sexual experience never happened. We both agreed that I needed to come out and record some more. My demo was already starting to sound dated and I needed new material. I set my sights on visiting New York City in July and told Chris I'd let him know once my plans were set.

Since Steph and I were inseparable, I asked her if she would consider flying to New York City with me for a week or two. We could share a hotel room and sightsee. I could show her The Statue of Liberty, Wall Street, the Twin Towers, Little Italy, China Town, the Fashion District, 34th Street, Times Square, Central Park, and anything else we could squeeze in before I hit the studio to write and record. Steph was automatically game but she could only take one week off from college and the bowling alley she was a bookkeeper at. She booked a round trip ticket and our hotel for one week, and I booked a round-trip that extended four extra days, figuring I could just extend the hotel stay when Steph went back home.

We touched down at JFK and took a bus to the A-train to Herald Square, where we checked into a room that was as small as a closet—just large enough to fit two tiny beds, a small box safe, a shrimpy side table and a chair. The single bathroom, to our dismay, was in the hallway and had to be shared with the rest of the rooms on the floor. I was a little embarrassed for encouraging Steph to book the cheapest thing she could find near 34th Street but Steph was the ultimate good sport and laughed it off. We didn't waste any time visiting as many of the places I promised as possible and eventually hopped the A-train to Clinton Ave in Brooklyn to meet up at Chris' apartment.

Going to Chris' place with a companion in tow emboldened me. I rang the buzzer, announced us, walked up the stairs and into his essential-oils-smelling apartment and confidently said, "Hello." He complimented me on how well I looked but was immediately attracted by my blonde bombshell of a bestie, so the focus fell from me. This was one time I was grateful to not command the room's attention. We sat with a couple of his friends—male and female—who also helped set the tone for a professional encounter and started brainstorming for our next song. Chris played a single he had just recorded with two female vocalists and said this was the next big hit for sure. Contrary to my stylistic chest voice and riffs, Chris' vocalists sang completely in soft falsettos. Following that lead, I started writing a song fit more for Janet Jackson's head voice than Mariah Carey's acrobatic chest one. By the time the session was over, we had a song on our hands and were ready to record, this time on my dime. Chris would set up studio time and we would meet again the following week when Steph was back home—something I equally looked forward to and feared. But I reassured myself that this was the new me. No one was ever going to get over on me like Chris did, again.

When it was time for Steph to go home, I accompanied her down to the hotel front desk and asked if we could extend the stay by a few nights. The man laughed in my face and said they were booked up for months—I would have needed to secure a room a long time ago. I played it as cool as a homeless tourist could, stuffed my luggage in one of the hotel's lobby lockers, and accompanied Steph to the JFK airport on the A-train to Far Rockaway and bus to an airport terminal before saying our goodbyes. I returned alone to the hotel in Herald Square, retrieved my small, rectangular carryon luggage, and started walking around to find a new hotel. Everywhere I went was either booked or too expensive, so I kept walking. The sun set and I had killed hours walking in dress shoes, which were actually more comfortable than the sneakers I brought, but still made my feet ache. I walked and walked until it was impossible to convince the remaining New Yorkers on the streets that I wasn't a lost tourist; so I got critically serious about my hotel search. I arrived at yet another hotel, where the desk person named a price beyond my means. I recognized that I was shooting way too high in terms of fanciness. I needed to find a dump.

I arrived at the run-down lobby of an ancient hotel in midtown, where I was immediately solicited for sex by an intoxicated man and his girlfriend. Luckily, they accepted my refusal with slurred words and laughter and stumbled their way to the elevator where the man had the last word, telling me I'd regret it. I turned to the desk person, who was barricaded in a box and who told me I have to be careful "out there." He named his price and I decided that I would be stupid to not haggle. I told him I had forty cash—take it or leave it. He told me he would take it because he felt for me but I had to be out by 8:00 o'clock in the morning. Deal.

I took the questionable elevator up to the even more questionable hotel room and hurriedly jammed my key in the door as if I was being chased by a killer and only had seconds to survive. Once in, I slammed the door shut and locked all four of the locks provided on the door: the handle lock, the deadbolt, and two chain locks as if one wasn't enough. I sat my bag down and looked forward to a shower before realizing that cheap rooms don't come with bathrooms in New York City—you have to share one out in the hall. But after my run-in with the crazy sex people, the last thing I wanted to do was step foot in anything that was shared. I changed into pajamas and went to close the window from where I felt a breeze. I opened the curtains to find that there was no window at all. Despite being fully inside of my room, looking down sixteen stories to the street below without glass between a death-drop and me scared me so much, I began to feel panicked and dizzy and stepped away from the window. If there was ever a time where I prayed that my five-year-old sleepwalking habit didn't relapse, it was that night in a sixteenth story windowless hotel room.

Despite my promise to leave by eight o'clock in the morning, I slept until eleven until the maid banged on my door. I apologized profusely for oversleeping and made my way to the shared bathroom to venture to clean up. The hotel wasn't nearly as frightening in the day and I took a shower only to find there were no towels. I made do with what I had in my luggage and decided that staying nowhere was better than staying in a place like that ever again. With that, I jaywalked through the boroughs like I used to do when I sold beepers until it was time for my session in the afternoon.

I was paying so I only had a couple of hours to get my vocals laid down perfectly and get out. Since I was in a professional recording studio with a professional sound engineer, whether or not I recorded quickly was up to me. In tennis, an athlete perfects their serve by practicing the same routine—a few bounces of the ball, a timed pause—over and over again until their muscles memorize a perfect serve. Recording artists do something similar. Some artists' creative process involves smoking weed, drinking, and socializing with their own personal studio squad before entering a soundproof recording booth. Others, like me, come prepared to get straight to business, practicing beforehand a song so much we almost never want to hear it again. Besides, I was never inclined to try any form of drug and the last thing I wanted to do was eat up my studio time socializing. Once in the recording booth, how people record is all over the spectrum. Some need the music volume loud and their vocal volume low. Some need the opposite. Most wear the headphones on both ears and get reverb applied to their vocals in real time. I always preferred using only one earphone. Wearing both earphones had some sort of psychosomatic effect and I would swiftly go flat. Hearing my voice through a headphone on one side, and leaving my other ear out in the open, was how I stayed on key. Some artists aren't satisfied unless their whole song is recorded in a single, perfect take. Others patch their vocals together in a series of "punches" (when an artist retakes passes and the sound engineer only presses record over parts that need to be fixed). With either method, you eventually get a song. But the more prepared you are, the better your chances of nailing it quickly.

I was never a one-take artist because, as important as singing on key is, singing with heart—a growl to underscore pain or a burst of volume to take a song to its peak—is just as contributory to a successful song as a good voice is. Sometimes one of my less than perfect vocal passes was kept on the merit of emotion alone. No matter what one's style or process, as long as the final product moves and resonates with the listener, it's a keeper.

Chris brought my attention to the fact that the studio owner, Arcenius, had also just started a record label called Hilltop Records. They played me the first single from the label—a mid-tempo dance song sung by a female African American RnB artist whose voice wasn't as nice as her body but I agreed that I thought the track would do well. I nudged Chris as if to signal to him to put a good word in for me with Arcenius and he looked at me in a way that told me he was already two steps ahead of me. I said my goodbyes as if I had someplace to go and the team at Noise in the Attic sent me home with a rough mix of my brand new song on a cassette tape that I could duplicate myself at home (as if there was anyone besides my friends and family back home who would care).

I had two more days to kill, less cash in my pocket than what it would take to stay at even the shabbiest hotel, and was wearing my last clean outfit consisting of a zip-up jumpsuit with patent leather boots that ended just under my knees and a patent leather (plastic) jacket that matched the boots. I thought I looked like a star but, in retrospect, what I'm positive I actually looked like was a prostitute.

I took a page out of the book of homeless people I used to see huddled in the corners of A-trains during my commutes in and out of New York City and hit the subway line for a nap in an air-conditioned train car that would only cost me a dollar-twenty-five. Instead of doing everything in my power to avoid the longest routes, I aimed for them. More time on the Subway meant less time walking. I spent that entire night on the A-train, riding it from the top of Harlem to the very last stop in Far Rockaway, Queens, where a construction worker who boarded just before the sun rose tapped me.

"Miss! Don't sleep on the subway. It's dangerous!"

I played it off like I just shut my eyes on my commute to work but my outfit and luggage said otherwise.

I emerged from the belly of New York City to eat and walk around again all day until settling at night in the main terminal of

Grand Central Station, sitting on the grandiose marble staircase and getting lost in the star constellations painted by hand in gold on the faded turquoise ceiling above.

"It's amazing, isn't it?" a voice beside me said.

"Oh, hi. Um, yeah. It's awesome," I replied to a short African American kid with messy braided cornrows, who was around my age and hanging out with two of his misfit friends—one with a huge afro and the other with the type of no-frills haircut a mother gives her son.

"I don't mean to be nosey, but what is a beautiful girl like you doing alone in the middle of the night?" he hit on me in the least assured way as if never expecting me to speak back.

"Well, what are *you guys* doing out this late?"

"Touché," He blushed at my forwardness.

By my deductions, after learning how to quickly read people through six months of selling beepers on New York City streets and one day of selling Hoover vacuums in Florida, these kids were major geeks. They weren't there to pick up women. They were there to study the ceiling and figure out for themselves why half of it was painted backwards. But after finding me, a member of the opposite sex who had clearly never given them the time of day before, they started studying me instead. A game of Q&A ensued and by dawn, just hours before I could finally take the A-train to JFK and get back home to a shower and a bed, I made three new friends.

The ringleader of the group asked if he could have my mailing address so he could write me letters. Letter-writing wasn't something I thought *anybody* would do, much less a teenager from the city. Nonetheless, I scribbled down my information for the young man. After that, I said goodbye to my three overnight companions, and New York City, until I could afford to move back.

# CHAPTER 18
# Record Deal

W HEN I GOT HOME, I GOT A CALL AND A LETTER. The call was from Chris with the most unexpected, incredible news anyone could have ever told me at the time: Arcenius at Hilltop Records was offering me a record deal.

"Tell him I accept!" I said as if recording contracts were verbal. Chris and I spoke just long enough to agree that I needed to get back to New York City stat. I estimated my return date and hung up the phone with a promise to circle back soon.

The letter I received was from the kid with braids from Grand Central Station. As I read the note that was handwritten in pencil, my heart melted. He wrote about how much he liked me, how much he enjoyed our time together, and how he hoped I would write him back soon. He was so innocent; so pure. I nearly fell in love based on that letter alone. But since I was preoccupied with my first record deal, I never wrote back.

As I drove around town in my drop-top truck, which was far more enjoyable when I wasn't sleep deprived in the middle of a tornado, Nick spotted me on the road and motioned for me to pull over. I pulled over and got out to say "Hi" and he looked me up and down.

"You lost weight," he noticed.

Indeed, walking all over New York City instead of resting comfortably in a hotel room shred another seven pounds off of my average frame. Nick proceeded to notice my new clothes and shoes, which I got for pennies on the dollar in New York City's Fashion District and which were light years ahead of the clothes available in Fort Collins. All of a sudden, Nick seemed a lot more interested in me. The only problem was, the only thing I was interested in was moving back to New York City and signing my record deal.

I declined the heavy chain Nick offered for me to "hold"—a sign that I was his girl—and set my sights on a savings goal: save fifteen hundred dollars and leave Fort Collins once and for all.

In the process of saving money from tips, I also managed to put together a showcase of four of my original songs at Tangz, where my coworkers and a handful of friends and strangers showed up to watch me sing. Steph and Jen (a girl I worked with) danced behind me and everyone clapped and supported, but nowhere near the massive audience and applause I received at the Lincoln Center back in high school. Still, I said I would do it and I did. For me, finishing things I started and being a decent person who didn't lie or cheat was of increasing importance. I hated the other me.

The clock ticked away and my giant money jar grew to over one thousand dollars. I was having the time of my life being back home in Fort Collins (this time with no rules) and hanging out with Steph, night and day. To take advantage of the record deal being held for me, I needed to get back to New York City ASAP. But the thought of moving back to The Big Apple without the trapeze net of friends was frightening. What if my blood sugar went low during the night? What if I was attacked on the subway? What if I ran out of money, or food, or insulin? Who would I call? I shrugged these things off nearly as soon as I thought of them. I survived my parents' houses. I survived the little old house of college girls. I survived squatting in my dad's property before bouncing to my grandparents' house. I survived living with mere strangers (who became great friends) in Queens. I survived Florida with Felipe's sister, who made it clear I was a piece of garbage she didn't want her brother around. What in the world was I worried about? I could do this.

Now that I was managing my own singing career, I needed to direct and fund my own stuff. I needed a new headshot before I met with Arcenius to seal the record deal. I needed to go in there ready, professional, and together. I had a firm enough command of English to write a decent one-page bio but I needed a headshot to complete my marketing package. At the time, Fort Collins, Colorado wasn't exactly set up for aspiring stars. So I headed to the mall to the most accessible place I knew of to take a headshot: Glamour Shots.

I walked in without an appointment to the hole-in-the-wall where a young woman greeted me and presented the many ways she could make me look absolutely ravishing. She would do my hair and makeup and select a feathered boa, or corset, or fancy jacket and then create the ultimate fantasy shot to capture my allure and sex appeal. I told her that all sounded great but I actually needed something a little more life-like. I asked if I could do my own hair and makeup and then I selected a black leather jacket that was three sizes too big (the only one they had) and made do. In the end, I came out with a convincing shot of a young girl with sun-kissed sandy brown hair, blue eyes, swollen lips that rested gently in a closed position over metal braces, and an oversized leather jacket. I took my prints to work and showed them to my night crew, only to find that the males all loved the photos and the girls all accused me of going to Glamour Shots, which I vehemently denied.

My glass jar of coins and cash became full, the night scene slowed down with most college kids hitting the books instead of the clubs on weeknights, and the clock was ticking for me to get back to New York City and do something with my life. Steph and I spent one of our last nights out together in Fort Collins at Perkins diner, where a sixtyish-year-old African American man named Henry—a psychic who found his way to our small town—caught my attention. I had stumbled across him before in town and knew that he did readings. I figured it was fate that placed him in Perkins and I jumped at the chance to get a glimpse into my future.

Steph and I invited Henry to our table and I asked if he would give us readings. He didn't do it for money. He just read people as a way of life. He took Steph's hand, examined the form and lines, and ran through some personal information about her, one of which things he refused to say out loud but confirmed with her through coded language. I could barely wait to find out if I was going to be rich and famous and happy and in love and have everything I could ever want in life, or even, simply just stay alive. He examined my hand more carefully than he did Steph's as if I was more difficult to read. He nodded at me knowingly without me necessarily asking any questions. I spoke up and prodded him with questions about where I would end up in life and he replied by telling me that my lines were straightforward but my path was not. I asked him if I would make it singing and he answered in a way that didn't rule it out, but also didn't confirm it.

I asked him if I would ever have children, and he pointed to the lines on the side of my hand that showed two, but then didn't answer when I asked directly, "So I'll have two kids?"

He let go of my hand and took a sip of the coffee Steph and I bought him as if he was bored. Since he seemed so disinterested, I didn't press him for more information. But he sipped his coffee contemplatively and connected eyes with me again and nodded up and down as if saying yes but not saying anything at all. The next week, I mulled over the reading, trying to figure out what all of Henry's head nods, eye contact, and ambiguous statements meant before deciding I was in control of my path. Whatever he saw in the past was done and whatever he saw in the future could be changed. If I could stay alive, I could do anything.

As if I wasn't confused enough from my psychic reading, I received a highly unexpected phone call at my mom's house: Felipe was calling to say "Hi." He was visiting his mom in New York City and she was "asking for" me. We exchanged guarded pleasantries and caught each other up on what one another was doing. He had continued on with the security job I got him, hooked up with a pretty girl, and partied with a new guy friend he found in Melbourne. I had done much more with my time.

"I knew you would do it," he said when I told him I landed a record deal.

I mentioned the irony of him visiting New York City since I had just booked a one-way flight there to move for good. I suggested we meet for lunch sometime and he countered by offering to pick me up from the airport. I hesitated a bit before accepting, not wanting to rehash any type of connection with him, but rationalizing that a ride home with Felipe still beat a ride with a smelly taxi driver or lugging all of my belongings on the A-train. Besides, at least I wouldn't feel entirely alone that first day back in the concrete jungle.

This time with my mom and Ricco's blessings, I said my last goodbyes to Steph—the best friend I could have asked for after the complete train wreck of life decisions in Florida; I packed a suitcase with my clothes, cassette tapes, headshots, and insulin; I handed my mom the keys to the truck my grandfather paid off with the marching orders to sell it and pay him back; and I boarded a flight to JFK International Airport in Queens, NY, where Felipe awaited my arrival.

I felt like coming to New York with my best foot forward so I dressed in a cute skirt and top, jacket, stockings, and heels. A month previously I got my long hair cut into a short bob that framed my strong jaw line in a flattering way that was both easy to style and fell naturally straight and spunky instead of long and messy. I stepped off of the plane and started walking to the greeting area when an airport worker showed up next to me and showered me with compliments that made me blush with no expectation of reciprocation. I thanked him and kept walking… right past Felipe who stopped me.

"Jenn! Hey!" Felipe greeted me.

"Oh, hi!" I hugged him instinctively.

"You look great! Wow! All I saw was legs walking towards me," he complimented me as if forgetting that I still kind of despised him for dragging me to Florida.

"Thanks. You too—you look great. Have you been working out? You look bigger."

He confirmed he had been bodybuilding with his new friend. His once skinny frame was now filled out with respectable muscles. It was hard to not find him attractive. He never failed in that department.

Before Felipe dropped me at my hotel, he talked me into stopping at his dad's apartment at South Street Seaport and hanging out for a bit. I didn't think it would be that big of a deal, so I accepted. I warned myself as we drove to not make any more mistakes. I had worked so hard to remain celibate, get into shape, land my record deal, and save up enough money to move to New York City on my own. The last thing I needed was a boyfriend—or worse, Felipe—to distract me. We arrived at his dad's house, sat down with a couple of glasses of sweet iced tea, and reminisced on the good times as if there were never any bad. And before I knew it, I was in bed having sex with Felipe. On one hand, I felt like if I wanted to have consensual sex with someone I once fiercely loved and had the craziest chemistry with, then I was well within my rights to do so without strings attached. On the other hand, I worried I just made another big mistake. Either way, I still got to my hotel that night and I marked off my stupidity as an inconsequential one-night stand that would go away as soon as Felipe returned to Florida.

I only planned to stay in the hotel a few days while I searched for a permanent apartment but the task was more difficult than I realized. Luckily, I had wised up about ways to survive without a place to stay in New York City and was less scared of everything so hit the classified ads for a room share. I secured a basement room with a bed in a multi-family house not far from the subway station at the corner of Nostrand and Atlantic Avenues in a dicey part of Brooklyn for one hundred and thirty dollars per week. I gave the landlord a heads up that I'd only be there one week, tops, but she still made me give her a deposit in addition to rent. Much like all the cheap hotels in the city, the basement apartment had two bedrooms with locks and keys, a shared bathroom that looked like it was built in a third-world country, and a fridge. I checked the bathroom and the only thing there was an old, used bar of rust-colored soap that was starting to split and harden. In the fridge, I found a half-filled baby bottle and a jar of pickles. I didn't hear a baby and stood in disbelief that anyone would have an infant down there.

I had previously arranged for my mom to come out and help me set up my apartment but, by the time she arrived at JFK, I still hadn't found a place. To avoid seeing Felipe, I took the three-hour trip from the N-train, to the R-train to the A-train to Far Rockaway to pick her up and then gave her an impromptu makeover and instructions before taking her back to Brooklyn.

"Earrings off. Lipstick off. Turn your ring around, big stone down. Put your purse over your torso and hold it in front. If the seats are mostly taken, let's just stand. Don't make eye contact with anyone," I prepped her.

We arrived to the empty room with a bed, and my mom (as good of a sport as she was) knew we had to get out of there ASAP and told me so. I searched my brain for ideas on where to find an affordable place and resigned to the fact that I really only knew Richmond Hill, Queens—where I stayed with Felipe's mom. With that, my mom and I got back on the train and hit the pavement around Lefferts Boulevard to look, in-person instead of in the classifieds, for a place for me to rent. When we didn't see any "for rent" signs anywhere, we got desperate and found a real estate office with an apartment advertised for four hundred and fifty dollars per month. The broker led us a few houses away to a multi-family house and up two flights of stairs to a tiny, L-shaped attic. One side was about five feet by seven feet. The other was five by ten, with a tiny fridge, make-shift kitchen, and just enough room for a toilet and tiny standup shower that were inches apart. The price was right, I knew where I was, and all I really needed was a roof overhead, so I took it. The only problem was, there was a one-month's rent realtor fee, one-month's rent deposit, and one-month's rent on the spot. I was short and the realtor didn't budge, so my mom saved the day and wrote a check—a gift I vowed to repay.

Mom and I stayed a night in Brooklyn before setting up my apartment in Queens before she headed back to the Rocky Mountains. After dropping her at the airport, I had a daunting task to accomplish: head back to Brooklyn and get my security deposit back. After what felt like an eternal train ride, I made my way back to the temporary room I was relieved to be rid of. I yelled back and forth with the landlord, who sent her son down to answer the door while staying at the top of the stairs, before finally getting my money back and finding my way back to the A-train to Lefferts Boulevard. Finally, in my own apartment, I was at peace. I did it. Well, everyone who helped me did it. But I did it, you know? And I sat very satisfied with myself before remembering that I was jobless and all alone.

# CHAPTER 19
# Noise in the Attic

WITHOUT THE SAFETY NET OF A ROOMMATE, family, or nearby friends, I knew it was game time. My first item of business was obvious: get a newspaper and get a job. I searched the classifieds and found an ad for seasonal cashiers at Century 21 (advertised in the newspaper as "NYC's Best Kept Secret") across the street from the twin towers in Lower Manhattan. The department store sold high-end, name brand clothing and accessories for a fraction of tag prices. I dressed in a suit and arrived at the Human Resources department early, but not the earliest. At least twenty people beat me to the punch. I looked around to find a melting pot of people of all ages, shapes, colors, sizes, and wardrobes—some too casual for an interview and others spot-on. I handed my resume to the gatekeeper of a woman who was responsible for screening and sending candidates in and out of a single room and she handed it right back, referring me to a clipboard and pen to fill out the store's application by hand. After transcribing my resume to the application, I was swiftly sent into a room to meet with a manger, foregoing the wait everyone else seemed to have. After answering only a few questions, I was told I was hired as a supervisor for a dollar more per hour than the cashier job I applied for. I didn't have any experience as a supervisor or cashier but was prepared to figure it out to secure the job. To my relief, the manager informed me that all supervisors go through two weeks of paid training and sent me away with an acceptance stamp. I felt sorry for everyone there before me, whom I was bumped ahead of. But I carried on, thankful for my privilege.

I didn't reach out to Chris until I had worked at my job for a full week. I didn't think it would do any good to sign a record deal with zero advance money if I couldn't support myself. After being satisfied that Century 21 was a sure thing, I proceeded to handle my music business. I followed Chris' instructions and called him to set up a face-to-face meeting with Arcenius, the owner of Noise in the Attic recording studio and founder of Hilltop Records. Naïve, it didn't occur to me to check before moving to New York City that the record deal was real. Luckily, it was.

I arrived after work to Noise in the Attic, which was located in the Garment District of Hell's Kitchen on 8$^{th}$ Avenue between 38$^{th}$ and 39$^{th}$ Streets. During the day, business bustled much like any other area in the city. At night, the scene changed. Neon signs that advertised twenty-five cent peeps shows were turned on and corners and dark alleys became populated with nightlife to the tune of scary looking men and street-walking women. As such, to get into the building, you either had to catch a person coming out and make a plea for entrance, make nice with the old Spanish maintenance guy, sneak in behind someone on their way in, or get buzzed in by someone who actually wanted you there. To my delight, Arcenius buzzed me in on my first try and I entered the old building with a trail of unannounced guests who snuck in behind me and assured me they just forgot to bring their keys, which I believed given they appeared to have showered that day.

The old building looked like it would come crashing down at any moment. The foyer was comprised of exposed, decrepit brick, metal pipes, and electric wire innards as if the builder forgot to finish the project. I hesitated to get on the elevator, which was loud, rickety like the ancient roller coaster at Coney Island, and looked like it was installed just after my mother's ancestors—The Coopers—sailed over the Atlantic Ocean on the Mayflower in 1620. But I proceeded to go in, following the herd of musicians who seemed unfazed.

As we ascended up to each floor, the elevator halted to an abrupt stop and pounded as if a dinosaur stepped in. The door rolled open with the smoothness of a jammed bike chain and music seeped in until a full volume song flooded our ears. Once the door closed and the elevator began moving again, the songs gradually faded away and blended with new sounds up above. Every floor seemed to have its own genre of music: second floor, Latin; third floor, Reggae; fourth floor, Dance; fifth floor: Alternative; sixth floor: random silence; seventh floor: Strings; and eighth floor: Heavy Metal. When we reached our destination on the ninth floor and the elevator door opened, bass boomed in, vibrating the walls as if an earthquake was taking place.

Thankful to step out of the elevator, I looked for the door with the Noise in the Attic sign and rang a buzzer that sounded like an electric chair. The huge, heavy door creaked open like a coffin and Chris appeared through creepy purple lighting and invited me in so professionally, one would have never known he once preyed on me. We walked through a tiny entrance past a coffee machine, water jug, and air freshener that failed to cover up the stink of the previous night's session and proceeded to make reintroductions before getting down to business.

The studio was more cramped than I remembered. Just beyond the water jug was a two-person leather couch that left a walkway that was two feet wide. At the end of the couch was a step up to a corner desk, cassette duplicating machines, filing cabinet, and a comfy office chair that Arcenius mostly manned. In front of the couch was the door to the studio production room and a window that was covered by a professionally printed poster with studio rates, as well as photos of Arcenius' latest artist—an older African American female R&B artist.

Chris broke the ice, reiterating how Arcenius was impressed with my music and how he "talked Arcenius into" signing me. Arcenius sat quietly with the calm presence of an old man in a rocking chair on a porch. Since I hadn't paid much attention to Arcenius during my demo recording, I took a moment to size him up and assess whom I was about to do business with.

Arcenius was a tall, thin, forty-something African American man with a clean fade topped by short, naturally curly hair, droopy bedroom eyes, a strong nose with pronounced nostrils, and big, puffy lips that were punctuated by a thin mustache and gapped front teeth. He wore a huge diamond earring in his left ear, gold chains around his neck, and a gold bracelet or watch on his wrist. His clothes were sharp and his loafers seemed brand new. If it weren't for him greeting me seamlessly, I would have thought he was shy. But it turned out he was just extremely relaxed, as if he had the world in the palm of his hands.

Arcenius skipped pleasantries and cut to the chase: he was prepared to sign me if I was prepared to sign. He handed me a contract with instructions to have my people look it over and return it to him so we could get straight to work on an album. But without a manager, much less a lawyer, much less my first paycheck from Century 21 in hand, "my people" actually consisted of one person: me.

Since I had received at least a few compliments on my decent command of the English language during my time in New York City, I had the audacity to assume I could easily read and understand a recording contract on my own. I didn't want to let anyone know that I didn't have a lawyer, so I played along as if "my people" would immediately review the contract; but I knew full well it would be me who negotiated anything. I left the studio after listening to my four songs on the loud studio speakers, somewhat reaffirming for Arcenius his decision to sign me (and hyping me all the way up), and headed back to the A-train for an hour and a half ride home on a local train—the only option late at night.

I found a seat in the train car that gave me space on each side so I didn't have to touch legs with strangers or smell strange scents or accidentally elbow someone when I was getting my Walkman and headphones out. Then, I pulled out my contract and began to read every sentence of the twenty-pages. I marked everything I didn't understand before circling back over my marks to reread confusing sentences until I felt like I understood what I was signing. I slashed all of the percentages down by ten percent, the contract time down to a year, removed the auto-renew clause because I had learned from the good citizens on the streets of the city that you always have to negotiate (even for a beeper price that is nonnegotiable). Satisfied, I hand-delivered the mark-up back to Arcenius within a week.

"You did this yourself?" Arcenius asked.

"Yeah."

"So who is my lawyer supposed to call; you?" he laughed in my face.

"I mean, it's my life, right?"

"You gotta get a lawyer, sweetheart."

"I don't have the money for it."

"Well find one who will do it for free."

"No. I'm confident in my markup," I replied, certain that I knew the exact price for "free."

"I'm not giving up these percentages. The whole contract is standard. You won't get better than this anywhere," Arcenius bargained.

"Fine, just give me what you want me to sign. But you only get one year of my life to make something happen. That's all you get," I said as confidently as an insecure, family-less, friend-less teenager could.

"Fine."

"Done deal?"

"Done deal."

I really didn't care that the contract bound me to things I probably didn't want to be bound to. I didn't care that I didn't have a lawyer. I read every word of my contract. I understood it. I knew that, from that moment on, my music wasn't my own. My image wasn't my own. My words weren't my own. And certain business choices would not be my own. In return, I had complete freedom to write and record whenever I wanted for a long as I wanted at Noise in the Attic, complete with a producer and sound engineer, and I wouldn't pay a single penny. I was signed and my label would cover everything. I recalled my mom's good advice that, if something was real, I wouldn't have to pay for it. I felt extremely confident that signing my record deal was a good decision, for once.

With the record deal sorted out, I now had a free pass to drop in at the studio any time I wanted (usually at night after work) and write or record in between paid sessions by various artists. If I scheduled an actual session with Arcenius, the studio was blocked off just for me. If I dropped in, I could always count on finding a new cast of characters within the heavy coffin door. Over time, I grew to be able to tell who was inside the moment the elevator door opened on the ninth floor.

If I was hit by a wall of body-odor-smelling smoke but no music was playing, I knew Frenchie was inside alone and I usually didn't bother going in because, while I liked Frenchie, I absolutely despised smoke of any variety, much less what I finally figured out was weed smoke. Frenchie was a light-skinned, average height, stalky African American kid who lived in a durag (much like almost every Hip-hop head at the time), Timberland boots, baggy jeans, and a t-shirt that either advertised his squad or was just trendy. He had the vibe of Dr. Dre—a little bit intimidating—but was professional (when he wasn't smoking blunts) and nice enough that he wasn't necessarily frightening. Still, he was someone I wouldn't want to upset. Therefore, I was always polite but tried not to get too involved otherwise.

If I was hit by a wall of body-odor-smelling smoke, and the brick walls were vibrating with bass, and a ruckus was being raised by male voices inside, I knew a rap squad was in the building. Arcenius' most loyal clients were Doo Wop and Da Bounce Squad, and Doo Wop's shorty, Uneek. Doo Wop was a short Puerto Rican kid who, like Frenchie, wore a durag, baggy (expensive brand name) clothes, Timberland boots, a fat gold chain weighed down by a huge medallion, gold teeth, a plentiful pocket of cash, and recreational weed at all times. Doo Wop was a mixtape king and always had a project he was working on, always had his team with him, and always seemed to sprint in and out of the building for quick mixes or cassette duplication or cassette labels or just a quick check-in if he wasn't there for a session. In either event, when he came to the studio, he was treated like a big deal and Arcenius trained me to stay out of the way and not act like a groupie—just play it cool like I belonged there.

Doo Wop's girl, Uneek, was a petite, medium-skinned African American girl from the Bronx (where, presumably, she met Doo Wop) and dressed nearly identical to her beau, in Timberland boots, baggy jeans, a tight shirt that exposed a sliver of cleavage under a big leather jacket, a perfect weave of long, red-dyed hair, huge gold hoop earrings, gold chains, gold bracelets, gold rings, and a sidekick in the form of a Shih Tzu dog with the hair on its head secured with a bow. The pup even had its own baby bag, filled with pee-pads, treats, food, and dishes, and during the listening portions of Uneek's sessions, it was not uncommon to find the dog attempting to hump a leg, which Uneek tended to by extending and straightening her own leg so the dog could satisfy itself on her boot. Uneek was pretty, feminine, charming, and interesting, yet outlandish, raw, rugged, and—for lack of a better descriptor—hood to the hundredth power.

"What up my nigga?" she would greet Arcenius with a hug.

Uneek was one of a kind in her time. She rhymed as well or better than the rest of Da Squad. She was a Lil' Kim meets Remy Ma before there was a Lil' Kim or Remy Ma (except that they made it all the way and she would eventually fall short of stardom). After seeing Uneek in the studio a few times, Arcenius asked her to take a listen to my music.

"That's you!?" she asked me in disbelief.

"Yeah."

"You black?"

"No," I said with a chuckle as if she was kidding.

"I don't believe that. You can blow, girl! You black!" she insisted.

"My grandparents say I'm British, Norwegian, Irish, German, and French. Anyway, I'm from Colorado. We don't really have black people there."

"See? You don't know. You probably *are* black! You gotta be with that voice!"

Even though Uneek's swag was thuggish and intimidating, I was enchanted by her. She was a strong, talented, tough, potty-mouthed, force to be reckoned with. She had that automatic star appeal—that aura that screams "one of a kind." She wasn't on TV yet, but she instantly gained my fandom after she took the time to check out my music. To my surprise, Uneek liked me so much, she invited Arcenius and me to an event that Ed Lover was hosting. At the time, Ed Lover was at the height of his radio career, starring on Hot 97's hip-hop morning radio show "Ed, Lisa, and Dre" with Lisa G. and his former co-host of *Yo! MTV Raps*, Dr. Dre (not to be confused with the producer from Compton). An invitation to an event with him was a big, unbelievable, break. Arcenius stuffed his pockets with my demo tapes and we hit the road with Da Squad. The only problem was, we didn't arrive at a red carpet like I imagined. We arrived at Ed Lover's house. And when we walked in, he grilled us, whispered a few words back and forth with Uneek, and then invited us in. I sat as quiet as a mouse on a couch, feeling extremely uncomfortable for crashing a family affair.

One of Ed's friends came out and ask, "Who are you?"

I explained my connection to Unique and sat for what felt like the whole night quiet until we left. I felt embarrassed for going and disappointed that, after all that, we didn't even get a tape into Mr. Lover's hands. Another lesson in the music business learned: don't crash people's personal events looking to sneak a cassette tape into a pocket.

If I stepped off the ninth floor and didn't hear anything at all, I sometimes found the studio locked with no one home or happened upon a rare sighting of a bigger name, like Big Kap, a local celebrity DJ who was known for mixtapes and appeared on Hot 97 frequently enough for me to know his name. We also encountered artists who were not famous but who just happened to be blood relatives of actual stars. For example, one night Arcenius woke me up out of a dead sleep in the middle of the night and sent a car to pick me up so I could sing the hook on a record for the brother of reggae star, Shaggy. When I got to the studio, the kid needed me to write a hook, sing the hook, lay background vocals, and then say a bunch of things with a sexy voice in Spanish. I aced the session and the kid's team was ecstatic. The only problem was, they didn't want to pay a respectable rate for my time and inconvenience. Truth be told, I was none the wiser. I was excited to have two hundred dollars of cash in my hand. Arcenius, on the other hand, was livid. He immediately and angrily pulled the manager aside and started a yelling match.

"You got this girl coming all the way from Queens in a car in the middle of the night and that's what you're paying her!?" he said more animatedly than I had ever seen him before.

He knew I'd have to go straight to work on no sleep, but more importantly, that I wouldn't get any credit on the track for my vocals. Despite going to bat for me, they refused to pay me more. I was still thankful for the work and unexpected cash but Arcenius regretted ever referring me in the first place.

If there was no smoke in the elevator bank on the ninth floor and I heard my own songs playing or random loops of music on auto-repeat, I could usually count on finding Arcenius there producing. Whatever he produced, I wrote and recorded to. After I signed with Arcenius, I noticed that he quietly pushed Chris completely out of the picture so Arcenius could maintain full production credit on my music. I never mentioned it because I frankly never wanted to see Chris again if I could help it.

When Arcenius and I worked together in the studio, he would sometimes give me a full song—music and lyrics—that he wrote himself and wanted me to record. But more times than not, he'd give me a musical track to write lyrics and vocal arrangements to, which I grew to excel at. Either way, I started singing more than I ever had in my entire life. With so much practice, I quickly mastered recording in a studio where, unlike live performance, you can start over and take breaths and punch in and out of lines and add background vocals multiple times over in your own voice and riffs and runs and audio effects. After each session, when my body was ready to collapse from exhaustion, I would still find the energy to pull out my Walkman and headphones and happily listen to my fresh recordings on the A-train ride back home in the middle of the night. I was living my dream. Even if it wasn't quite as glamorous as I had imagined, the experience was not lost on me. I was an actual recording artist. Now, all I needed was to get all of us paid for it.

# CHAPTER 20
# Rookie Mistake

ICLOCKED IN AT CENTURY 21 EVERY DAY FOR EIGHT to ten hours of standing on heels (which I quickly learned to replace with sneakers) and oversaw one of the many cashier lines on the main floor of the store. I didn't ring anyone up. My job was to walk back and forth across the line to fix cash register errors, resolve any disputes, pitch in with bagging during rush periods, count the money, "cash out," and transport money bags to the safe room buried deep beneath the store, where a multi-point check system was followed to ensure the cash didn't leave in employees' pockets.

As busy as the cashier line was, I had the opportunity while doing my job to come into contact with a lot of New Yorkers. It wasn't uncommon for the cute girls on our line to get hit on or flirted with. But one day I overheard one of the girls shooting the breeze with a sharply dressed, well-to-do-looking African American man who, when the cashier asked him what he does for a living "to look so fine," replied that he was an Artist and Repertoire for Island Records, one of the major labels at the time. I barged in on that conversation like a pit bull vying for a dropped chicken leg. I grabbed the suit the man was buying to prep it for purchase and butted my way into the conversation.

"Island Records A&R, huh? Can I give you my demo tape? I can really sing, I promise." The pressure of the customers waiting behind the man forced the conversation to be quick.

"Take my card and have my assistant set up a meeting," he handed me his card. "And here's a card for you, pretty lady. You can call me direct," he handed a card to the cashier.

Even if I did just completely insert myself into a love connection in the most desperate, sorry way, I was ecstatic. I was signed to Arcenius and Hill Top Records. But I had learned enough in my short time there, that if you get signed by a major label, everyone—especially Arcenius—will get paid a ton more than what a little rinky-dink independent label could offer. I called the assistant at Island Records immediately and got a sit-down meeting scheduled for the next week.

Arcenius was all for me pursuing the opportunity I landed myself. If either I, or the songs he produced, were picked up by Island Records, we would both be in very good shape. The day of the meeting arrived and I got dressed in what I thought was a star-quality outfit: black, lace-up boots that went just above my ankles; nude stockings (that camouflaged the scar on my left shin enough to prevent people from blurting, "Oh my God! What happened to you!?"); a short, cheerleader-like skirt; cute shirt topped with a black leather jacket; and my short hair (which Arcenius continued to be upset I cut) pulled into an up-do and wrapped with a leopard printed scarf with some bangs hanging out in front. Even though my metal braces completely killed my vibe, I felt pretty and presentable until I asked directions from a straphanger.

"You're not from here, are you?" the stranger said.

"Not originally. I'm from Colorado."

"I can tell."

*Ugh. There went my confidence.* Still, I had the most important meeting in my life to get to. There was nothing I could do about my look now. I prayed my voice would be enough.

I arrived at what was known as The Music Building in Midtown, where numerous major labels lived. I walked in and saw a group of rap artists trying to get past security, to no avail, and I realized even more what a big deal it was that I was there. I approached the security desk and stated my name.

"Jennifer Johnson. Uh, JJ. Here to see Will Knight."

To my delight, they phoned up to confirm my invitation and handed me a visitor sticker to stick on my jacket with instructions on how to take an escalator up to the elevator to Island Records.

I arrived at Will's office with ease and was somewhat struck by how small and regular it was. He welcomed me in and asked me a little about myself before I handed him my tape cassette, which had around eight songs on it by then. He listened to pieces of each song, fast-forwarding the tape cassette until he had heard everything.

"So, who wrote and produced all of these?" he asked as anyone would.

I told him that Arcenius produced all of the tracks, and I wrote, vocally arranged, and sang everything.

He cut to the chase. "I'm not in love with the production. It sounds kind of dated. But you can definitely sing, girl. Let me ask you something," he eased in. "Would you want to write for us? I have a new group I'm working with. What do you think about writing some joints for us?"

I didn't even let him blink before I told him no. I was a recording artist, not a writer. I was in New York City to get signed—my own deal—and become the star I was born to be. I needed to focus on my project and, if he signed me as an artist, I would not let him down. He told me it wasn't that easy. They don't just sign artists. There's a process too lengthy for him to go over with me. Bottom line, though, he did have the power to put me on his project as a writer. He asked if I was sure I didn't want to write. I told him I was positive, thinking he would fold and hand me a record deal, not realizing that was the last time I would ever see the man again. But before I left he had one more question.

"So what's good with your friend?"

"My friend?"

"Yeah, your girl at Century 21."

Truth be told I didn't even know that girl. Cashiers were temp hires and switched around all the time.

"Oh, she's great. I'll definitely have her call you, OK?"

"Sounds good. Hey, good luck out there. You're going to need it," he said with a wink.

I walked down 8<sup>th</sup> Avenue and stopped in at Noise in the Attic. When I recited to Arcenius how the meeting went, he told me I screwed everything up for myself.

"Missy Elliot writes! Mariah Carey writes! Every single artist you hear on the radio, either writes or has someone else write what they're singing! That's where the money is, J! Oh, wow! You just turned down the opportunity of a lifetime. Call him back!"

I called and called but got no response. I one thousand percent destroyed a once-in-a-lifetime lucky break. I mourned my rookie mistake from then on, learning the hard way that I would probably sooner be hit by lightning than to ever get invited up to a major label like that again.

From there, my life became a robotic regimen of working during the day, singing and songwriting in the studio all night, and stealing four or five hours of sleep if the A-train cooperated. I was around plenty of people every day but I didn't have any friends because, if I got a break at work, I used it to get a quick bite, obsessively listen to my recordings, and write new songs on scraps of paper. Nights were lonely and the only person I could just call up any time I wanted and feel like I was talking to a friend I knew forever, was Felipe. I told him about all of my happenings and invited him over to my attic apartment after work one day to spend some time together. I was grateful for his companionship and his trek out to Queens. Instead of going back to Florida, he landed a job as a concierge in a hotel on Fulton Street just a block away from his mom's job and a handful of blocks away from his dad's apartment at the South Street Seaport, where he stayed. The minute he came over it was as if two of the greatest friends were back together. We were never short on conversation, always found ways to joke and laugh, and always found ourselves in bed with one another. That one night turned into every night and before I knew it, Felipe was moved in and we were back together. Except this time, in my apartment and on my terms.

My seasonal job at Century 21 was up and I scrambled to find a new gig before rent was due. I despised sales jobs but found a telemarketing job in the city that was an easy slam dunk so took it and ran. All of the telemarketers at the job worked independently in little cubes, cold-calling people all around the United States to attempt to get them to switch to an AT&T long distance plan. Every now and then, I would hear odd sounds on the line, usually indicating a supervisor had tapped in to monitor my selling technique. When that happened, I followed the textbook sales process they taught us to the letter. Otherwise, I really didn't care or put energy into it. I got paid the same hourly wage whether I switched people over to AT&T or not. For some it was the easiest kind of job. For someone like me with a hyperactive brain, it was torture. Sitting there repeatedly giving the same spiel over and over only to get hung up on, cursed at, mocked, and more, wasn't just annoying, it was life-wasting. What was I doing here? I hated it.

I managed to make a friend who turned me on to a Tex-Mex lunch spot that sold a stuffed burrito for three bucks. We started going to lunch together every day until she disappeared never to be seen again. I kept going to Noise in the Attic at night but, with less money and a boyfriend at home, I was less aggressive with my singing and writing. It felt great having Felipe back in the picture now that we were completely on our own. But then his whole family moved back to New York from Florida and his sister resumed her position as Godfather of the family. At first, she was indifferent to me. But soon, she made her hatred for me extremely known.

While telemarketing one day, I started daydreaming during dial tones and realized something: I hadn't had a period in as long as I could remember. I started trying to count the months but couldn't figure it out. The rest of the day, I kept going to the bathroom, expecting to find blood as if I could wish my period to reality. Nothing.

I went home and realized I hadn't bought feminine products since I landed back in New York. How could I overlook that? Pregnancy was an obvious thought but I kept thinking about how, when I got diabetes, the doctors warned against having babies and I always interpreted that to mean I simply couldn't get pregnant. When I did get pregnant previously, I lost the pregnancy before the first full month. Maybe I was just working so hard, my period stopped. Maybe my body was adjusting to my new life in the city. To be safe, I went to the Woolworth down the block and under the A-train and bought a pregnancy test. The cashier made a comment about me being really young to be buying such a test. I laughed it off, letting her know I had been on my own for years—I was practically an old woman at twenty years old. She said no more and handed me my receipt, change, and bag.

I didn't bother waiting until morning like one is supposed to. I took the test right then and there. Normally you have to wait to see two lines develop but no sooner did I pee on that stick did I have a very positive result. I told Felipe when he got home but he was impartial to the whole thing. I told him I needed to get checked out as soon as possible. I had gone months being pregnant and moving so fast in NYC between work and the studio that I didn't even realize it. No throwing up. No symptoms that I hadn't already attributed to lack of sleep. I couldn't believe it. I called information to get the number for Planned Parenthood, which I had heard of since a lot of the girls in Fort Collins got their basic gynecological care there. They quoted me one hundred and thirty dollars for a full exam and pregnancy test. Felipe had the money and took me in.

Planned Parenthood got me straight in when we arrived. I weighed in, got undressed, and waited in a hospital gown in a room for a doctor. It had been over four years since I saw a doctor because I didn't have health insurance. I figured whoever was about to come in would reprimand me when I couldn't rattle off my hemoglobin A1C numbers or provide a chart of my blood glucose and eating habits. I didn't have enough money to test more than a couple times per day, much less see a doctor out-of-pocket. To my surprise, the doctor came in, asked some basic questions surrounding my symptoms, and went straight to the pelvic exam to handle the most important thing first: whether or not I was actually pregnant.

"Oh yeah. You are very pregnant. At least three months already."

Felipe somewhat panicked after the pregnancy was confirmed. When we got home, he brought up abortion. We weren't married. We were living in an attic. We could barely support ourselves, much less a child. I didn't even have all of the medical supplies a type 1 diabetic should have and I hadn't had "tight control" of my diabetes like one should when they're pregnant. There were a million reasons why it was a bad idea to have a baby.

"It's a boy," I lied through my teeth.

"What?" Felipe questioned. "They told you the sex?"

"Yes." I lied again. "We're having a little boy."

Felipe got quiet. I said it because I knew that would change his mind. He had confided in me that he had a complex about his family never having a boy again. He was the only one—the "Golden Child" they called him—and any prospect of him carrying on his father's name was too good to resist.

"I guess we're having a baby!" he said happily.

"I guess so!" I replied, not at all ashamed of lying and hoping like heck a boy was on the way.

Given my last miscarriage, I worried history would repeat itself. However, this time I was already in my second trimester. I was well past the miscarriage window. This baby was coming. The doctors told me that, diabetes or not, there wasn't any reason why I couldn't give birth to a healthy baby. As for singing, I would give it up. This was more important. I knew what I had to do. I called Arcenius to break the news.

I told Arcenius I was pregnant and that I was so sorry for wasting his time—the deal was off. He told me to hold up. He felt strongly that I could still write, record, and fulfill my record deal while pregnant. We would work around it. Taken aback by the complete opposite of how I thought he would react, I hesitantly agreed. I honestly thought everything was over but Arcenius wasn't all that concerned.

At home, I found Felipe highly perturbed. He had just gotten into an over-the-phone fight with his sister because he passed on coming to a fancy family dinner to celebrate someone's birthday. He declined because he didn't have the money for both he and me to go. His sister was enraged, saying he could leave his worthless girlfriend at home and come by himself. He said no again but then she went off on him, saying if he didn't go she'd never speak to him again. She would pay for him to go—but not for his sorry girlfriend. To keep the peace he agreed. But when he told me the story, I felt like the stupid, worthless, good-for-nothing, wretch that left Florida and asked myself, "Why did you get involved with this boy again?" What's worse, now I was going to have a child with him, meaning I'd never escape his family.

Felipe went to the dinner and then came home and told me all about it. He said things were going great until his sister started talking about me. She had the whole table laughing at jokes about how pathetic I was, what a piece of garbage I was, how stupid her brother was to be with me when he could get so much better, how I couldn't even afford to eat dinner with them. To add injury to insult, his sister selected his ex-girlfriend as her youngest daughter's God-parent. So Felipe's ex-girlfriend was at the dinner laughing along. However, when everyone noticed that Felipe wasn't laughing at all, his sister joked.

"What, did you go behind our backs and marry her or something?"

"Jenn's pregnant, Marta. She's like five months pregnant. She's having a boy," Felipe replied.

Purportedly the whole table went silent, Marta started crying out of disappointment, Carmela started crying out of happiness, and everyone else knew well enough to stay completely quiet. Then Felipe started laughing. Fuming, Marta told him to send me the message that, as soon as that baby was born, she was going to take it from me. She didn't care if she had to call Child Protective

Services every day of my pregnancy until I gave birth—she would be damned if her nephew was born and raised in an attic (as if she had much more in the way of a borrowed apartment by the airport).

The same knots in my stomach and tension in my nerves I felt as a teenager came flooding back. My heart started to hurt, I lost my appetite, and I could barely sleep. Why couldn't Felipe's sister just leave me alone? Yes, I shouldn't have come to Florida. But I got a job while I was there, paid them rent, and gave them a check for their mattress when I left for good. I hadn't even seen Marta since Florida, much less done anything to her. What Felipe and I did was our business. How dare she talk about me the entire dinner and then threaten to take away a baby I was working extremely hard to keep. I was monitoring my blood sugar every hour, taking extra shots to get my blood sugar just right, drinking water and eating as well as a person with little money could. I tried to think of ways to cut ties with Marta. But Felipe was a package deal. It was either him and his entire family, or nothing. Marta may have been a strong person, but I knew I was stronger. No one was going to take my baby away from me.

# CHAPTER 21
# Hard Knocks

I WASN'T SURE IF MARTA HAD A CHANGE OF HEART, or if she was trying to scam me, but she invited me over to her house for a get-together with her family and friends. She picked Felipe and me up, and just as we had piled into the back of her car and closed the door, the person in the passenger seat turned around.

"Hi, I'm Keisha," she said, extending her hand out to me and staring me straight in the eyes with fake green contact lenses over her naturally brown eyes.

Keisha was Felipe's ex-girlfriend, Marta's husband's cousin, and the Godmother to Marta's second daughter. Keisha was the girl Felipe seemed to have cheated on with me when he was in the Air Force. But to me, Keisha was just another person I didn't want or need to deal with.

We made it to the party and I felt completely out of place, as usual. Someone offered me a drink and I passed, letting him know I don't drink alcohol. When he pushed some more, I was blunt.

"I'm pregnant."

"Oh, wow. I'm so sorry to hear that."

"I'll be fine," I said, annoyed that a complete stranger automatically deduced it was a bad thing.

I watched as Marta and Keisha pranced around like besties. I started to feel like they invited me there to rub in my face the fact that Marta absolutely adored Felipe's ex but hated me. *OK, Marta. You win. I'm nothing to you. You've made it clear. You're still not getting my baby.* I decided I was done letting Marta infiltrate my thoughts, my self-esteem, and my life. In that very moment, I decided to walk with my head held high. She really didn't know jack about what I had been through in my life. I had faced far greater challenges. I was mad at myself for ever letting her get to me.

I started looking Marta in the eye when I spoke to her and conducting myself in the way my mom taught me to: cordially. After the party, Felipe, Carmela, and I stayed back at Marta's house to help clean up and Marta invited me to watch a video about babies by myself in the living room. She had a VCR tape she used for her first pregnancy that helped her out. I figured it wouldn't hurt and watched it. Marta and Carmela appeared after the video and wanted to have a look at my belly.

"You're not really showing," Marta said.

"Well this lump wasn't here before," I replied naturally, not stopping to think they may be questioning my pregnancy. After a little more show-and-tell the pair seemed to concede I was, in fact, pregnant. I mean, who in their right mind would fake that with a Marta in the family?

As the weeks passed, Marta started becoming my advocate instead of my enemy. She got on Felipe's back about how a man should operate when a woman is pregnant. Namely, the woman shouldn't have to work so she can focus on baking a healthy bun. Felipe agreed and told me to quit my telemarketing job. He would take care of us. Normally, I might have insisted on working. Coincidentally, just a few days before I had fallen down the entire length of the subway stairs after work, exhausted and not paying attention. I feared my stubbornness might hurt my baby so I agreed.

Felipe was an extremely hard worker but we still weren't making ends meet and I was worried that I hadn't had any prenatal care. Wasn't I supposed to be taking vitamins or something? Didn't they need to check the baby? I had so much time at home I worked myself up into a frenzy, hopped on the train, and rode it all the way up to the fanciest hospital in the city: Columbia-Presbyterian on the Upper West Side. The only way I could afford a doctor was through the emergency room, where they take you with no questions asked and send you an astronomical bill that will kill your credit and control your life. But my baby deserved the very best and I calmly walked myself through the emergency room doors.

When they asked me what was wrong, I didn't have anything in particular to discuss so I asked plainly if they could check on my baby. I emphasized that I was broke, barely had medical supplies, hadn't had prenatal care, and needed help. They gave me a courtesy well-check and a bottle of insulin but couldn't do anything more, like monitor the baby or anything, unless I had symptoms and a real emergency. Somewhat defeated but grateful I at least got a bottle of insulin, I left and treated myself to McDonald's cheeseburgers (which I craved with a passion during pregnancy) before heading back home. And all seemed well until I woke up the next morning.

I woke up well after Felipe had left for the day to the completely risen sun. As soon as I was awake, I noticed immediately a dull pain in my lower back. This was a pain I hadn't felt since Colorado but knew well because it tended to be the last signal before my period came. I stood up and tried to convince myself that the pain was just something random. I checked my blood sugar and took my morning's insulin but felt something. Was my underwear wet? I walked slowly to the bathroom, terrified I would find blood. And I did.

I called Felipe at his job and told him I was bleeding. He told me to call 9-1-1 and he would meet me at the closest hospital in Jamaica, Queens. I dialed 9-1-1 and got an ambulance in-route, got my things together, and Marta called. Her husband was in school to become a physician's assistant at the time and she ran through a list of questions he dictated before scrapping the home-diagnosis and saying she'd meet me at the hospital.

The ambulance arrived and I told the two EMTs who came up to the attic to retrieve me that I had just taken insulin and would need to eat in a half hour. They said the hospital would give me something but I needed to go now. As I walked down the stairs, my landlord came out of his first-floor apartment and asked me if I was ok.

"No," I was honest.

I was wheeled into Jamaica hospital and left in a corner because all of the stations were filled. I asked for juice and a snack from every worker who passed by, knowing my blood sugar was on a downward trajectory and starting to feel shaky. As I continued to get ignored, I started hallucinating a bit and I felt a huge splash of fluid explode from my underwear, wetting the stretcher with what looked like clear water.

"Hello? Anybody? I think my water just broke. Hello?" I tried to get someone's attention.

Meanwhile, beads of sweat formed on my head, my vision blurred, my body began to shake, and I went into full insulin shock. And just as I was about to pass out, I heard Marta scream.

"Oh my God, Jenn! Somebody get their ass over here now! She's dying! Get over here now!" Marta screamed, uncaring about what anyone thought of her.

A nurse brought me juice and crackers that weren't nearly enough to cover the meal I was supposed to have eaten and I was wheeled into a room for further evaluation. Still delusional with barely detectable blood sugar, I sat in the room confused while my abdomen cramped and I started bleeding again. I refused to allow myself to cry but I wanted to. Marta and her husband, Nikolai, came in and I showed them the blood accumulating under me. Nikolai assured me that, since the blood was bright red, it wasn't period blood. We all could still survive this. Marta once again got a nurse, who got a doctor, and Nikolai debriefed her on a not entirely accurate but excellent attempt at my health history. Marta and Nikolai were excused and the doctor sat at the end of the examination table and had me assume the position of a pelvic exam. I laid there with my legs open as she sat, calmly, and chugged down an entire can of Coke before she examined me. She apologized but she was running on fumes. She stated the obvious, "you're bleeding," and then less obvious things that

I would have needed a medical textbook for. Then, without warning, I felt her pull out something and I prayed it was not my baby. She spoke clinically, with zero emotion.

"OK, I just pulled out your fetus."

I didn't hear a baby crying. I didn't see the doctor scrambling. She didn't hand my baby to me.

"We'll send it to the lab and see if we can figure out what happened," she said as if she had completed a routine exam with an affable patient.

Since the doctor wasn't upset, I didn't allow myself to be. I had grown to love the baby inside of me. I had done all I could, even without medical care, to bring it into this world. And I didn't even get a chance to absorb the enormity of losing it. I didn't get to say goodbye. I didn't even get a chance to feel. Without seeing Marta, Nikolai, or Felipe, the latter who had since arrived in the waiting room, I was wheeled straight to Radiology for an ultrasound.

Marta tracked me down after my ultrasound and asked if the baby was OK so sincerely, after being so kind and basically saving my life, I let my guard down and I started crying. I told her I lost "him" (even if "he" was really a "she," which I will never know).

They wheeled me down to an empty station in the ER, where I found Felipe extremely angry. He wasn't one to show emotion so, in retrospect, he was probably extremely sad. But my read on him at the time was that he was upset. I failed him. I failed everyone.

A nurse came in and advised us that because I was so far along, I would need a D&C—surgery to remove the placenta—and, therefore, needed to stay overnight. With that, Felipe and the whole family left the hospital and I stayed all alone that night, sobbing and mourning the loss of the baby none of the hospital staff had the decency to let me see or talk about.

I stayed up most of the night staring into darkness since I didn't have money for optional television service and wouldn't have wanted it if I did. My time for surgery finally came and the anesthesiologist greeted me in the hallway to get my stats before mixing up the potion to knock me out. I was wheeled into the operating room and a needle was inserted into my arm, only halfway into a vein, making whatever liquid he was pushing in extremely painful. I tried to tell him the needle was wrong but it must have been just correct enough to knock me out.

I woke up from anesthesia feeling like death. I knew where I was and what had just happened despite wishing it was all a terrible nightmare. I looked at my arm to find a strange, abnormally huge bump where the anesthesiologist only half-hit my vein and looked down to my belly, which was still swollen as if I still had a baby in it. A nurse told me they had to observe me for several hours before they could send me home. All I wanted was my own pillow, my own bed, and for everyone in the world to go away.

With so much time to pass before Felipe would come to take me home, I got restless. It was too soon to talk about everything I just went through but I just needed to hear a friendly voice. I called Arcenius and told him the devastating news. His voice automatically changed to a sincerely sorry tone as he apologized and sent his deepest condolences to Felipe and me. Then, he made a mistake. He handed the phone over to a woman he hired to promote me.

"I overheard your conversation with Arcenius. I'm sorry for your loss," the woman said plainly.

"Thank you," I replied without really wanting to talk to her.

"You know what you have to do now, right?" she asked.

A couple of thoughts flashed through my mind: Take it easy. Take some time off to mourn.

"Lose weight," she said.

I hung up the phone. If I could have jumped through the phone to fight her, I would have. What kind of vile individual says that after a person has just lost a baby? I blamed the rat race of a music industry for people like her. But I accepted it, certain I would eventually beat everyone to the finish line.

When Felipe came to pick me up, I still felt absolutely awful, as if I was dying. I was dizzy and nauseous and in pain and devastated. He helped me into the back of a cab and we were home within minutes. When we walked through the front door, our landlord popped out and asked if everything was OK. He was such a polite and sweet old guy from Guyana, we couldn't help but say everything was fine, despite it being the furthest thing from the truth. He told us to not worry about paying the rent on time—we could pay it a few weeks late.

A week passed and I had to get going and find a new job. I found an ad for a car dealership seeking a receptionist in Brooklyn for an hourly wage that beat my old telemarking job. I called to inquire and was transferred to a man named Kevin who wanted me to come in the very next day. I agreed, got my game face on, and squeezed into a dress that barely fit the next morning.

Kevin was a fast-talking, skinny, good-looking, salesman extraordinaire from California who was only at the dealership to hire a bunch of people to man the phones and implement a sales system he personally designed and sold to the dealership. In short, I (and three others) would answer all of the dealership's calls and then follow a script to get people to walk through the doors. Instead of getting paid hourly, which the ad I saw lied about, I would get nine dollars for every appointment I made *if* the person I spoke to actually came in. I hated sales jobs, I hated Kevin's vibe, I hated a job based on commission with no benefits, I hated the A-train ride to Lafayette Avenue followed by a long bus ride down Nostrand Avenue, but I settled and took the job.

"Can you start right now?" Kevin pressed.

"No. I'm diabetic and I don't have my insulin with me. I'll start tomorrow," I said without giving him a choice.

I started and excelled at the job where I worked with two African American women and a thirty-year-old Italian man who was not shy about announcing his ties to the mob. One of the women, Sondra, treated me like a child and would say "sweet baby" the way a loving grandmother would each time I entertained the office with self-deprecating jokes. The other woman was so conservative, prim, and proper, I wondered if she had ever let down her hair in her entire life. The Italian guy was quickly promoted to manager of the used car lot—a position I was thrilled to be overlooked for. I worked that job for nine months before convincing myself I deserved better. During my time there, I had witnessed a mugging at my bus stop and I was almost attacked by a man on the bus who insisted I was a "white devil." I needed to come up with a game plan. I needed to take control.

I soon found that every position that was better than a sales job, but entry-level enough for me to qualify for, required computer skills. I could type quickly thanks to all of the work I did in my parents' businesses and high school speed-typing class. But I didn't have a computer. I called my dad and asked him for a loan. I needed two hundred dollars to buy a basic computer that I would learn Microsoft Office on. All of the employment agencies in the city warned candidates not to come without expecting a test of computer skills and I had no other way to brush up than with my own computer. Dad was supportive of my aspiration to do better and quickly agreed to the loan but refused to be paid back. He just wanted to see me succeed.

The second call I made was to my mom. I needed her to write me a letter of recommendation in the fancy "business speak" she was so good at. She needed to write as if I was a valued secretary who knocked her socks off and who she whole-heartedly recommended for future employment. She needed to use her Italian married name so there was no hint of family ties and I needed to lie through my teeth to avoid slipping and admitting to any interviewer that the shining recommendation came from my mom.

As soon as I received Dad's money in the mail, I bought a computer and started studying on my own the ins and outs of Microsoft Office and speed-typing newspaper articles until I felt I was typing extremely fast without errors. With the few dollars

I had left, I went to the Everything Under $10 clothing store and picked out the closest thing they had to a dress suit: a bright blue top and matching skirt. It wasn't as professional as I had hoped but it was better than the more casual items in my closet.

I took a day off from my job and headed to an agency in the city, passed my computer competency test with flying colors, and interviewed with an agent who immediately picked up the phone and arranged an interview for me, a "grad-like" candidate she said. I went on three interviews and by Friday had two job offers. One was from an insurance agency where I complimented the big boss on how lovely she was because I felt sorry for the huge black eye she couldn't hide. Was she an abused wife or something? I didn't know but I really didn't want that job. The second offer was from the manager of the Tech department at Grey Advertising on the east side of Midtown. The building was beautiful. The employees were super hip. The pay was more money than I could have ever imagined making on my own—nearly triple what I made at the car dealership. And the final kicker: the job came with health benefits. I accepted the job with a zealous "YES!" Bye-bye, sleazy car dealership. Hello, wonderful job and stable, respectable employment!

# CHAPTER 22

# Grammys

LIFE IS DIFFERENT WHEN YOU HAVE A JOB WITH A livable salary and benefits. You never search the floor of the closet for the couple of extra cents you need to buy a subway token. You don't have to figure out how many days of peanut butter and jelly sandwiches before payday. You dress well for work and have extra money to buy cheap outfits and shoes for the weekend at the Conway on 34th Street. You give all of the singles floating around in your coat pockets to homeless people without first checking the currency to ration out a portion for yourself. You go to the doctor when you're sick, get blood test strips, have enough syringes to use a new needle with every injection, and have enough insulin to forget about the days of skipping shots altogether or guessing blood sugar based on how fast your heart is beating. And when you don't outspend your rather loose budget, you have enough room to slide into your next paycheck like a homerun.

My new boss demanded perfection. If I didn't deliver, I was sure his brain would combust and splatter computer-coded brain matter everywhere. I worked twelve-hour days, arriving before and leaving after my boss until he was caught conducting personal business on company time and was fired within three months of my start date. I was moved temporarily to support three executives—two finance officers and the agency's Chief Technology Officer—and afforded the opportunity to earn the seat permanently. I figured the role out quickly and landed it permanently after successfully completing the Microsoft Mail Merge project previous assistants failed to figure out, marking the second or hundredth time I lied and said I could do something I had never done before, only to end up doing the something with flying colors. Sometimes we don't have to know what we are doing, so much as we have to know we can do anything.

Without the distraction of poverty, I had time to reflect. I blamed my miscarriages on karma since I was living in sin with Felipe and we began to talk marriage and plan a wedding with his mom, entirely skipping a proper proposal. But when the pressure of putting on an elaborate, Puerto Rican dream wedding became too much, we eloped and I got married, not in a gorgeous gown, but wearing a sweat suit on a random Friday morning at a courthouse in Queens. The officiator might as well have been a cattle-caller he spoke so fast and unintelligibly. And we might as well have been on a conveyer belt the way couples were moved in and out of our small courtroom, saying "I do" before being hurried out to a hall where they took wedding photos against the bare, brick wall bowels of the building.

I continued to excel at the ad agency, receiving another promotion to executive assistant to the CFO and earning a huge, forty percent pay raise (in part, as a reward for recovering sixty thousand dollars of debt for the company when I discovered employees were using company cards for personal purchases). My raise enabled Felipe and me to move one floor down to a two-bedroom apartment and feel as grown up as I had been acting since I was seventeen.

I always wondered if my tubes were tied against my knowledge during the surgery after I lost my baby, or if something else happened, but I never got pregnant again despite never trying to avoid it. Life became a stable mix of a full day's work during the day followed by studio sessions at night. And despite Felipe's mom confessing to me that he was cheating on me before we were married, he was faithful during our marriage until I got distracted by a mysterious chat friend on AOL. Felipe and I took a "break," and Felipe flew to San Francisco for a weekend with the girl he had the fling with while we were dating. We ultimately stayed together while I signed a second record deal with Laundry Room Records, an independent subsidiary of Sony. However, the label ended up dropping me because I looked like a secretary instead of a star one day when the CEO visited the studio unexpectedly. After that, Arcenius told me to never show up at his studio again unless I showed up looking like a star.

Arcenius hired various promoters to increase my exposure but none of them were able to do more for my career than get me into Tamia's album release party in 1998 (which only made me envious and annoyed that I wasn't on the stage instead of her); get me a backup singer gig in a choir behind Isaac Hayes for a Christmas show that same year; get me a solo three-song set at a random Mother's Day event; and form a girl group that never went further than a single song recorded. Arcenius and I by ourselves, on the other hand, were more productive. That year, mp3 digital files emerged as the way to share music and MP3.com was born. Arcenius took me to a digital music conference where we met the owners of MP3.com, who gave us a spotlight for my music. That spotlight garnered thousands of downloads and shot three of my songs up to MP3.com's Top 10 List, including the number one spot for several weeks on end. After that success, I personally booked myself to sing the National Anthem back home at a Colorado Rockies baseball game at Coors Field, and at a Colorado Rapids soccer game at Mile High Stadium, respectively. Lastly, Arcenius landed an opportunity for me to tag along with one of his clients on a trip to Los Angeles during Grammys week (so long as I came up with travel money myself).

Celeste, a girl whose claim to fame was singing a raunchy hook on a rap song that reached the 127th spot on the Billboard 200, booked a session at Noise in the Attic to record a demo to take on a trip to Beverly Hills for Grammys week. She didn't have tickets to the Grammys, per se, but booked a hotel in the heart of Grammy-related happenings with the sole plan of hustling. Arcenius played my music for Celeste in case she had any connections that would get us further. Impressed by my songs, Celeste told Arcenius that I could tag along on her trip, saying she would cover the hotel room at no cost if I could get my own airline ticket.

Despite having never laid eyes on this girl or hearing her song (which was too graphic for mainstream radio play) I couldn't resist the opportunity to potentially meet someone who could elevate my career from "noise in the attic" to smash hits on the radio; so I agreed to go. However, while I was keeping up with rent and bills, I wasn't so well off as to afford an impromptu trip with only a couple of weeks' notice. Going on this huge gamble of a trip was going to require some fundraising. Since I didn't have any friends, I cut to the chase and called my dad. I explained to Dad the opportunity, leaving out the part about me never having met my host. I also didn't mention that I would fly to Los Angeles on a complete whim with no other information than "stand on the street outside of baggage claim when you land—she knows what you look like." I promised him I'd never ask him for another cent again. If he could lend me two hundred dollars, I might very well secure the dream I had been chasing since childhood.

Dad's check arrived in the mail a few days later and came with a surprise: fifty extra dollars to go on a date with my new husband. Also—no paybacks required. Dad saw how I turned his computer donation into a job at New York City's largest advertising agency. His money was literally on me to turn this last contribution into my dream come true. He was a seasoned entrepreneur, a risk-taker, and a spontaneous adventure-seeker. He was more than happy to place his bet.

I touched down in Los Angeles in February of the year 2000 with a carry-on of clothes, makeup case, clip-on ponytail extension, sparkling polyester dress that didn't require ironing, a pair of heels and a pair of sneakers, a couple bottles of insulin, and my game face. I stood outside as directed, making eye contact with every female African American driver who crept by the passenger pickup area before hearing, "JJ!" from afar. Two African American girls honked and waved frantically at me and

I ran to the car and got in as seamlessly as I would have, had I actually known them.

Celeste introduced herself and her co-pilot, June, an aspiring actress, and headed to Rosco's for fried chicken and waffles—a must-do recommended by locals. June immediately claimed the shot-gun passenger seat in the rental car for the entirety of the trip, which I conceded to as if she cared how I felt about it. As we drove, I sat quietly in the back while the pair hooted and hollered up front. Celeste then announced that she was prepared to do anything—and she meant anything—to make this trip worthwhile.

"Don't ask questions. Just watch and learn while I get this money," she directed.

Celeste was petite with a pretty (albeit weathered for her age) face. She wore her hair in long dreadlocks and tended to live in tight sweat suits and trendy sneakers. Her scent permeated a four-foot radius around her and struck me as a more flowery version of what the studio tended to smell like: scented oils, incense, and weed. Before I could learn much more about Celeste, June stole the show with a monologue about her strategy to make industry connections at our hotel by hook or by crook. June's claim to fame was appearing on MTV's *Say What Karaoke*, where she sang Destiny Child's "Say My Name" and finished runner-up. It automatically annoyed me that an actress made it onto a singing show that I, a bonafide singer, was turned down for.

The pair didn't bother asking me about myself. I guess Celeste already knew all she needed to know before she invited me: I could sing and write. She probably assumed I could also schmooze but I had no idea how to hustle in Hollywood. Nonetheless, I was down for anything that didn't involve breaking the law, smoking or drinking (I wasn't into either and doing any form of drug was a mistake I never made), or cheating on my husband. I already knew what being a cheater felt like and nothing was worth that. Therefore, even if I was a rebel by Colorado standards, I was the Miss Goody Two Shoes of the Grammys trip. And since these two women were in complete command of everything, I was happy to take a back seat and ride along.

We got our fried chicken and waffles to go as Celeste and June pointed out all of the famous people they recognized eating in the restaurant. I was not a person who ever knew the names of B-list superstars or below. If someone didn't reach Top-40 radio, I was oblivious to them. June, on the other hand, could rattle off names, roles played in sitcoms or extra appearances in movies, songs written, music videos shot. She was like an Encyclopedia Britannica of artists—known or not. It immediately struck me that I probably should have been paying way more attention to people's names. In fact, June was probably on this trip with me because she knew that Celeste sang the hook to a song I hadn't ever heard of. I ultimately concluded that my trip mates were a force to be reckoned with and I was just lucky to tag along.

When we arrived to our hotel room, June immediately called the couch (Celeste obviously had the main bedroom) so that left me on the floor where I belonged given I wasn't contributing anything. We ate, June went to the restroom, and then reappeared completely naked.

"I'm an exhibitionist," she announced.

Feeling uncomfortable and out of place, I contemplated if I should cut the trip short and go home but stayed with the hope that I could sneak into the Grammy Awards. To my surprise, something even better happened: we got into Clive Davis' annual Grammys party.

Clive Davis, the founder of Arista Records and a Rock and Roll Hall of Famer, was infamously the most important record executive in the music business for decades on end. He was lauded for numerous accolades, including signing Whitney Houston and P Diddy, among others. His party was more important than the Grammy show. At the Grammys, you could sit and watch performances and award acceptance speeches. At Clive's party, you could literally rub elbows with the biggest stars, producers, and Who's Who in the industry.

June schmoozed with an industry head she met in our hotel and earned an invite to Clive's coveted party. And since Celeste ditched us to go spend the night with a famous producer, I became June's honorary wingwoman.

We arrived at Clive's party, walked the red carpet where no one wanted to take our photo, entered the front doors and made a bee-line for the first star we saw: Dark Child. DC was producing Destiny's Child at the time and I wasted no time introducing myself, handing him a card, and all but forcing his agreement to work with me. He wiggled his way out of my groupie-grasp and I turned around to find Brittney Spears and 'N Sync standing ten feet away from me. Before I could go make a fool of myself, June pulled me aside like a mother dragging a kid by her ear and gave me a talking to.

"You can't act like a groupie, JJ! You're going to get us kicked out. Play it cool!"

I was embarrassed that June felt the need to school me and I completely retreated into my Cancerian shell for the rest of the night. But that didn't stop me from basking in the starlight of every superstar I cared about.

We went down a grand staircase to hear a bunch of ruckus from a loud-mouthed woman only to find Whitney Houston in a tight gown and fur shawl barking random things and pulling and tugging at family members who seemed to escort her outside for a break. I stopped in my tracks and stared as anyone in my shoes would, completely floored that my childhood idol was within feet of me while simultaneously shocked that she was clearly and severely intoxicated with something. From there we proceeded to our table, only to find that Rod Stewart and another one of my idols, Lauryn Hill, were sitting one table over. June completely abandoned the speech she gave me and ran up to Lauryn in the same way I ran up to Dark Child.

"Here, take our picture!" June shoved her disposable camera into my hands.

Lauryn obliged and despite wanting so badly to also get a photo with her, I decided to leave her alone (but not without telling her in a few words that she was my favorite artist).

In somewhat of a permanent shock, I headed to the bathroom only to find myself standing in line directly behind Jennifer Lopez. Once again, I was awe-struck, examining her from head to toe and marveling at how truly perfect she was. I wondered if she felt me staring because she turned around briefly, made eye contact with me, and grinned with a closed mouth before turning back around. I smiled back with a closed mouth in return (despite being proud of my teeth that no longer had ugly silver braces on them) and refrained from tackling her for an autograph or photo.

We spent the rest of the night at the table, staring in shock as Whitney gave the breathiest, most strained performance I could have ever imagined. As I watched, I caught the attention of a man sitting at a table beside me, who was aggressively flirting and going as far as to touch me, uninvited.

"Work that," June told me.

"No thanks," I replied as she shook her head at me as if I would never go anywhere in life.

The man who got us into the party invited us to come and see a friend's mansion, which June was entirely impressed with but that I couldn't have cared less about. Although he clearly wanted to get June into bed, my status as a third wheel killed the vibe and got us both sent home. Within a couple of hours after arriving back to the hotel when I was already changed into my conservative two-piece pajama set, Money Harm and Product G&B knocked on our door to come hang out. They were nominated for a Grammy for their vocals on "Maria Maria" alongside Santana, who played lead guitar on the track, and Wyclef, who produced it. Celeste made the connection and invited them over as if it was no big deal.

When I first laid eyes on the young male recording artists who walked through the door, I feared that, at any given moment, there would be drugs and an attempt for sex—things I wanted no part of. To my surprise, Money Harm was *harm*less. I flashed my wedding band right away to emphasize my married status but they didn't even try to hit on the single girls. We all had a genuinely great time talking and laughing before they turned in for the night and won a Grammy for their song the next day.

I didn't get into the Grammy Awards show like I had hoped. In fact, despite rubbing elbows with superstars, my trip to Beverly Hills did absolutely nothing for my career. But I learned some lessons. First, we're all human. "Stars" are human. Second, you can be arguably the world's greatest singer, rich and famous, and still make a complete mess out of your life (read Whitney Houston). Third, don't put anyone on a pedestal. Even JLo uses a restroom. Lastly and most importantly, I learned that opportunity is highly a product of hustle. The Clive Davis party gave me new perspective. I realized that the only thing separating celebrities from me was a little more elbow grease.

Returning back to NYC with my eyes opened, I knew that anything was possible. But I also knew that it wasn't going to happen with a team I highly doubted. I had to split from Arcenius. I needed a better team.

# CHAPTER 23
# Full Force

ARCENIUS DIDN'T GAMBLE ON A BUSINESS BREAKUP when I returned from L.A. but that's what he got. He warned that if I moved on, our contract guaranteed he'd still get a decent percentage of anything I made if I blew up, even if he had nothing to do with it. I agreed because he meant no malice by it and the contract had an expiration date that ensured that, at worst, I'd have complete freedom in a matter of months.

With Arcenius' backhanded blessing, I started auditioning for anything I could find: a huge cattle call in the middle of the day when all I could do was run ten city blocks over from my job on my lunch break to drop off my demo package (only for it to be thrown back in my face because a whole day of singing and dancing was required for consideration); another cattle call for singers who could also act, where I blew away the casting agents with my voice but couldn't act to save my life; a one-on-one with a self-proclaimed superproducer who became irate when I wouldn't let him record my original songs during the audition; an audition with a random man who claimed to have worked with the Spice Girls, who needed a fifth member of a new girl group whose four members I slam-dunked vocally but who wanted me to shed five pounds to get to "fighting weight" and into the group; and lesser auditions that were obviously completely novice attempts by wanna-be producers to make a dollar out of absolutely nothing.

After several auditions, I started recognizing fellow singers waiting outside mystery doors for auditions with mystery people. A handful of us girls—always girls—were bonafide singer/ songwriters who were not beneath auditioning but who knew deep down that, if given the opportunity to work with someone who knew what they were doing, we would hit it big. Whenever we spotted each other among obviously less experienced dream-chasers, we exchanged approving nods.

I felt like I had become extremely skilled at auditions—the look, the headshot, the demo tape, the hellos, the humility, the brief and articulate preface of what I was prepared to sing *a capella*, the review of my biography and accolades, the hoop-jumping, the gracious weathering of ridicule, the goodbyes, the mulling over the opportunity at hand, the adrenaline rush of a perfect performance, and the defeat of not receiving a call back—but I was growing disenchanted and wondered if I was wasting my time. Still, I had already broken ties with my label and I knew deep in my heart I had to move on to move up, so I continued to scour classified ads.

*The Village Voice* was a racy, independently published newspaper that filled most of its pages with articles as uncensored as the New Yorkers who read them, but reserved a small section in the back for downright filthy classified ads and a few scattered G-rated job offerings for performers. Upon opening up the back page of the newest publication to search for auditions, my eyes connected with a quarter-page ad. A team of "hit songwriting," "platinum-selling," "Grammy-nominated" producers were holding auditions for a female pop singer. I had been in the game long enough to know that people tend to lie. So the ad seemed too good to be true. I honestly thought I would go to the audition and get hustled for a one hundred dollar photo shoot or one of the many scams I had come across during my time in the city. But I went anyway.

Normally I would obsess over every detail before auditions: what to wear, what to sing, what to say. But since I fully expected this audition to be some sort of fraud, I took it less seriously. For my outfit, I picked out a long, polyester powder blue-colored dress with Adidas-inspired white stripes down the sides. The dress hugged my body just enough to show my figure but not so much to read sexy and came with a matching jacket, which I zipped up because the tighter fit around my waist drew attention to the hour-glass shape Seventeen magazine told me I had. I completed the look with white platform sneakers that made me feel relevant and in the know, my wispy brown hair half-up in a ponytail, fancified eye makeup, and vanilla-scented lip gloss that made my lips look plump and kissable despite being gooey and tar-like. I printed out a single-page collage of my best photos and a bio I wrote myself, and I grabbed a cassette single of "Tell Me Your Name," a one-hit wonder of a remake of LL Cool J's "Who Do You Love." I figured I would be more impressive effortlessly singing over the vocals of a hit song than I would attempting an *a capella* original the producers had never heard.

Arriving at SIR Studios was a big deal in and of itself because that's where all of the stars used to practice and you couldn't step foot in the place without label money or a personal invitation. Just beyond the entrance, around thirty girls waited for their turn to audition. I wasn't early like Grandpa Cooper taught me to be and I was so sick of auditioning, I didn't care. I sat for a while and watched with a huge chip on my shoulder as certain girls came out of the audition looking oblivious, while others starting cheering for themselves as if they had just received a golden ticket to a chocolate factory. Confident in the only way I had ever been, I assumed without any proof that I was the best singer and songwriter in the building but the wait was still getting to me. Dead-last in line and certain the entire thing was a complete sham, I got up and left. But as I was opening the front door to walk out, a middle-aged African American man wearing a backward fitted ball cap with a single braided tail covered with beads hanging from the nape of his neck was simultaneously walking in.

"You're staying to audition, right?" Bowlegged Lou asked me as if he was a walking advertisement.

Caught off-guard in the quickness of the moment, I said yes and headed back to my last place in line until it was finally my turn.

I entered the audition room to find a spacious, barren rehearsal space with a microphone on a stand on one side of the room and a make-shift production area on the other side, where four bald African American men seemed to be working on something as if I had walked into a session instead of an audition. Baby Gerry, who sat behind a portable keyboard and drum machine, greeted me first in an uncannily human way that made me feel like he was honored to meet me and not the other way around as it should have been.

"Hey, come on in!"

"Hi guys, I'm JJ," I said as I handed Gerry my press kit and audition tape.

"Nice to meet you. I'm Gerry. This is Curt, Junior, and Lou."

The men all said "Hello" as if they weren't legendary celebrities, which fact I was completely unaware of. In fact, Full Force had been dominating as recording artists, producers, artist developers, actors, songwriters, and music businessmen for decades. Unbeknownst to me at the time of my audition, I grew up listening to Full Force hits. Lisa Lisa and the Cult Jam's "Head to Toe," which was the smash hit I remember roller skating to at Roller Land as an eleven-year-old; Samantha Fox's "Naughty Girls Need Love Too" and "I Wanna Have Some Fun," which I sang along with into a hairbrush with fellow sixth-grade girls at slumber parties; "Ain't My Type of Hype," Full Force's own song used during a dance challenge scene in the classic film "House Party" (which Full Force also starred in); Backstreet Boys' smash hit "All I have;" Brittney Spears' demo tape that launched her to stardom; Nicki Minaj's demo tape that launched her to stardom; and a huge laundry list of work with scores of superstars over the years, were all a result of Full Force's songwriting prowess and power production.

"Wow, I'm digging the photo page—nice," Gerry complimented.

"Thanks, um, thank you," I said awkwardly before taking my place behind the microphone as robotically as a dog sits for food.

"Tell us about yourself," Gerry prodded.

"Sure. Well, my name is JJ. I'm twenty-two years old. I'm originally from Colorado but moved to New York City five years ago or so. I've been singing since I was five, I write all of my own songs, and I speak Spanish," I said, making sure to talk about qualities I knew the industry valued at the time.

"Nice, OK. Is this the tape you're singing to?" Gerry asked.

Having determined over a few seconds that this was an actual audition with obviously serious musicians, I grimaced, disappointed that I brought such a stupid song to sing to instead of a proper audition tape.

"Yes. I'll sing over the vocals if you don't mind. I meant to bring my original tracks but grabbed the wrong tape," I lied.

"Yeah, yeah. Do your thing."

The music started and, as planned, I hung with the lead vocals without much effort but, with all eyes on me, knew I had to kick my performance up a notch. Since my ten years of dance classes failed to produce an R&B or hip hop dance aesthetic, I avoided dancing and instead walked from one side of the room to the other, inserting jokes into the song to appeal to the obviously easy-going spirit of the group.

"Most guys they come a dime a dozen. And they're always trying to get with me [especially the fifteen-year-olds]," I sang and joked as the guys chuckled ever so slightly.

I sang the rest of the song with all of the vocal prowess I could muster, being sure to nail somewhat complicated riffs to ensure my audience knew I wasn't new to the game. The song ended and Gerry resumed speaking on behalf of the group.

"Good, OK. You have a nice tone and I liked the riffs. Let me ask you something: can we hear one of the original joints you were talking about? Do you have anything Spanglish?"

"Yes, of course!" I replied as if I had a million Spanglish songs when in actuality I only had one. But one was all they wanted so I went for it.

"*Papi*, I see that you're making moves, breaking rules, *para mi amor*. Now here from my perspective I've got nothing to lose, I'm feeling you, *ven mi amor. Ven papi chulo*, uh-huh, *bailes conmigo*, uh-huh, *yo te quiero*, uh-huh, *en mi vida. Ven papi chulo*, uh-huh, *bailes conmigo*, uh-huh, *yo te quiero*, uh-huh, *en mi vida. Y ahora*, brothers always sweatin' me, these lines they feed, if you know what I mean. *Pero, yo no se*, what you could do to me, can't wait and see, *verdad mi dulcera...*"

I ran out of breath and I apologized, quickly pointing out it was hard to sing the lead and chorus with only one person as if I wasn't in front of a group of seasoned, wickedly talented vocalists who could have sung the same without a missed breath or beat.

"I'm digging it," Gerry said, starting to hum and dink around on his keyboard. "Yeah, that's really strong."

Hearing that someone—anyone—liked my original song was like winning the audition in and of itself and I breathed a sigh of relief until Gerry spoke again.

"Ok, are you ready to dance?"

"Yes, of course," I replied as my heart started to race.

I mean, as a kid at the performing arts academy, I tap-danced, clogged, jazz-danced, and performed dance routines to every song we sang. But as a solo artist, I tended to just walk back and forth on stage with exaggerated hand gestures and, well, not a lot more. I was terrified that I would blow the entire audition with my cheesy dance moves.

"Do you want a choreographed dance or just freestyle?" I stalled.

"Whatever you got," Gerry encouraged.

"Let's go with freestyle." I figured moving to the beat was better than performing the one hip-hop dance routine I knew, which I didn't pull off all that convincingly at class so would surely bomb at this audition.

A song with a booming bassline filled the empty room with life and I channeled my club-hopping days and hours spent dancing on top of speakers to attempt to sell myself in my long athletic dress getup as a real entertainer: a singer, songwriter, decent-looking girl who no longer had ugly steel braces on her teeth, and if it killed me, a dancer.

The guys all smiled politely as I did my best to showcase every move I had ever learned in the clubs, only for them to have mercy and shut the music off. Gerry thanked me for auditioning and the rest of the men waved goodbye as I left with a fat piece of humble pie.

They were so kind. They were so human. Gerry not only understood my song concept, he started playing his keyboard to it on the spot. I was simultaneously hyped and hurt that, when I left the room, I didn't have the slightest urge to celebrate like a few of the other girls before me. Even so, I concluded that that was the best wasted time yet.

Back home I started to tell Felipe about the audition but, after so many audition debriefings, he was unenthused and quickly changed the subject to something that was far more important in his mind. His dad called that day and proposed a "once-in-a-lifetime-opportunity" for us. The deal was this: we would go live rent-free in the South Street Seaport with Big Felipe and save our rent money to eventually buy a two-family investment property in the Bronx; thereby achieving the greatest thing Big Felipe conceived we were capable of.

"No way," I didn't even blink an eye.

"Why not?" Felipe countered.

"That will end up in us getting divorced," I said plainly, not explaining the long list of other reasons I had, the most important of which were: one, I never wanted to live with anyone, much less a relative of Felipe's ever again—period; and two, I didn't do well getting favors from people I love, much less people I felt completely hated by.

Felipe was smart enough to put the discussion on the back burner until I calmed down, even if it took weeks for me to calm down. During the interim, I got a very unexpected phone call from Gerry of Full Force.

"You know, the guys you auditioned with last week?" he reminded me.

"Of course! Don't be silly. How could I forget?" I replied.

"Well, I'm calling to let you know we didn't choose you for the spot you were auditioning for."

My heart sunk. That was a *real* audition. The one I really needed to be the most prepared and first in line for. And I blew it.

"Thank you so much for the opportunity. I really appreciate it. But please do keep me in mind if you need a writer," I said having learned that songwriting was not the sell-out I once thought it to be.

"Actually, that's also why I was calling. We didn't pick you for the spot, but there's something about you. We can't quite put our finger on it. If you're up for it, maybe you can come down to our studio sometime and vibe out, see if we can work on something," Gerry offered.

"Yes! I mean yes, of course. I write original songs, you know. Everything that's popular now—I can write it. I have at least a thousand songs written. I'm a spot-writer. I write songs in five minutes. You won't be disappointed if you try me on a track. I promise." I spoke a mile-a-minute as if I was selling him a beeper or a Hoover.

"No, we gathered that," Gerry replied as calmly as a church usher.

Gerry gave me the address to Full Force's studio, located in the basement of a home in Brooklyn, and invited me to stop by later that week.

I wasn't fazed by the train ride, followed by bus ride, followed by short walk in Brooklyn but I still didn't like it. I rang the doorbell hoping like heck I had the correct house and a tall, teenage African American kid answered the door.

"Hi, I'm JJ here to see Gerry," I somewhat stated and asked at the same time.

The kid let me in as if I knew where I was going and finally said "downstairs" when it was clear I was lost. I stepped slowly down a tight staircase and knocked on the only door in sight until it creaked open and Gerry's friendly face appeared.

Gerry introduced me to the handful of people who were there and chatted briefly with me about writing in between getting pulled away from time to time into the various endeavors going on in the room—a recording session, a powwow in the back room to pick out the best photos from a recent photo shoot, and the arrival of a food order. During the gaps in our discussion, the walls of the room, which were plastered with photos of Full Force posing with every superstar ever known to man, caught my complete attention. Here I thought I was special for seeing people like The Backstreet Boys in-person at Clive Davis' Grammy party. Meanwhile, Full Force not only had a photo with them, they had a platinum plaque on the wall for writing a hit for them. If that didn't put me in my place, the rest of the photos did. James Brown, La Toya Jackson, Patti LaBelle, UTFO, The Real Roxanne, Ex Girlfriend, N'Sync, Selena, Rihanna, The Black Eyed Peas, Da Brat, TLC, Brandy, Allure, LL Cool J—the photos went on and on. Full Force even had a photo with basketball star Michael Jordan, who they starred with in a commercial alongside Kid 'n Play. Here I was in this random basement in Brooklyn with a team whose hit songs I grew up to. No one in a million years could have imagined finding their big break in a random basement in Brooklyn. But that's exactly what I did.

Gerry was busy but sent me home with a couple of "throw-away" tracks—tracks that sounded good enough to be on the radio but weren't good enough for him—to write to and report back to him with. It was my one shot to really show my stuff and I took it and ran.

When I got home, Felipe congratulated me on my opportunity despite not fully understanding it and pressed me again to move in with his father. I was so high on a cloud after getting two of the best tracks I had ever had to write to, Felipe could have told me he wanted to move into a tin can and I would have agreed. Despite my previous rejection of moving to the city, I caved, we gave notice to our landlord, and we moved to the South Street Seaport.

# CHAPTER 24

# Lower East Side

IT DIDN'T TAKE LONG TO FIGURE OUT THAT LIVING with Felipe's single dad was the marriage-wrecker I knew it would be. Big Felipe breathed down my neck for being notoriously messy but refused to speak to me in person, instead sending messages through Little Felipe that I needed to clean up the master bedroom I shared with his son, and the bathroom and kitchen I shared with them all. Beyond that, John Street, which was mostly made up of warehouses, office buildings, and shops catering to tourists, was not an ideal location for residences. Unlike the rest of the city, the only thing that was open in the area after work hours was a single deli a couple blocks away. The closest supermarket required a drive and a person who was remotely interested in cooking instead of surviving off of bagels and cream cheese from the deli (which person I was not, much to Big Felipe's disgust). Big Felipe came from a long line of macho men with subservient women. I was unlike any woman he had ever seen. I expected everyone in the apartment to stay out of my way and serve themselves. My singular focus was on cooking up a career that finally showed some real promise.

I figured the train-ride to work would be easier in the city but, between walking several blocks up to the Fulton Street stop, then walking from New York Port Authority across and up town, the time to commute was about the same. I continued to dutifully arrive at my job supporting the CFO of Grey Advertising while getting ducks in a row to record reference vocals for the two songs I wrote to Gerry's tracks. I searched the paper for a cheap studio and found one buried in the projects on Clinton Street in the Lower East Side within walking distance of our apartment on John Street. Since I didn't have rent to pay and was already miserable living with Big Felipe, it was easy to brush off the house-savings deal and invest all of my income into my music instead. I fully believed my music career would blow up to the level of buying any house I wanted, anywhere I wanted. I had zero interest in saving for what I considered to be Big Felipe's low bar of a dream.

I called and booked a session at the dirt-cheap studio with a kid who sounded as professional as someone who spoke in informal street vernacular could. The next day I arrived at a storefront ready to handle business. Two twenty-year-old kids were at the studio and showed me down ladder-like stairs to a five-foot by ten-foot basement which was normally used by businesses to store bulging black garbage bags ahead of trash collection day. I spotted a kid sitting in front of a modest mixing console and speakers, assumed correctly that he was the engineer, handed him my CD, and asked where the recording booth was. The engineer introduced himself as Slick and asked if it was OK for him to listen to the tracks before we got started. I said sure but warned I didn't have time to waste and insisted on getting microphone levels from the booth worked out simultaneously. I overheard Slick and the other kid, who introduced himself as Kord, comment about how good the tracks were and wonder aloud who I was and where I came from.

"I heard that guys," I said through the microphone from the booth.

"Oh, sorry. I didn't realize my mic was on. Dope beats. You produced these?"

"No, Full Force did. I wrote to them. Let's get started by recording a dummy-lead straight through. Then I want to circle back and record sixteen tracks of background vocals, two tracks of adlibs, and a final lead track," I said decisively.

"You heard this girl, my nigga? She knows her shit," Kord said to Slick.

I paused for a second, perplexed to hear a non-African American person using the n-word. But I didn't have time to ponder it further. I had songs to record. I completed what Slick and Kord considered to be perfect takes, only to rerecord them several times over until, a couple hours later, I was personally satisfied with my recording. I blasted out of the recording booth, where the guys were playing and rough-mixing my song out loud, only to push Slick to the side and start adjusting track volumes and EQs myself.

"Shit, OK. She's gonna mix the shit herself, too," Slick said as if I wasn't in the room, obviously annoyed that I pushed him out of his own engineering seat.

"Sorry, guys. I need this to be right," I apologized without the required sincerity of remorse.

I left the studio with one song recorded, paid my fifty dollars, and set up a session for the following day to complete my second song.

The next day I arrived at Basement Recording Studio on schedule and Slick and Kord were better-prepared to accommodate the most demanding female singer—or only female singer—to step foot in their recording booth. I approached the second session the same way I approached the first and started recording vocals when I spotted from the corner of my eye someone coming down the stairs. A kid around Slick and Kord's age landed on the bottom step, got a huge smile on his face, and started bopping to music he didn't realize I was recording live to. I stopped singing from the distraction and immediately told the guys to retake the last pass without so much as acknowledging the kid who I felt shouldn't have been walking in and out of my paid session. I finished the song and burst out of the booth, ready to mix, when the kid started raving.

"You're an amazing singer, miss. A really amazing singer," the kid said with a thick, New York accent.

"Oh, thanks," I said only marginally politely because I truly didn't want anyone in my way.

"Oh, JJ. This is JayUno," Slick introduced. "He's an up and coming rapper."

"Hmm, OK," I replied, holding my tongue because everyone in the world is an up-and-coming something. I wasn't impressed.

"His dad is responsible for starting the Terror Squad, and actually, for us having this studio," Kord boasted.

My ears perked up. "You're Fat Joe's son?"

"Nah, nah. My step-pops is with the whole Terror Squad thing. I'm nobody," JayUno replied.

"Well, let me hear something," I said, curious about what a kid who had surely rubbed elbows with Big Pun (whose rap music I adored) would sound like.

Slick opened a folder on the computer desktop, pulled up a half-finished rap song by JayUno, and pressed play.

"No, don't play that one," JayUno interjected.

"Let it play," I demanded.

The couple of verses finished and I turned to JayUno, "You sound just like Pun, man. Just like him. Wow. I really love this."

"Thanks," JayUno blushed. "I wish I had you on there singing the hook."

"You want me singing the hook, huh?" I laughed. "Sure, you got it."

JayUno was dumbfounded. He acted like a teenager who had just been asked out on a date for the first time. He was smiling from ear to ear, laughing, blushing, and thanked me over and over again.

"Thank me *after* I record it. It might suck," I joked.

"It won't. No way," JayUno insisted.

When I made it back to Brooklyn and played the two songs I recorded for Gerry, he was impressed enough to want to work with me some more, but not so impressed that he intended on doing anything with either track. Even so, my foot was all the way in the door. With the blessing of Full Force's five other members—Shy Shy, Curt-T-T, Paul Anthony, B-fine, and Bowlegged Lou—Gerry and I started songwriting together for real. No more auditions.

When I wasn't at work or in Brooklyn building a business relationship with Full Force, I was in that bathroom-less, amenity-less, squat box of a recording studio in the Lower East Side. As promised, I wrote and recorded a hook for JayUno's song that I genuinely loved. I was convinced I would hear it on the radio one day. Then, I wrote and recorded a hook for JayUno's second song. And then yet another. In fact, my hobby, if you will, became going to Basement Recording Studio, unleashing my love for hip hop and singing, getting huge amounts of overzealous and exaggerated praise from kids who were on the verge of fanatics, and walking on cloud nine as if I was already a huge superstar.

Kord was the bravest out of the city kids who hung out at Basement Recording Studio. He let me know straight-up he had a crush on me and that he would do anything to woo me, husband or not. I was his "future wifey" and I just didn't know it yet. At twenty-four years old, I should have known better. But instead of the past when a creepy producer made me feel indebted to him, Kord made me feel like a goddess. He shamelessly enumerated the ways he would obsess over my happiness, break me off sexually, care for me, and love me eternally. He would make a million mini-JJ babies with me and we would hold hands and skip down sandy skirts above ocean tides into blazing red sunsets and make passionate, *real* love until our dying day.

As unrealistic as any of his sales pitch was, it still gave me butterflies in my stomach and sent chills down every nerve in my body. I got caught up. I "got got" as they say on the Lower East Side. I convinced myself that Kord, not Felipe, was my soul mate—the person who is meant to be with you and whose chemistry is so right, anyone else is wrong. Kord was broke; Felipe had a job. Kord was average looking; Felipe was gorgeous. Kord was a drop-out; Felipe attended the most prestigious high school in New York City. Kord had a baby mama and little son; Felipe had hope that he and I would have kids one day. In short, the obvious choice was Felipe. But I chose Kord.

When Kord and I finally made lackluster love on the futon in the five-by-ten studio without even a bottle of water in sight, much less a bed of roses, it was immediately apparent that my overactive imagination had created a fictitious expectation of what life would be like trading in a decent husband for a hood rat. But it was too late. I cheated on my husband. Not just my boyfriend. My husband. And it hurt inside more than anything had ever hurt before.

Felipe was on to me. My countenance changed. I was overcompensating for my sin by swinging on a pendulum between way too mushy or all the way a jerk. Part of me figured I could take it to my grave and just start fresh with my husband. But the lie was eating me alive. I started being mean and dangling the D-word around recklessly and Felipe warned me.

"If you say the word 'divorce' one more time, it's over."

"Divorce," I called his bluff.

"We're done," he settled it.

And that was that. Maybe I was wishy-washy but, when Felipe said something, he meant it. And if I didn't get the picture with words alone, Felipe's new Asian girlfriend made it clear. A year earlier when I caught the pair flirting at Felipe's job, he swore she was a lesbian and that I was imagining things. Turns out I was right all along. Drama aside and lucky for me, Felipe still had a heart. He let me stay in the apartment as long as it would take me to find an apartment.

Work-wise, I continued to do a good job at the advertising agency. Music-industry-wise, I continued to impress Full Force with my writing and leveled up to recording my references in their private studio. Otherwise, I was a mess. Even though I was a charismatic, talented, somewhat happy-go-lucky young woman, I hated myself to the core. And life has a way of putting things into perspective or downright pounding messages all the way home until you get it.

My sister, Cindy, called my cell phone as I was getting in an hour nap between my day's work and a studio session and told me something was wrong.

"Are you OK?" I immediately asked.

"I think Grandpa Johnson died," she said.

"What!?"

"Well, I don't know that for sure. I just have a feeling. Aunt Cheryl called me and asked if someone was here with me because she needs to come by and tell me something in person."

"Oh, man. Well, let's think positively," I attempted to blindly console.

"I mean, Grandpa is the oldest, right? That makes the most sense, right?"

"Yes, definitely. But Grandma Johnson has been telling us she's dying since we were kids. I mean, we're all dying, right?"

"Yeah."

"Oh man. Hopefully it's nothing. Maybe it's nothing?"

"No. It's got to be something. Why would she come all the way over and want me to have someone here if it was nothing?" Cindy reasoned.

"You're right. Well, I'm just going to stay on the phone with you until she gets there, then."

"Are you sure? I don't want to bother you."

"I don't have anywhere to go," I lied. "I'm going to stay on the phone with you."

We chatted, attempting to piece together what may or may not have occurred until we had explored every obvious possibility and resigned to sitting in silence. Then, Aunt Cheryl arrived.

"She's here. I'll call you back," Cindy rushed.

"OK, love you."

"Love you."

The wait wasn't long. My phone rang again within five minutes and Cindy choked through sobs.

"Jenn, are you sitting down?"

"No!" I panicked. "Just. What is it?"

"Dad was in a terrible car accident."

"Oh no. Is he going to be . . ."

She interrupted me, telling me "he didn't make it," before crying inconsolably.

"No!" my knees buckled and I fell to the floor crying, gagging and fighting the urge to vomit.

"I'll…I'll call…I'll call you…later," Cindy hung up.

Unbeknownst to me, Felipe arrived home from work and appeared in the doorway.

"What happened!?" he yelled, deeply concerned as if he still loved me.

"My dad was in a car accident…and…he didn't make it," I repeated verbatim what Cindy said before crying inconsolably.

Felipe hugged me tight, saying he was sorry for my loss. I held onto him, fully aware of how undeserving I was of his kindness.

# CHAPTER 25
# After the Storm

I SWALLOWED MY PRIDE AND SECURED THE FIRST flight out of New York City back home to Colorado with a loan from Big Felipe. The reduced bereavement fare was still more money than I had floating around since I constantly invested everything I had into my music. Even though I knew I would pay Big Felipe back with my next paycheck, his willingness to help me out in my time of need was not lost on me. Once in flight, the pilot announced that there was an unusually severe thunderstorm in Colorado and our flight would be redirected to the nearest airport. Once there, we would need to speak to a gate agent to be placed on another flight when the storm passed. After we deplaned, fellow passengers and I flocked to a line the length of a city block where it seemed like twenty planes worth of passengers waited to speak with one of two gate agents. Given my state of utter shock and despair, I made a beeline to the front of the line and asked the agent if I could be tended to first, explaining I just lost my father in a terrible accident and needed to get home. The agent told me I had to ask the permission of the next passenger in line, who looked me dead in the eye and shook his head no.

"Get to the back of the line!" A woman yelled from a few people back, obviously not hearing why I was attempting to cut in the first place.

Adrenaline rushed through my body and my heart started beating so fast, my breath became short. The fighter in me was ready to go to blows. But something happened. A stroke of logic. I was a grown adult and if I beat that woman into the bloody pulp she deserved to become at that moment, I would surely go to jail. For the first time, in a very long time, I made a very sound decision to stay put.

"Who said that!?" I yelled nonetheless. "I hope you're treated like this when someone in your family dies!" I said, as if anyone cared.

I walked to a pay phone area in tears and the people there parted like the Red Sea to offer me an available phone booth—no questions asked. I called home to report that I would be home about twelve hours later than I planned, distraught as if getting there earlier would have changed anything. But reality sunk in. My dad was gone. Gone forever. No picking up the phone to say "Hi." No one-of-a-kind chuckles when I shared small successes with him. No redos. No goodbyes. Just darkness.

I fell into the company of two women—a twenty-one-year-old hottie and a frail, fifty-year-old admitted prescription pill addict who spoke with a raspy smoker's voice and whose bony body and deep wrinkles read more like one hundred—in an airport waiting lounge. The pair kept me company and served as a makeshift overnight support group until cheerleading me on to my flight the next morning.

Once in Colorado, Mom and Ricco picked me up from the airport and lent me Mom's truck to drive while I was there. Mom was devastated for Cindy and me and supported us in every way she could. But given years of estrangement from my father and his family, she knew better than to cause a distraction by attending his memorial service.

I drove straight to my dad's farm, which I had only visited once before at Christmas time a year and a half earlier. During that visit before Dad died, I remembered him gathering Cindy and me at the doorstep of his home, with the Yellow Labrador he bought my stepsister when she was eight-years-old and a newer Black Labrador he bought for himself. He gave us a tour of his dream retirement home, where he planned to live happily ever after with his sweetheart. Cindy and I "oohed" and "ahhed" together as Dad showed us the masterful craftsmanship of the house he designed and built from scratch with my then eighty-year-old Grandpa Johnson, Great Uncle Bud, and Betty

Lou, the latter who miraculously cheated death when she fell from a ladder during the house's construction.

The house sat on several acres of farmland and was positioned perfectly so that the most picturesque view of Colorado's Rocky Mountains was in full sight through large windows across from the couch in the living room and breakfast table in the kitchen, as well as the porch out back. Dad then gave us a tour of the mini-barn he built for the lot of miniature donkeys Betty Lou convinced him to buy for fun as a hobby before realizing a lot of donkeys is just a lot of work. He created a system to keep the animals warm, clean, and fed in the harsh snow-packed winters, and shaded and blissful in the perfect temperatures of colorful Colorado's sky-blue and forest-green summers. Cindy and I instinctively grabbed shovels to scoop snow and poop from the corral before being pulled by Dad to come check out Betty Lou's landscaping, and an area the size of an acre or so that was reserved for Dad's next hay crop, which he was intent on not losing to rain like he did the last batch. At the end of our tour, Betty Lou's ex-husband, Travis, stopped by to say "Hello"—something I found peculiar since my own two parents would sooner eat miniature donkey doo than intentionally seek each other's company even after over a decade divorced. Dad invited us all to the back porch to drink plain iced tea and kick the tires. It was a beautiful sunny day, but below freezing, and the trendy jacket I brought as my main coat was utterly insufficient for the weather. Travis looked at me.

"You definitely came from New York City," he laughed.

It didn't occur to me until he said that, the contrast between my outfit and everyone else's was extreme. I wore black boots, shiny polyester pants, a black shirt, and a poor-excuse-for-a-ski-jacket fashion statement of a matte black jacket with obnoxious, oversized faux fur collar. Everyone else, including Cindy who traveled from Seattle, wore hiking boots, jeans, all-weather Columbia jackets, ski gloves, and hats. Travis was right. I was laughable.

Sparing me of further embarrassment, Travis left and Dad invited Cindy and me in to see the rest of the house—the most impressive of which was a massive master bedroom with a connected bathroom with the type of huge jacuzzi bathtub I had only seen in movies. I purposely rubbed Dad's ego because I loved seeing him smile and laugh. I praised him for an incredible job well-done before heading to Denver with Cindy for the Cooper's annual Christmas Eve gathering at Grandma Cooper's house— the single chance every year to see aunts, uncles, and cousins. The next morning, Cindy and I arrived back at Dad's farm and exchanged Christmas gifts. Dad (or more likely, Betty Lou) got Cindy and me each a robe that I thought I didn't need but kept and used forever, Cindy made me the most meaningful scrapbook of the few childhood photos of me that survived Dad's many moves and crawl space flood, complete with a poem she wrote about the child me "singing like my life depended on it," and Dad (himself without anyone's help) got Betty Lou a set of eggshell colored graduating ceramic jars with green moose hand-painted on each jar to display in the kitchen and store dry ingredients in. He was thrilled with himself for finding and buying the set because the moose symbolized a special time he and Betty Lou shared together. Betty Lou, on the other hand, hated them. She absolutely detested the jars from the moment she opened them. Cindy and I thought it was funny until it became clear that Dad's feelings were hurt. Dad was unfazed by taking lumps from anyone other than his "Darling." Her happiness was his joy, too.

A couple of weeks after that trip I received a small, bulky envelope in the mail. The return address showed Betty Lou's hand-written name and address. I opened the envelope up to find a pair of worn, unwashed women's underwear. Confused, I sat for a moment to consider why on earth she would send me such a thing before realizing she probably found these underwear after Cindy and I left and assumed they were mine. Even though I had made amends with Betty Lou and let a whole river run under the bridge, that envelope made me feel like a despicable, unwanted stepchild again. It made me feel like my face was being rubbed in a puddle like a dog's nose in wet carpet. Anyone else would have thrown the underwear away or at least washed them and figured out whose they were before sending them back. Betty Lou was either innocently tone deaf or purposely a complete jerk. Whichever it was, I resolved to keep my distance from her even if that meant keeping distance from my beloved Dad, including passing on a family trip to Lake Powell that summer—a breathtaking and unforgettable experience that Dad never stopped talking about and that would have been my last time seeing him before he died.

Now, I would arrive to Dad's house and be let in the front door, not by a smiling and chuckling Dad who side-hugged his kids and rarely said "I love you" because he showed it instead, but by Betty Lou's sisters who greeted me with sunken faces and instructions to please be quiet because Betty Lou was in the master bedroom, barely holding on to life without Dad. I was selfish. I was dealing with my own hurt and remorse. But I felt for Betty Lou. So I dropped all of the things I once tallied against her. Life was fragile. Fighting was frivolous. All of the things that I thought mattered so much—the injustices, the wrongdoings, and even the accomplishments and the success—didn't matter anymore. Any of us would have swallowed our pride and made anything right or sacrificed any of our greatest personal successes to have Dad back. But life doesn't work that way. Once you're gone, you're gone. And anyone left behind is left with the burden of reconciling their own conscience.

Cindy and I stayed in the same room we shared during our last visit at Dad's and tried to stay out of the way. Mourning was exhausting and it wasn't in either of our nature to lay down and be overcome with the trials we faced so we tried our best to think about the good times and indulge in a single distraction of Cindy's new boyfriend. Cindy had just started dating the man of her dreams: a huge, handsome, muscular member of the Army's Special Forces, whose irresistible charm and uncanny sense of humor was only elevated by a thick, Boston accent. When the mourning alone in our room became overwhelming, Cindy called Ed. Within seconds, Ed had both Cindy and me giggling as Cindy held the home phone receiver between both of our ears so we could all hear. But no sooner did we laugh did our door burst open and Betty Lou's sister blasted us for, not only making noise, but laughing of all things. HOW. DARE. WE.

Cindy apologized to Betty Lou's sister, and I without blinking packed my bag, got into my mom's truck, and headed to Horsetooth to go stay with my mom. However, after an hour of driving, as the truck huffed up the last remaining mountain climb to Mom's house, I stopped and turned around. I refused to be a runner. I wasn't a kid anymore. I was an adult. And I fully intended on starting to act like it. Moreover, I admitted to myself that laughing with my sister while Betty Lou suffered downstairs was in extremely poor taste—poor spirit. I was wrong.

I learned that night that the hardest part about swallowing your pride is, well, swallowing your pride. After that, the rest falls into place. I drove back to Johnstown, let myself in the unlocked front door, slipped into bed with my sleeping sister, and paused for a moment to acknowledge that I was exactly where I needed to be.

I woke to Betty Lou hugging and sobbing over me, telling me she was sorry and thanking me for coming back. My heart sunk. I had never seen her so low, so desperate, so humble. She told me she loved me and I felt even worse. I had made this woman out to be a monster. I had built brick walls between us. I had missed the opportunity to spend time with my dad to spite her. And all this time, she loved me. I told her that I was sorry for being so inconsiderate—so unbelievably inconsiderate—that it was my fault, and that I couldn't imagine her loss. We hugged and she disappeared down the stairs and back into her room, where she sunk to the deepest depths of despair for the rest of the day and many days to come.

Cindy woke and was glad to see me. We each were far more cognizant of the need for reverence and I took the opportunity to read some things I jotted down (in the notebook I carried around to write songs in) when I was on the flight home. I flipped to three pages of chicken scratch that oddly amounted to a eulogy. I reminisced about how Dad was a jack-of-all-trades. How he turned a lawn mower into to a go-cart. How he was a thrill seeker, entrepreneur, positive thinker, dedicated family man, and dedicated husband to his soul mate, Betty Lou. I wrote about how much Dad gave to the world—many times to his own detriment (according to the neighbors, who borrowed so much water for their crops that Dad's lake ran dry and he had to pay to have it refilled)—and that his example, especially as a single father to Cindy and me, largely shaped who I am and made me want to be even better.

Cindy insisted that I let Betty Lou's sisters, who had taken control of all arrangements, read my letter. Perhaps I could give the eulogy at Dad's funeral (if they had one). We were in the dark. When my aunts and grandparents called to inquire about arrangements, one of Betty Lou's sisters said, "It's none of your business!" before hanging up. Ultimately, the sisters had mercy on my grandparents and arranged a viewing of Dad's body before he was cremated according to the wishes outlined in his will. Having learned the hard way what a bad idea viewing dead bodies is, Cindy and I declined, opting instead to remember Dad well and alive. And a few days later at a brief memorial service at a funeral home just a few paces from the mortgage company Dad owned, I delivered a eulogy to a group of friends and our tiny family.

# CHAPTER 26
# All In

WHEN I ARRIVED BACK TO NEW YORK CITY, I HAD no choice but to head back to work at the ad agency. Life doesn't stop, bills don't go away, and dreams don't disappear when you lose someone. If anything, I felt an increased sense of urgency to work harder and faster before my own days were up. Moreover, I knew my dad wouldn't want us to dwell on his death. I knew Dad would be best memorialized by his children living full and rewarding lives. For me, that meant continuing to sing and write songs. I quickly made my way back to Full Force's studio in Brooklyn, where Gerry welcomed me home with a condolence card signed by every member of the team. It was the most sincere, human gesture I had ever experienced in the music industry. These guys got it. They knew what really mattered in life. I had just learned, but they already understood. Full Force's collective realness and sincerity left a lasting impression on me. This was what a true business relationship was supposed to be like: straight-forward, professional, even lucrative; but still sensitive to the fact that not a single day is promised to any of us. Work can never come before life. Alas, Full Force's secret recipe for success: family first.

Even though Full Force was a family-focused business, they still let a select few outsiders in from time-to-time. I, myself, was one. After me, came another: Gerry's girlfriend, Kelly. I'm not sure if I was the only person who didn't know Gerry had a girlfriend or if everyone didn't know. Either way, I finally got the message loud and clear. Kelly was given a management position on the team and pulled me aside privately to warn me to stop working with her boyfriend because he needed time to work with other songwriters. I wasn't the type of person to be bullied and concluded that I would work with whomever I wanted. But I somehow started working with Paul Anthony instead. Logically, the move didn't make sense since Gerry and I were a producer-singer-songwriter dream team and Paul Anthony and I were a singer-songwriter duo who had to go out and fish for producers. But this I knew: if you work with one of the six members of Full Force, it's as good as working with any or all of them. I also knew battling a jealous girlfriend to work with the best producer I knew would probably not end well. So I stepped back and invested more time elsewhere.

I decided to take up an offer to accompany June (the naked girl from the Grammys) to a meeting with a producer she met through a friend. That meeting at The Orange Factory ended badly for June, who didn't pique their interest, and splendidly for me, who was sent home with a bunch of songs to write. Soon after, I logged a handful of recordings with the team and expanded my catalogue of Pop, R&B, and Hip-hop songs, with The Orange Factory's signature Dance music.

At the height of my business relationship with The Orange Factory, I was called in to record a vocal reference for a dance record for the legendary Donna Summer. Donna shot to fame in the 70's with such hits as "She Works Hard for the Money," "Hot Stuff," and "Last Dance." Over her career, Donna scored forty-two hit records and five Grammy awards. I got to meet Donna (who was around fifty-two years old at the time) briefly at the end of the recording session. I was never good at knowing artist's names, especially if an artist wasn't from my era. So much like when I met Full Force, I didn't realize how legendary the disco queen was until long after meeting her.

Weeks later after another late-night Orange Factory session, JayUno called.

"JJ, I need you to come to the studio now," he sounded stressed.

"Are you OK?" I checked.

"Yeah, yeah. Cuban Link is here working on a song for his album and he needs a singer. I told him I got the best one in New York City coming. Can you do it?"

I paused, knowing that agreeing would mean I'd be in the company of the kid I cheated on Felipe with—a kid I never wanted to see again for the rest of my life.

"Eh. I don't know, man."

"JJ you gotta come through," JayUno practically begged.

"For you, I'll do it. But no funny business," I said as if JayUno had ever acted funny, which he had not.

"Thanks, JJ. You're gonna kill it," JayUno boasted.

I arrived at the studio, was introduced to Cuban Link, and got straight to work. He had a song with rap verses and no hook. He had a rough idea for a melody but it sounded like something a kindergartner would sing—monotonous and lacking any resemblance of a chorus. I got to work writing, coming up with ninety percent of the hook in around ten minutes before getting stuck on a line. I needed the hook to have street savvy. I needed it to be abstract and creative in ways no one had ever heard. Cuban's team was insistent that this was an album single (meaning a song that would be released on the radio and pushed heavily). Since my name was attached, I had to bring my A-game. Pressed by the team to get in the booth and record, I jotted down a line I heard another writer from The Orange Factory use, and I used it in my final hook. On one hand, I thought it was a slimy, shady, no good, awful, crappy, violative, plagiarizing thing to do. On the other hand, I figured we could work out the credits later and that The Orange Factory might be appreciative of getting writing credit and making money on a song they never even had to show up for. I recorded not only the hook with full background vocals, I also recorded an intro and adlibs throughout the entire song. When I stepped out of the booth, everybody in the studio celebrated the birth of "Sugar Daddy," a song they were certain would become a smash hit. And while they celebrated, I went home to get a couple hours of sleep before work the next morning.

Given my dad's death, Felipe agreed I could stay at the John Street apartment a few more months so I could squirrel away enough money for my new life alone after the divorce. In the meantime, instead of continuing to share a bed, I insisted on sleeping in a tiny extra bedroom with the only things I cared to hold on to: three cardboard boxes full of clothes, a few mementos, and the same desktop computer Dad bought me before I landed the job at the ad agency.

The internet had come of age by the year 2000 and I was up-to-speed with new technology. I owned a handheld digital recorder and taught myself how to use one of the very first DAW (digital audio workstation) software applications to record vocals and produce beats at home. Once I mastered engineering my own recording sessions using only my computer's keyboard and built-in microphone, sharing my song ideas with the team became as easy as sending an email. However, since attempting to produce instrumentals with keyboard plunks could never stand up to the production prowess of my all-star team, I quickly learned to stick with recording vocals. Recording my songs in full, with several tracks of background vocals at lightning speed, gave me an advantage over most songwriters. I would record and email Gerry my original, *a capella* songs, and Gerry would wave his enchanted wand and bring those songs to life with his musical genius, which we called "magic." Before I knew it, Full Force started asking me to submit ideas for every project that was placed in their lap—from Brittney Spears' pop songs to Method Man's rap hooks; Gerry started introducing me as the team's "secret weapon" when we met stars outside of high-end studios; and Paul Anthony started devising a plan to get me some money, starting with signing me as an official songwriter for Full Force. While I had plenty of impressive works-in-progress, I wouldn't get paid until the songs I wrote were on the radio and making sales.

When I wasn't submerging myself in songwriting, I was hanging out with JayUno around the Lower East Side to avoid

"The Felipes" at home. After singing several hooks on records for the young, unsigned artist, JayUno's music not only grew on me—he did. The kid was a humble young man with good looks, bad self-esteem, and a ton of promise as a rapper. He became a little brother figure in my life and a personal hype man who constantly told me in his heavy New York accent that I was the best "singah" in the whole wide world. He was convinced that I was going to be a big star one day, he constantly rubbed my ego, and we always had a lot of lighthearted fun.

Chasing opportunities and masterminding new ways to make it big with JayUno made me forget about all of my personal problems and shortcomings. JayUno and I drove aimlessly around New York City in an old BMW that I bought for three hundred dollars off of a guy who couldn't afford the daily parking tickets he was getting in Queens. JayUno affectionately named the car Mango—pronounced in his Nuyorican accent "mahn-GO"—in honor of its horrid orangish color. Eventually, we grew close enough for JayUno to not be too embarrassed to bring me to his mother's run-down apartment on 10th Street in Alphabet City, where the elevator always smelled like a neglected bathroom at a gas station.

Eventually, I became aware that JayUno's teenage brother, Nicco, not only dropped out of eighth grade but also had a hard time reading. I immediately empathized with Nicco. Illiteracy was a dirty-little-secret like bedwetting; except worse because it was more difficult to hide. I quickly concluded that any dysfunction or hardship I had known was nothing compared to what I observed at JayUno's house. With eyes more widely opened, I counted my blessings and I got to work.

Nicco's mom, Marisol, told me that Nicco's dad, Nelson, was to blame for Nicco dropping out of school. Everyone knew Nelson as the Lower East Side's drug-dealing kingpin whose money got the Terror Squad record label off of the ground. He didn't have even the remotest form of a visitation schedule with Nicco, but when Nelson came around, he took Nicco for the night—no questions asked. And taking Nicco for the night meant Nicco was kept awake all night in smokey recording studios, earsplitting nightclubs, and various gangster hangouts before being delivered to school in the morning without sleep, breakfast, a packed lunch, or homework done. This, Marisol claimed, caused Nicco to routinely fall asleep in class, never have food to eat at school, and constantly underperform. Moreover, Marisol gave up trying to advocate to get Nicco bused to a school in Brooklyn that could help him. Floored, I asked for Nicco's information, spent a day making calls, negotiated on Marisol's behalf to not get her thrown in jail for not having her child in school, and Nicco was picked up the next week by a big yellow bus to Brooklyn. And since I couldn't just mind my own business, I started visiting once a week to teach Nicco how to read.

I didn't realize it at the time but I was at the top of my game in the music industry and I grew to love songwriting. I could say anything, be anyone, and sing any way I wanted without the buzz-killing critique of managers who always painstakingly make sure every song, every outfit, and every word that comes out of an artist's mouth is in compliance with the synthetic image that has been created for them. I found that songwriters, on the other hand, have full creative liberty. Our songs either fit an artist's vibe or they don't. Our songs either hit or they don't. And as long as I was basking under the umbrella of a platinum-selling powerhouse (namely, Full Force), there grew to be a steady stream of opportunities for me to get placements—songs placed—on superstars' albums. And I never turned a single one of those writing opportunities down. However, despite my growing potential as a songwriter, I still couldn't shake wanting to sing my own music, on my own album, my own way. So whenever a song I wrote for a project didn't go anywhere, I banked it for myself. And when I wasn't writing for others, I was plotting on how to send my own singing career into orbit.

I decided I needed to go the extra mile to get noticed as a recording artist. I decided I needed a music video. But since making a decent video couldn't just be done from a smartphone back then, I needed to hustle. I told JayUno my plan for a video and asked his stepdad to chip in a grand for a stretch Hummer with a hot tub in the back since JayUno would have a huge cameo—and big exposure—in my video. Next, I rounded up a couple of secretaries at the ad agency, who always talked about dancing on the side, to choreograph a routine and appear in the video with me. After that, I figured out a way to get free makeup for everyone on the day of the shoot by scheduling a bunch of free consultations at the MAC makeup store in the village instead of paying dearly for an actual makeup artist. I sent a save-the-date to a few people I knew, including my Full Force team, and JayUno invited Tony Sunshine, a singer from the Terror Squad, and around a bazillion kids from the Lower East Side. With all of my ducks in a row, I searched the classified ads and arranged to pay heavily for a seasoned videographer.

No sooner did I venture to record a music video did I receive word that my sister and I were the beneficiaries of one of the IRAs my dad had been contributing to for years. If we rolled our respective shares over, we would each retain eighteen-thousand dollars in a new IRA. If we cashed out, we would pay thousands in tax penalties. Young, dumb, in need of a new apartment, and in the process of launching my singing career to the next level, the choice was clear: cash out.

I made a mental promise to Dad that I wouldn't squander away the money he painstakingly saved but by the time I paid for my music video (minus the thousand dollars Nelson paid entirely in singles to the stretch-Hummer-limousine driver), loaned Felipe's mom around three-thousand dollars to buy a new house in Florida since she had always been so good to me, and earmarked several thousand for when I found a new place to stay, my bank account was soon unimpressive again. Song placements didn't come with cash advances and none of my song collaborations had hit radio yet. But I never regretted the investment. My music video started playing on local cable TV and word got out that some new singer named JJ was a force to be reckoned with. Now, I just needed a record deal.

Taking a page from the book of JayUno's impressively large squad, I realized I couldn't keep putting all of my eggs into one basket. I started marketing myself to everyone I met and somehow landed in the company of Steve Mac, a young man not much older than I who worked at a jingle house. He claimed to be a producer who would be able to get me a record deal but then shied away once he found out I was signed to Full Force as a writer. Nonetheless, he had a project for me. The singer Brandy was the new face of Cover Girl and he needed me to take a poem that an ad agency wrote (ironically, the same ad agency I worked for as a secretary in the Finance department) and turn the poem into a thirty-second song. On the spot, I created a song, recorded reference vocals and backgrounds, and soon after, watched in awe as Brandy sang in a commercial her own rendition of the vocal arrangement I wrote. I was really doing this. I was writing for superstars.

From there, my career as a moonlighting songwriter took off at a breakneck pace. Steve Mac landed a deal with Warner Brothers for his teenaged girl group "Trace" and offered me a sizeable chunk of royalties to "fix" six songs originally written by the legendary Carole King for the project. While King could still write a good song, her lyrics and melodies were dated. Steve wanted me to remake the songs—and write a couple of new ones of my own—to give his girl group a fresh sound and fighting chance. From there, I worked several nights per week writing for and vocal coaching a trio of girls, on top of several nights per week writing for Full Force. To keep up, I borrowed from sleep. I began a steady regimen of working twenty-two-hour days and sleeping from 4:00 a.m. to 6:00 a.m. before reporting for work at the ad agency in the mornings and hitting the studios again every night. Even though I had completely arrived as a songwriter, I still needed health insurance and I still needed the big music industry paychecks that everyone around me was getting before I could quit my day job.

A born procrastinator, I put off getting an apartment until the very last minute when living with The Felipes was utterly unbearable despite hardly being at the apartment. Big Felipe didn't understand how a young lady could stay out all night, barely sleep, shower, and leave every single day for months on end. The old man was convinced I was up to no good and told Little Felipe to let me know he wanted to talk to me. Since I was never around to talk to, I came home to a small blue sticky-note stuck to my bedroom door from Little Felipe. The note advised me to stick around before work the next morning so Big Felipe could have a discussion with me. Knowing there wasn't a single thing Felipe could have to discuss with me other than telling me to get out, I spent the day before our talk locating an apartment rental in Jersey City that was "close to bus transportation to New York City" and "way better than living in the city" according to June, who still popped in and out of my peripheral vision from time to time because she saw me making some ground in the music business and unabashedly tried to hop on my coattail. In fact, on at least two occasions, I arrived at major, secretive recording sessions to find June somehow there waiting for me, playing groupie to the superstar I was supposed to be writing with. Still, since I knew June couldn't compete with me, I didn't waste energy calling her out.

I waited the next morning until 7:30 a.m. when Big Felipe appeared from his bedroom for coffee. I sat quietly on a kitchen bar stool waiting for him to say something but he never said a word. Once it was clear we weren't going to have the talk I had worried the whole previous day about, I got up and started to leave when the old man spoke:

"Jennifer?"

"Yes?"

"Talk to Little Felipe when you get home."

"Ok."

Big Felipe honestly didn't have to say a word. I got caught up in my dreams and overstayed my welcome. The only talk Little Felipe and I had that night was to ask him for the quick favor of driving me to see my "new" apartment in Jersey City since I wasn't confident enough to find my way to New Jersey on my own. I realized after the fact that I just needed to drive through a single tunnel under the Hudson River.

The ancient, one-bedroom railroad apartment was shown to me by a quiet, middle-aged, balding man with dark brown hair and eyes, who was firm in asking me for information for a background check while simultaneously being apologetic.

"I'm sure you are fine. I'm sure you'll be OK. I just have to do this, you know, because a lot of people lie. I'm sure you're honest. You understand. I just have to check."

The man didn't have to explain anything to me. I was there with a pocket full of cash, average credit that was finally on the rise, and full intent on renting the underwhelming apartment. Granted, the place was far more spacious than my second apartment in Queens, but still what one could expect to find in the city. The apartment was a perfect rectangle, with a rather scary bathroom with broken tiles and a drop ceiling on one side; a fairly large kitchen with high ceilings, vintage sink and oven (and out of nowhere, majestic original tin tiles on high ceilings) in the middle; wooden wall panels covered in white paint and cheap thin carpet that looked like it was a hand-me-down from an old office building further in; and a room with two large windows facing the street and a single, small closet to house my three boxes of clothing at the end—just like a train car the style earned its name after.

My credit check came back fine and I arrived with my boxes and my computer on Christmas Eve—a day when the bustling city did, in fact, sleep. Without furniture, a television, or even a single dish to eat from, sitting quietly in a lowly-lit, empty apartment on Christmas Day and looking down upon a quiet, snow-covered street outside, was serene at first before it became maddening. I used my new Sprint flip-up cell phone to call my mom, grandmother, and sister for ten cents per minute but otherwise sat in silence. When the street started buzzing and stores began to open the next day, I wasted no time walking to local stores that lined my street for a full mile, to purchase some of life's basic necessities: a few dishes, eating utensils, towels, curtains, and a computer desk and chair so I could get back to work. Then it dawned on me that I should have at least taken the TV Felipe and I bought together since he was living in a fully furnished apartment with several of them.

Back then, it was somewhat normal to arrive places unannounced. And since Felipe and I were still able to be completely amicable, and Big Felipe went to the Bronx on the weekends, it didn't occur me to knock before I unlocked the door and entered the apartment at John Street. But as soon as I barged in, I realized it was a bad idea. The air was damp with the familiar fragrance of the hair products I left behind and the hallway was wet with the mist of a recently-taken shower. Still, I carried on. I went to the master bedroom to retrieve the TV I came to recover and found Felipe and his freshly showered girlfriend primping in the reflection of closet doors made of mirrors. Extinguished tea candles were spread throughout the room around the unmade bed and despite the pair being fully dress, the room reeked of sex.

"Oh hey!" I said as if we were all old friends. "I just came to grab the TV." I looked at Felipe with squinted eyes. "Ya'll don't waste any time. The day after I moved out, huh?" I picked up the VCR and walked out of the room with it. "You know, I think I'll also take the couch, the lamp, this VCR," I said.

Felipe said nothing but was visibly fuming. He started collecting all of the things I itemized and threw them into a pile next to the front door. I was killing his vibe with his new lover and he wanted me out.

I managed to stuff everything into Mango, except the couch, which Felipe delivered to me with his dad's mini-van a couple of days later when he calmed down and realized how dumb he looked for getting mad when he was the one with the coworker he claimed was a lesbian in his bed. While he was there, I asked him for the favor of taking a few photos for me. In actuality, I really *did* need some "artist" photos to continue to push for a record deal. But I also felt inclined to entirely disrespect his new girlfriend. I got dressed (or undressed), wearing only a sweater and underwear to attempt a knock-off version of a magazine cover I saw Jennifer Lopez on. I then changed into a bikini and posed on the cheap, white laminate tiles in my kitchen for as many photos as it took to finish the film in my camera. Before Felipe left, he told me his new girlfriend had a dream that we would get back together. I smiled, happy that she was worried.

"We'll see," I said before wishing him a good night and officially starting the next phase of my life, alone.

# CHAPTER 27

# Missionaries

NEW YEAR'S EVE ARRIVED AND JAYUNO FELT sorry for me that I didn't have anywhere to go or anyone to spend it with so he invited me to tag along to Jimmy's nightclub in the Bronx with his girlfriend and him. Jimmy's was a well-known hangout for the Terror Squad, who "walked around the metal detectors" like Remy Ma's rap lyrics. For this reason, it was no surprise when news spread months before that Cuban Link, the famous rapper who I wrote "Sugar Daddy" with, got his face sliced there over a disagreement. But the noise from that event had passed and the nightclub was going to be a million times more fun than working at home, so I accepted. One can only write so many songs before entirely burning out.

I spent a few hours painstakingly curling my dead-straight pieces of long, black-dyed hair into a huge nest of spiral curls, carefully constructing the perfect smoky eye and pale glossy lip, and squeezing into a stretchy-jean body suit that left no room for imagination before completing my look with knee-high black leather boots and a very convincing faux fur coat. I came outside just before 9:00 p.m. when the streets were already dark and I muscled close and locked the heavy, steel door that kept strangers and vagabonds out of my building when I heard the nauseatingly happy voice of an obvious out-of-towner.

"Hi there! Would you like to hear a message about Jesus Christ?"

Normally if I heard a voice within a few feet of a door I was locking, I would instantly take a defensive stance and prepare for any number of scenarios: a robbery, sexual harassment, or worse. But I turned around calmly instead, having a solid hunch about who was behind me. Two teenage boy missionaries stood before me with parted hair, grey wool coats with tags on the left lapels, scarfs wrapped around starched white shirt collars, sharply ironed dress pants, and worn dress shoes, wet from the snow on the ground.

"The Church of Jesus Christ of Latter-day Saints, right?"

"Yes! How'd you know?"

"My childhood best friend was a Mormon. I've been to your church a lot, actually. Most of my childhood, really."

The two missionaries only had seconds to round the corner and make it to their apartment by their curfew—nine-o'clock—so hurriedly gave me a card and invited me to church on Sunday before disappearing into the darkness.

I arrived at JayUno's mom's apartment and he and his girlfriend piled into Mango for a ride up to the Bronx. There, we saw the whole crew from the Lower East Side, including Tony Sunshine, an up-and-coming singer from the Terror Squad, who had been increasingly flirting with me over several months. Once through security, we found a table outside of the main club and JayUno's girl ordered a drink while JayUno and I, natural non-drinkers, ordered sodas.

Tony Sunshine visited our table and grabbed my hand to pull me off to "talk to" me but it was clear to everyone he wanted more than that. Still, I went because having my ego rubbed felt better than tagging along with JayUno and his girlfriend as a pathetic third wheel. Tony pulled me away and led me down a dark staircase to a pitch-black basement that was closed to the public that night but otherwise seemed to serve as a reception area for parties. Tony pushed me up against a wall and started kissing me, forcefully sticking his tongue down my throat. Not totally committed to the little romp, I turned my head and laughed before Tony turned it back and tried again. I loved the attention but I didn't need any more bad decisions under my belt. Luckily, security came, hit the lights, and broke it all up.

Soon after that night, I got word that Gerry—the most talented and successful producer I knew by a landslide—was moving to a fancy apartment on the water in Jersey City. I was elated because I thought that meant I would work with him much more often as a result. Much to my dismay, the move didn't change a thing. If anything, I saw Gerry less. Still, I hustled to keep pumping songs out of my desktop computer at home and even drove to Brooklyn for a couple of writing sessions with Paul Anthony, whose eccentric, in-your-face personality could be easily misconstrued for flirting. But such idiosyncrasies were just the authentic hallmark of Paul Anthony—a born superstar.

Back home, an unexpected predicament occurred: it seemed like every single time I stepped foot out of my apartment, I bumped straight into the same Mormon missionaries who invited me to Church on New Year's Eve. At first, I made one hundred excuses as to why I couldn't talk—had to run. Then I started accepting their card with hand-written church times every time I saw them. Finally, they got me to agree to actually come to church one Sunday, which promise I broke several times before feeling utterly ashamed and finally giving it a go.

I arrived at an old grey office building near Journal Square and thought I had the wrong address before seeing muted grey letters that spelled out The Church of Jesus Christ of Latter-day Saints, fused to the concrete wall. I barely made it up the stairs when the missionaries who had been stalking me for weeks, Elder Kaupert and Elder Leader, met me and invited me in. I attended sacrament meeting and, even though the place lacked the grandeur of the churches back home with high, glorious, embellished wood ceilings, stained glass, beautifully upholstered pews, and a packed congregation of handsome families, I still felt nostalgic. As a kid, I always thought that the Leethams' church was their own. I thought that some people were born with a God and some people, like me, were not. But here I was, being invited to be a part of the thing I looked up to so much as a child—the thing I never thought I was good enough for. And then, as I sat there in awe, one of the missionaries nudged me.

"Sister Johnson?"

Elder Leader handed me a sacrament bread tray, signaling the "Sister Johnson" he was talking to was me. I took a piece of bread, ate it, and handed the tray over to Elder Kaupert on my other side, just like I did as a child when I went to church with the Leethams. I listened to everyday people, unpaid clergymen and women, give talks and testimony. I saw more white people in one room than I had in all of New York City in six or seven years. Jersey City was the cheapest area to live in within commuting distance to the city. Most church members I met there were only staying temporarily for school or work. I somewhat felt out of place because I had long past assimilated with city culture. But being in a room with so many Midwesterners reminded me of home.

Between juggling my day job, songwriting, and teaching Nicco how to read, I squeezed in time to have "discussions"— formal lessons about the gospel—with the missionaries. During our first lesson, a missionary asked if I knew who Jesus Christ was.

"Um, our Lord and Savior?" I stated uncertainly, recalling what many stars said during Grammy acceptance speeches.

"Right! Now, do you know who God is?"

"Our creator?" I replied and questioned at the same time, again quoting award shows.

The truth was, I didn't know those answers. I stopped going to church when Mom left, and I didn't pray because I figured having type one diabetes and a bladder that still failed occasionally were curses so bad, I was immune from worse. But the missionaries kept coming over and teaching me precept upon precept. One week, I was challenged to read certain scriptures from The Book of Mormon. Another week, I was challenged to commit to the "Word of Wisdom," which mandates that one must abstain from coffee, tea, smoking, and alcohol (things I didn't consume anyway). And the real kicker: I was eventually challenged to accept the "Law of Chastity" which meant no sexual anything outside of marriage. The further one could stay away from the sinful edge, the better.

I agreed to it all and then had a lesson that sealed the deal for me.

"Did you know that we can live eternally with our families?" a new missionary, Elder Griffiths, who replaced Elder Leader, asked.

"Wait, what?"

"If we endure until the end, we can live together forever in heaven," Elder Griffiths rephrased before testifying, "I know you will see your dad again, Jenn."

The kid might as well have given me a record deal, a million dollars, and a million puppies on the spot. Hearing from someone who was tight with the God who I never thought belonged to me, that I would one day hang out with my dad again and that all would be well and right, was enough to intrigue me to take their advice and pray.

Late that night, standing alone in the quiet of my empty kitchen, I folded my hands, bowed my head, and prayed.

"Dear Heavenly Father," I prayed the way the missionaries taught me. "I thank you...um, thee for this day that you...uh, thou has given me. I thank thee for my home and food and insulin and a job and music. I thank thee that I'm still alive. I kind of can't even believe it. God, if I could talk to my dad? Well, OK, I'm sure Dad is up there, so Dad? Can I talk to you? Dad, I'm sorry for being a bad kid. I'm sorry I didn't realize how privileged I was. I'm sorry I thought I had it rough in your house. Now I know better. I've seen much worse. Dad, now that you're up there, can I please ask a favor? I can't say this out loud but I can say it to you here. Will you please tell God that the cursed bedtime bladder he gave me is one of the most crushing things in life that I have to go through? Worse than diabetes. Can you ask him to please remove the curse? I'm sure I deserve it. But it would be the biggest relief to never have to worry about it again."

I had to stop praying because I felt an area the size of a large palm on my back left shoulder blade heat up and tingle, radiating through my torso and, seemingly, through my heart to the front of my chest. Scared, I opened my eyes and stopped praying while the feeling took several seconds to go away. Earlier that day, the missionaries encouraged me to pray to know if The Book of Mormon was true. But I had a bigger test. If there was a God, then surely he could take away the single most burdensome anomaly in my life. I didn't know if the prayer would work. But, with tears streaming down my face, I knew that I had just felt my dad. And I didn't need any more convincing than that, that there was, in fact, a God and a heaven. And if being a member and attending the Mormon church was how I personally got there, then so be it. The denomination never mattered to me. The feeling did.

The next day, I told the missionaries I wanted to be baptized. And it took me several weeks to notice, but I realized that, after my prayer, I never suffered from a bladder problem again.

I told my mom and sister about my plans to become a Mormon, figuring they would think it was wonderful that I was going to church every Sunday and that I learned how to pray and think twice about decisions and keep commitments and be honest and such. But only my mom was genuinely happy for me. My sister, not so much. She was confirmed as a thirteen-year-old in the Lutheran church and extremely sentimental when it came to carrying forward family traditions. But for me, Mormonism was the only tradition I had an example of. My experience was vastly different. I didn't feel a connection to the Lutheran church other than sitting confused by my grandparents' side every Sunday when I lived with them.

After taking the big dip in a hot tub sized baptismal font in Jersey City's branch of the Mormon church, I wrote Grandma Cooper a letter telling her about my decision, scared to call her myself. Once she received the letter, she called my sister crying. And once my sister had to console her beloved grandma on my behalf for a decision she detested, Cindy stopped speaking to me for a while.

I never imagined that doing something so positive, healthy, and uplifting for myself would cause me to be somewhat shunned. Perhaps no one knew how many innocent girls I had beaten up in high school, how promiscuous I had been as a teen, what a rotten wife I was, or what a filthy liar I had become to get ahead in the world? Even my Full Force family and contacts in the industry passed on attending or hearing about my baptism or newfound faith. In fact, some were concerned I wouldn't have the same sass, same punch, or same uninhibitedness that was a huge part of my appeal as a songwriter. But I quickly proved them wrong.

# CHAPTER 28
# Blaque Out

OTHER THAN SUDDENLY ABSTAINING FROM swearing like a sailor, with respect to my music, not much changed after I was baptized. I still banged out songs. I still stayed up all night in various studios. I still hung out with JayUno in the Lower East Side. But I started attending church without fail every Sunday and took more pride in what I grew to recognize as "righteous" endeavors. For one, I continued to work with Nicco on his reading, which had improved so much since our first lesson that he grew to be able to read sentences out of the Wall Street Journal. And after a reading session one week, I went further and found other ways I could help, like washing the family's dishes.

As I washed dishes, my feet ached from working all day in my trendy, high-heeled boots, and beads of sweat formed around the baby hairs that lined my forehead since Marisol's apartment building was always kept hot. As I wrapped up my good deed, I heard the pit bulls bark at a guest at the front door before a stranger behind me spoke.

"Wow. You're a lot shorter in person."

I turned around to see a kid JayUno's age—around three years younger than me—standing in the doorway of the kitchen.

"I'm Charlie. And you're…"

"JJ," we said together.

Charlie introduced himself as a longtime friend of JayUno's. They grew up together in the 286 building on Clinton Street. The story goes, when Charlie's mom was walking out to give birth to him, JayUno's mom was walking in with her newborn (JayUno's little sister). Charlie lived in that building until he turned sixteen when his dad borrowed from the 401K he earned over twenty years installing cable and bought a home in the Pocono Mountains in Pennsylvania. Now, Charlie only visited the city to tag along as a marketer and hype man for all of the rap stars that were emerging from the Lower East Side.

I didn't think much of the meeting. It was a little strange to have my first fan experience, meeting someone who knew of me when I didn't know a thing about them. But other than that, I passed the meeting off as a routine hello between friends of friends.

Life went on at an even faster pace than before. Since only one relative was speaking to me, I didn't take time out of my busy schedule to call anyone other than my mom. My day job still sped by in a blur every day and my studio nights were still filled with what felt like millions of hours of creative brainstorms, hits and misses. Church on Sundays felt like a huge sacrifice of three hours of time but I always came home feeling glad I went. And as soon as I took my church clothes off, I hit my computer to write more songs.

This particular Sunday, Full Force called shortly after I got home from church and said they had an urgent assignment. A group called Blaque—a trio that boasted a hit first album and were in the process of recording a second—still needed a title track for their record. Paul Anthony tapped me to submit something entirely brand new and hit-worthy within a few hours. By that time, I was well-versed on handling high-pressure songwriting situations. It was not uncommon for me to write full songs in a matter of five or ten minutes. There was no doubt in my mind that I could write the smash hit they were looking for and I was right: the song "Blaque Out" came to me as seamlessly as running comes to a gazelle. I sent my *a capella* vocals via email to the team, and by early morning, Gerry produced a hit-sounding track to accompany my hit-sounding song.

I called out from work the next morning because the team needed me to come to Brooklyn to record a high-end demo of Blaque Out, recorded and mixed as tediously as a song that would actually go to radio would be. By night, the label not only accepted Blaque Out for the album, they dubbed it the title track. Paul Anthony called me to give me the great news, saying he heard that many prominent songwriters tried and failed to get a track on the album.

"I bet they're pissed, J!" Paul Anthony said followed by a booming laugh that was reminiscent of the way Dad used to laugh when he was tickled with one of my accomplishments.

Later, I received a voicemail from Gerry while I slept.

"Yo, J. I heard the good news, man. Congratulations! Now don't get gassed, son!" Gerry teased, reliably speaking to me as if I was a male homie instead of a young lady.

Alas, I had arrived. I was now the songwriter in the industry that the artists I grew up listening to had to watch their back for. I was the person who, after all of the years of paying dues, was the go-to man for a hit record. I was living the dream, even if it was a songwriting dream I didn't set out to have. I was making it. Working my body and soul to the bone had finally paid off. It would only be a matter of time before the hits started piling up and "JJ" would become a household name. In the meantime, I got an unexpected phone call.

JayUno's friend, Charlie, got my number from JayUno and unabashedly gave me a call one Saturday afternoon.

"Oh, hey. Yes, of course I remember you. What's up? Do you need something?" I asked, totally confused as to why he would be calling me.

"No I'm just here at drill washing dishes so figured I'd give you a call," Charlie replied.

"Drill? Are you in jail or something?" I questioned with a laugh.

"No. Army National Guard drill. I'm in the Army," he clarified.

"Oh, ok!" I laughed at myself. "I mean, are you trying to *talk* to me?" I asked, getting straight to the point and wondering out loud if he was poised to ask me on a date or something.

"You could say that," Charlie replied, making us both laugh.

From there, the calls came more frequently until we were both so madly in love with the idea of being in love that we couldn't wait to see each other again. But given my jam-packed schedule, meeting would have to wait.

After not speaking for several months following my baptism, my sister sent me an email. She saw an ad on TV for a medical alert bracelet—a bracelet that said "diabetic" that I could wear daily as a safety net in case I ever had a medical emergency. Unlike the ugly stainless steel bracelets they sold at pharmacies, this beaded bracelet was less of an arm-sore. Cindy wanted permission to buy one for me because despite being disappointed in my baptism, she still worried obsessively about my wellbeing like the fiercely protective big sister she had always been. I was wise enough by then to know that that email was likely the easiest opportunity I would get to resume speaking with Cindy so, despite not wanting to swallow my pride, I did anyway and accepted her gift. After that, we started speaking again like nothing ever happened, with me making great efforts to tiptoe around the topic of Mormonism. And thankfully, we started speaking just in the nick of time because something that required full family togetherness was about to transpire.

# CHAPTER 29
# The Swiftness of Death

TWO PROSECUTORS CALLED ME TO INFORM ME OF the sentencing hearing for Jack Arnold (the man responsible for the accident that took my dad's life) and I booked my flight home without a second thought. Betty Lou and Cindy both previously declined to speak or attend the hearing and Cindy seemed shocked when I told her I planned to go.

"Wait, you're going? I thought we weren't going." Cindy said over the phone.

"No, *you* said you weren't going. I was always going," I replied decisively.

"Well, now I wonder if I should go. Do you think I should go?"

"I think you should do what's right for you."

"I don't know. I'll call you back."

Cindy took a week or so to call back, which wasn't unusual for sisters who could go a lifetime without having the opportunity to speak and still pick up as if we never missed a second. In that week, she not only changed her mind and decided to attend, Betty Lou did, too. And not only did they plan to attend, they decided to join me and speak.

I arrived in Colorado on schedule and arrived at the courthouse in unison with Betty Lou, Cindy, and Grandma and Grandpa Johnson. We entered the courtroom and sat on polished wood benches that reminded me of the old church pews at Gethsemane Lutheran Church. We sat quietly while the courtroom slowly filled with people: the lawyers, the transcriber, the bailiff, random onlookers, and a family consisting of a man and his girlfriend (a woman without a wedding ring), another young lady, and presumably, their parents. They smiled and shot the breeze as my family and I sat still and cold with anxiety, with lumps in our throats and knots in our stomachs.

Once I figured out who Jack was, I didn't take my eyes off of him until the judge arrived and Jack was asked to come forward and join his attorney. The judge verbalized what I assumed was routine legal jargon before allowing the prosecutors to review the details of the case. The two-man team summarized police reports, witness accounts, and the only thing I had not had access to: my dad's autopsy. The rest of my family seemed to be in a trance, not particularly listening to what was going on and perhaps planning out in their minds what they were going to say. I, on the other hand, was shocked. The lawyers stated that Dad's cause of death was "asphyxia" from his seatbelt. I didn't know what that word meant until the lawyer proceeded to explain how after my dad's truck was t-boned, it rolled several times down a ravine before landing up-side-down and Dad, completely knocked out with every bone in his body broken, suffocated. I felt my veins fill up with the familiar fight that's lived inside of me my entire life before I realized something. As terrible as that death sounded, Dad preferred such an ending over nearly every other scenario. He was extremely vocal about wanting to go fast when it was his time. He never wanted to become a vegetable or be a burden to anyone. For my own sake, I continuously reminded myself of this quirk of his. If he had to go, he went his way.

Before I knew it, the judge looked our way and asked our family if any of us would like to make a statement.

"I do," I said before anyone else could respond.

I decided months before that when I finally had my day in court, I would be strong. Dad didn't raise a victim. Dad didn't raise a copout. Dad raised a tough kid. And there was no way I was going to leave that courtroom until I looked Jack Arnold dead in his eyes and said everything I had rehearsed over and over in my head for the year leading up to that moment. It was show time. And I was standing in front of the most important microphone of my life.

"Jack, I'm Jennifer Johnson. Frederic Joseph Johnson's youngest daughter. Do you know who my dad was?" I looked straight at him until his head rose and our eyes connected. The smile he had before the hearing was replaced with flat, closed lips and apologetic eyebrows.

"No, ma'am."

"I heard you said in the last hearing that you knew he was a computer programmer."

"Yes, ma'am."

"He wasn't just a computer programmer, Jack. He was a son, a brother, a husband, a best friend, an inventor, an adventurer, a philosopher, a comedian, a philanthropist, a fishing buddy, a guy who refused to say even a single swear word, and the best father I could have ever asked for. Fred Johnson served honorably in the U.S. Army and built from scratch over several decades many businesses and even a dream home with his own two hands. He was a Big Brother to needy kids, a self-taught scientist and friend of the environment, an animal lover, an avid reader, a farmer, a volunteer professor at a community college, and yes, if that weren't enough, he created a computer program that processed in seconds what it used to take loan officers hours to accomplish, lending to an incredibly successful mortgage company that he spearheaded and that provided for many employees who are now left to figure out their future. He wasn't just a computer programmer. Do you understand that, Jack?"

"Yes, ma'am."

"Jack, I want you to look behind you right now. I want you to look into my grandparents' eyes and see for yourself the hurt and the pain." Jack turned around while my grandparents stared blankly ahead and then turned back around to me. "My dad was their only son. My dad was their livelihood. Do you get it?"

"Yes, ma'am."

"No you don't." I spoke over him. "You can't. Because until my dad was taken from me, I didn't get it, either. How does a person measure the value of a lost life? A taken life. It's impossible.

# CHAPTER 30
# Payday

I ARRIVED BACK FROM COLORADO AT JFK AIRPORT IN Far Rockaway, Queens, and Charlie—the kid I had managed to fall madly in love with over the phone—met me at baggage claim, marking the first time we had laid eyes on each other since meeting in JayUno's mom's kitchen.

"Why are you so tall? Are you wearing heels?" he asked, preoccupied with my five-foot-four frame, which was only an inch shorter than his.

"Yeah, I have a few inches on you at the moment," I laughed, unconcerned.

I grabbed my carryon from the baggage carousel and unabashedly held Charlie's hand as he led me to the parking garage and gentlemanly opened the passenger door of the car he borrowed from his dad without asking. His parents were in Alaska visiting his older brother, sister-in-law, and newborn nephew at an Army base at the time. Once buckled in, Charlie reached behind my seat and pulled out a dozen roses cradled in the cheap plastic wrapper that covers all flowers that are purchased at gas stations. I leaned over and gave him a quick peck on the lips as if we had been married ten years and were saying goodbye for work. Then, once we exited to the Van Wyck Expressway back to Jersey City, Charlie said he had a song queued up that was just for me before pressing play on the car's CD player. A guitar-like synthesizer with bell-like chords in the background introduced Genuiwine's "Differences"—a love song that said everything Charlie wanted to say to me.

I listened and sang along in my head to the song and I smiled, blushed, and gave Charlie an awkward side hug from the passenger seat as he drove. Charlie turned the music down and reiterated his strong feelings for me as I sat stunned. I had never been the recipient of such a sincere and romantic gesture before and my stomach bubbled over with butterflies. Through our phone calls, I had become a huge fan of Charlie's sense of humor, communicativeness, spontaneity, and reliability. And I definitely loved him. But I had a knack for falling hard and fast for even the worst choices in men. To feel so much love coming from someone who was actively courting me filled my whole soul with euphoria. Charlie might as well have proposed to me right then and there. I would have said yes.

We arrived back at my apartment and the reflex after such a touching and deeply loving car ride was to rip each other's clothes off and make deep, passionate love. But as soon as I dropped my bags, invited him in, and found myself wrapped in his arms on my bed, I reminded him of the disclaimer I gave him over the phone after we started talking more regularly: now that I was a Mormon, I couldn't have sex, or do anything remotely related to it, save I destroy what I thought was a perfect record with God following baptism.

"Well, can we kiss?" he asked seriously.

I laughed and we connected lips, wishing it was far more but satisfied by the mere presence of each other.

After officially becoming boyfriend and girlfriend, Charlie and I carried on a long-distance relationship between Jersey City and the Pocono Mountains where he lived with his parents while trying to figure out what he wanted to do with his life. Beyond serving in the Army and "repping" hard for rap artists emerging from his childhood projects in the Lower East Side, he didn't have much direction. But whatever he lacked in clarity he made up for in drive. More importantly, he was extremely uncomfortable in life, desperately wanting more for himself. I, on the other hand, couldn't care less about what he was or wasn't professionally because love, commitment, loyalty, and stick-to-it-ness were worth more to me than any amount of money or success. I didn't mind carrying us with my success until he found his niche and caught up. In the meantime, I invited him to church.

I was overjoyed about my newfound relationship with Heavenly Father—the name Mormons use as a sign of reverence and respect to our Creator and to avoid overusing the word "God." My greatest hope was that Charlie would convert to the church, keep all of the commandments I promised to keep, take me to the coveted temple for an "eternal marriage" where we could be sealed forever, make some babies, and live happily ever after rolling in my music industry dough. But my realistic expectation was that he'd eventually press me hard enough for sex that I'd be unable to resist, utterly fail at Mormonism, and go back to square one of being a young woman I didn't entirely like or respect.

To my utter surprise and delight, Charlie not only came to church, he kept coming to church. He got baptized. He abstained from everything I abstained from. He paid his tithes. And after a year of regular attendance and church activity, he took a temple class so he could receive the same endowment I did—a temple ordinance that is performed when one feels responsible enough to make stricter promises with the Lord. The catch was, if you were endowed and then made a mistake, the spiritual consequence was higher.

While I was inclined to pressure Charlie to move up in the church's hierarchy, I didn't have to. He took full initiative in his church membership, which action only made me fall more deeply in love with him. He was my "one." No courthouse wedding in a sweat suit. No funny business on the side. Just a man who seemed to do everything in his power to be a mate worthy of my full trust, unconditional love, and abiding loyalty—things I thought I was incapable of ever getting or giving again.

To be closer to me, Charlie asked JayUno for a spot on the FedEx truck JayUno worked on to secure a weekly paycheck on top of his Army National Guard pay and moved himself back to New York City, sleeping on the floor of his best friend's room in the projects until talking JayUno's mom into renting him a room.

Once there, the whole family benefitted from Charlie's timely rent payments (which covered the entire rent bill), military grade housecleaning, and stellar example to the kids who lived there. The greatest beneficiary of Charlie's presence was Nicco, who was in desperate need of the example of an invested and consistently responsible man in his life. Charlie set a high bar and demanded respect, courtesy, and goals from a kid who had learned previously from the hood that hustling on the street was the best he could hope for.

Back at my apartment in Jersey City, I still hustled during the wee hours of the night to keep climbing in the music industry. As I kept racking up song credits on albums, Paul Anthony stepped in and made some calls to his contacts at ASCAP and SESAC to fish for an opportunity for me. I had yet to decide about which performance-rights organization (a company that tracks your airtime and collects money for such on your behalf) to join. Typically, one could sign up with one of these organizations for free. But Paul knew that a songwriter like me, with a Cover Girl commercial on TV, songwriting credit on the title track on Blaque's album and alongside Carole King on virtually an entire, soon-to-be-released album, vocals on a dance single with Donna Summer, credits on Full Force's new group's album, a possible hit with Cuban Link, and new opportunities being presented every day, could probably not only get signed, but also get a royalty advance. Before I knew it, I was in a meeting with Trevor Gale at SESAC, signing a contract that was sure to benefit everyone, and receiving an eighteen-thousand dollar advance on anticipated royalties.

I took my check to work the next day and showed one of my bosses, who called a bunch of people into his office to show my check and me off as if he was a proud father. Everyone seemed interested but quickly headed back to their desks, rolling their eyes. I had been "reported" before for talking music industry business on my ad agency phone and several employees were not shy about complaining about me, asking why I don't just go and do music for a living.

"Because I need health insurance and more money," was my honest answer. But after I got my check, I sat down with my boss and said, "Maybe it's time to cut the cord. Maybe I can actually quit and go for it." As proud as my boss was, he encouraged me to stay at the agency (but to keep my music business to myself). Health insurance was invaluable and a conservative Finance guy would hate to see me go without it. Since I was managing OK the way I was, I kept the day job and kept getting only a few hours of sleep every night, which had become my personal norm.

Back home, I had something new to work into my schedule: a "Home Teacher." The Mormon church is big on looking out for one another so assigns every member in good standing with a list of people to visit every month to share a spiritual message with and check the needs of. My Home Teacher, Joel, was an extremely straight-laced, dare I say uptight, faithful, clean-cut, cookie-cutter-of-what-I-imagined-a-Mormon-was-supposed-to-be man, married to a more easy-going but equally faithful wife, Sarah, who worked as a secretary to keep the couple afloat while Joel completed law school in the city. The couple came by like clockwork once per month to share a spiritual message and encourage me to stay on the straight and narrow path. This particular visit was about tithing. The scriptures say that tithing—a tenth of one's income—should be given to the Lord. I was familiar with the concept since I saw Grandma Cooper place her tithing envelope in a golden plate that was handed down the aisle in the Lutheran church. I just hadn't thought of it otherwise. At the conclusion of the "message," Joel challenged me to pay my tithing, which challenge I accepted and assured him I would do.

I soon learned that paying tithing hurts. Writing out a six-thousand-dollar check for what I estimated to be sixty-thousand dollars in earnings for the year after earmarking seven-thousand dollars for income taxes left me with less than one thousand dollars in my pocket. That big check I got from

SESAC felt like a free pass to buy a house or a car but it went as fast as it came. As I handed the cashier's check over to the bishop, I winced a little inside, thinking to myself how expensive having a God was. But I believed all of the promises made in the scriptures about keeping the commandments. More importantly, for the first time I could remember in my life, I was doing something the right way. Going to church every Sunday. Keeping all of the promises I made including completely abstaining from sex with Charlie. Paying a full tithing. Not swearing. I was Mother Teresa in the making. Except one thing: I was still in the music business, which was kind of the equivalent of a male-dominated, sex-driven, scandalous, cut-throat, and often times completely gratifying hell. I pondered this dichotomy and made a decision: I would no longer write risqué songs for purposely racy acts. I would take a different direction and start writing songs that contained morals to stories.

Shortly after signing to SESAC, Paul Anthony called me with great news. Trevor Gale submitted my song catalogue for consideration by a producer in Japan who was in charge of the album for Namie Amuro, the Japanese equivalent of the US' most famous female singer at the time. The producer, Tiger Michiko, fell in love with one of my songs, which was produced by a Full Force team member, and offered us an international publishing deal for the single. We signed without hesitation and logged another placement, never really thinking about it again. Meanwhile, Trevor Gale called me personally to ask if I would be willing to work with three of SESAC's best producers. I had learned by then to never turn any opportunity down so I said yes while still being completely loyal to Full Force.

In the midst of my songwriting career blasting off, I walked to the bus stop to head to work one morning and suddenly didn't feel like going because my stomach hurt. I questioned myself, reminding myself of the fact that I was already dressed and on-time, and that I had managed to rarely call out sick despite never getting enough sleep and juggling the demands of work, music, church, and my love life while managing diabetes. I thought about how taking a day off would mean I would have to explain to all of the inquiring minds the next day the gritty details of the "illness" that kept me from showing up and reaping the judgment of a Finance department full of workers who regularly slacked off themselves. But this time I didn't care. I walked back up the hill to my apartment, called out sick, threw a pillow and blanket on the cheap pleather couch I took from Felipe, ate cereal, and checked my blood sugar to make sure I was safe to go to sleep. I turned on the TV with my remote control for some background noise, only to find that every channel produced a screen full of black and white snow. I adjusted the rabbit ears of my dollar-store antennae to no avail, concluding the TV didn't work at all since watching TV wasn't a habit of mine (or of anyone who wants to be productive with their life). Determined, I tried for another fifteen minutes or so when the vague image of a newscast crossed my screen. I made out that there was some sort of fire at the twin towers and I ran outside to look to the sky since they were only a few miles away. Sure enough, I saw smoke in the clear blue sky above and went to call Charlie before realizing my phone wasn't working, either.

Within an hour, one channel of my TV started working and the unbelievable story of how two planes sequentially crashed into the Twin Towers, unfolded. And along with everyone else in America, I watched in horror as live video captured each tower crumbling to the ground in real time. My phone chimed with a single text message. Charlie, who had since transferred to New York City's Army National Guard's 1st Battalion and 69th Infantry known as the "Fighting Irish," had been activated. Charlie was ordered to arrive in uniform at the armory on Lexington Ave and be ready for anything.

By lunchtime, my family members, friends, fellow church members, and even my dad's former assistant reached out to check on me, each praising God that I was OK. In actuality, my bus commute wouldn't have taken me in the path of Ground

Zero, but going into the city without my insulin (which was normal for me back then since I took a long-lasting shot in the morning) could have definitely posed some problems. Perhaps after walking uptown, across the George Washington Bridge, and back down to Jersey City the way the rest of the New Jerseyans I knew were forced to do during the state of shock and emergency, I might have suffered from low or high blood sugar (or any other number of things that could go wrong during such a crisis) and fallen into grave danger. One way or another, I too, thanked God for my safety.

Rarely did I ever use all four locks on my door but that night I did. I kept imagining foreign soldiers bursting through my apartment door with guns, fighter jets dropping bombs above my building, and random rapid-fire on the street. Never in my life had I imagined such things. But that terrible day, anything seemed possible.

September 11th, 2001 changed everyone in and surrounding New York City. For a few weeks after, everyone seemed nicer, more willing to help, more patriotic, and more cognizant of their mortality. But after that, it seemed like those of us who were fortunate enough to have not lost someone or be directly and personally affected by the attack, resumed hyper-speed as if the whole thing had never happened.

Part of getting back to normalcy for me was reaching out to the producers I was referred to by Trevor Gale. The first producer I called was ecstatic to hear from me until I found out he was tight with a girl who saw Blaque in-person at a restaurant one night and lied, saying she wrote *my* song for them. Once I mentioned that slight, the producer chose sides and I never heard from him again. The second producer I called, who went by the handle "Fury," was known for a couple of Hip-hop hits and was so successful at the time, I didn't get to speak to him directly, but rather, to his manager who set up a meet-and-greet. Fury lived only a few miles away from me in Jersey City and after a brief meeting and demo of his work, I was sent home with an assignment to write to one of his tracks. I finished a song the same night and emailed it to his manager, and by morning they wanted me to come back to record a clearer version using their more expensive microphones and equipment.

I arrived at Fury's house and studio and was ready to work when he started rolling up a cigar wrapper. Even though I had never touched drugs in my life, I knew from my Noise in the Attic days that he was rolling a blunt. Being a freshly baptized Mormon who was insistent on living my religion to the letter, I stopped Fury.

"I'm sorry but I can't do sessions with smoke," I said, attempting to avoid bluntly saying that I absolutely despise the body-odor scent of marijuana and already paid dues in the industry so refused to have smoke-filled sessions.

"I mean, smoking is standard," Fury replied.

"Look, I know it's your house and I don't mean to be rude. But I don't want to be around drugs," I said a little more honestly.

"Drugs?" he laughed. "It's just weed."

"I realize that. I know it's your house but I don't do sessions with smoke."

"Then you can leave," Fury said more aggressively, clearly fuming while marching me to the front door and slamming it behind me when I walked out.

Public transportation in Jersey City was as excellent as all East Coast transportation tends to be, except between our two houses, so I walked home. And the whole time I questioned myself. I wondered if it would have really been that bad to record this smash-sounding record and work with a decorated producer in exchange for tolerating smoke? Then I thought to myself, firmly: *No! I made a decision that I would not compromise my personal morals or religion for anything or anyone.* By sticking to what I believed, I felt I would be blessed. Quandary over. In my book, I did the right thing.

The next day Fury's manager called and explained to me how ridiculous it was of me to not record. In return, I explained to him that I had worked long and hard in the industry and long-past paid my dues. If I didn't want smoke in my sessions, that was my prerogative and I had plenty of options in the form of other producers who would be happy to work with an up-and-coming writer—a spot-writer who could turn around a sure hit, including a fully recorded reference, in a single night. Fury's manager hung up and then called me back minutes later saying that he spoke to Fury and they were willing to comply with my no-smoking policy for the sake of recording the one song. I really wanted to drop the whole thing but figured if I could forgive the man who took my dad's life, I could forgive something as silly as a disagreement. I went back to Fury's smoke-free studio, recorded the song, and not too long after that, Fury's manager placed it with an up-and-coming artist. And after that, much to my surprise, Fury asked me to write and sing (meaning, sing as an actual recording artist) on a single he landed on Nick Cannon's sophomore album. He said he knew I would nail the writing and he hadn't heard a better singer than me in a long time so wanted to put me on the actual track *with* Nick. It was his song and his call, and I couldn't have been happier. If that single hit, I would all but certainly land a major record deal. Maybe Fury wasn't so bad, after all.

# CHAPTER 31
# Big Shot

AFTER RECONCILING WITH FURY AND TEAM, we collaborated on song after song until Fury proposed signing me as an artist and landing me a major record deal. After consulting with Full Force, who I had a writing contract with, I got the green flag to go for it. While Full Force knew I was capable of being an artist, they never signed on to manage me because they had their hands full with their own group, who had just signed a major record deal. Full Force wished me well with my artistry with the expectation we would still write songs together as frequently as they were used to.

Fury's team didn't waste any time scheduling me for multiple performances in front of various crowds to practice my recorded music live since singing in real time takes a ton of breath and stamina. (Recording, on the other hand, is kind of like bicycling instead of running a marathon.) They also got me a media trainer who doubled as a makeup artist and stylist, who taught me to never say anything out loud that I didn't want to appear on the front page of the New York Times; the imperativeness of full and laser-sharp eyebrows; and how to elevate my fashion sense. After that, the team landed me a meeting with an A&R from Jive Records, who landed me a meeting with all of the big shots *at* Jive Records, where I would be signed on the spot, or not, depending upon my performance.

My team rehearsed me to the point where, like an Olympic gymnast, the only possible way I would so much as falter on a note was if I got nervous. Managing my emotions the day of the audition was way more important than managing my voice. My voice was there. My vocal cords had been trained over and over again, gaining an almost natural reflex to follow the exact blueprint of a song through its completion. The challenge was staying calm, thinking fast if a curve-ball was thrown, and making my highly constructed "package" appear to be completely authentic.

I arrived at Jive Records with the team, who gave me a final lookover before we entered the building. I wore expensive boots I borrowed from the stylist, tight blue jeans, a nearly see-through, iridescent brown top with pink and white squiggly lines that formed an eye-catching pattern, and a brown newsboy cap that laid gently over my long, straight, auburn-dyed hair. I insisted on doing my own makeup with a natural eye, modestly doctored brow, and pale, shiny lip. Once we cleared security, we were greeted by the friendly face of Keisha, the A&R responsible for the once-in-a-lifetime shot at a make-or-break live audition in the 10th floor Executive conference room in front of bigwigs.

I entered the conference room with my team, expecting to find an empty room where we would wait indefinitely for the executives to arrive. Instead, I walked in on a packed room of highly acclaimed businessmen and women wrapped around a long conference room table, each with a bottle of water, a notepad, and a pen. This was it: curtain up, lights lit—show time.

I immediately smiled and said "Hello" politely as if I expected to see everyone right then and there, the way I had been trained since I was a singing tyke and my hair was naturally blonde. The team reciprocated my salutation and the room went silent. I filled the air with a brief introduction to my first song, being sure to highlight the fact that it was original, produced by Fury, and written and arranged by me. My team stood in a line on the left side of the room, holding the wall up with their backs, as someone pressed play on a boom box and my background music began to play.

The first song I performed, which would make or break me, was a Caribbean-inspired Hip-hop beat that I sang my original Jazz-inspired song over in a vague likeness of Blu Cantrell. The song was called "What I Need" and detailed how a girl like me didn't need a man with a million dollars or even a college degree. Rather, I appreciated nice smiles, street smarts, and loyalty. The song was inspired by my relationship with Charlie, who at that point (unbeknownst to me) was plotting to ask for my hand in marriage in a matter of months. When the group started clapping at the end of the song, the climax of which required a perfectly executed run in a booming chest voice, I only knew I nailed it by looking over at my team, who said nothing but squeezed their eyes, scrunched their noses, and ecstatically fist-pumped their arms on the side the executives couldn't see.

The next song was what the team considered to be a home-run ballad. I wrote the song over a track submitted to Fury by a producer in Georgia. The dramatic bassline coupled with a smooth piano and live drums immediately read "Baptist church" to me (despite the fact I had never once stepped foot in a Baptist church but deduced, from a wide range of music exposure, what such a sound might be) and I wrote accordingly. "Follow His Lead" was a song about how judgmental the world is, how we are quicker to be nosey and knee-deep in everyone else's business than to lend a helping hand, how imperfect I know I personally am, and how I learned that, if you want to be better than your best self, follow a perfect example. Without naming Jesus Christ by name, I heavily implied him. The song marked my effort to write more meaningful music and the producer of the track was elated when he heard my finished song. The label executives around the table burst into applauds and halleluiahs as if they absolutely loved it.

Finally, Keisha asked me to come prepared to sing Lauryn Hill's version of "His Eye is on the Sparrow" for the group. Keisha's thought was that, by comparing my singing skillset to Lauryn's, the group could hear for themselves that my demo tape was hardly doctored and that my voice is what she told them it was. The only problem was, my voice wasn't Lauryn Hill's. We had a totally different tone and style. And even though I technically nailed every note and riff and breath and belt, my performance was doomed from inception to be a knock-off of a one-of-a-kind talent instead of my own, original sound. Still, they clapped.

My songs were followed by an unexpected Q&A session from the big boss, an older white man who engaged with me as if I was interviewing for a job at his company.

"So, where are you from, JJ?" he asked.

"Colorado, originally. Jersey, now." I replied.

"Have you ever skied?" he threw me off.

"I was born on skis," I clapped back.

"So, clearly you're a gospel singer," he suddenly switched topics.

"Not necessarily," I said.

"Well, two out of three of your songs were clearly gospel songs." Theoretically, this was where quick thinking was supposed to kick in. I only had one gospel-like song in my entire demo package. Keisha tipped the scale by specifically asking me to sing the second. In actuality, my music was a clean, allegorical, commentary on society aimed at applauding normalcy and goodness while making people dance. But I didn't get a chance to say that.

"Send her down to our gospel division," he directed Keisha. "They'll eat this up."

With that, the meeting ended and the team and I went out of our way to continue to appear gracious and grateful despite feeling entirely disappointed. I wasn't a gospel singer. At all. We blew our shot.

Not long after that disappointing audition, I took a rare night off to hang out with Charlie, my childhood best friend, Jenny, and Jenny's younger brother and friend. The Coloradoans were staying with me on their first sightseeing trip to New York City. We started in Little Italy, where the food and ambiance were enough to sweep anyone off of their feet but which virtues were entirely overshadowed by awkward silence. Charlie had a stomachache and Jenny was quiet, so I exerted all of my energy filling the air with self-deprecating jokes and random chit-chat before our food arrived. We stuffed ourselves with fresh, handmade mozzarella and pasta with marinara sauce and meatballs that were so good, one would have thought someone's little old Italian grandma was in the back making it all. After passing on cheesecake and cannoli because our belts were about to burst, Jenny randomly said with a smirk, "I smell chicken," which I found odd since all I smelled was delicious Italian food. We left the restaurant and headed to Times Square so my guests could catch a Broadway show while Charlie and I sat in a McDonald's lounge to recuperate from playing tour guides.

Once we all reunited, Charlie led us to the middle of Times Square where there is a perfect, three hundred and sixty degree view of many of New York City's novelties: the illuminated tower from which a sparkling ball is dropped every New Year; a running stock market ticker; a lit up Sean Jean ad that spanned across the space of two buildings with Sean, Puff Daddy, Combs serving as the model; yellow taxi cabs that reeked of the scent of overworked drivers; packed herds of tourists grasping their purses with one hand and taking photos with the other; double-decker buses with Jamaican tour guides describing on a microphone loud enough for a block to hear the scene you're personally standing in the middle of; hot dog stands that sell hard "soft" pretzels that are held in aluminum foil over coals before they disappoint your mouth and scent your hair with smoke; young men dressed as the Statue of Liberty with green painted faces that perfectly matched their satin, emerald-colored costumes; street drummers, and singers, and dancers, and more. The center of Times Square is why anyone comes to the city at all. The center of Times Square is a place one connects their expectation of New York City with a far more astonishing reality.

"Well, I haven't been feeling well all night because I've been nervous," Charlie grabbed my hand. "Tonight's one of the most important nights of my life," he continued.  "JJ? Excuse me, Jennifer? You're the best thing that's ever happened to me and I love you so much," he got down on one knee and opened a ring box. "Will you marry me?"

I immediately crouched down to Charlie to say "Yes!"

Truth be told—and I told Charlie constantly until he finally proposed— I would have said yes to marriage the second time I saw him. For a year and a half, Charlie and I honored our baptismal covenants and church standards, which included abstaining from sex, abstaining from spending the night (even though I had my own place and could have easily moved him in), abstaining from drinking and smoking (which we both naturally hated and abstained from anyway), and keeping the many commandments we learned about every Sunday. Charlie never left my calls unanswered. He was reliable, consistent, on time, and never thought twice about putting in his best effort to see me, be there long car rides, messy subway and bus connections, or any amount of obstacles in his way. Charlie didn't just tell me he cherished me, he showed it. Never had I felt so loved, so honored as a woman, so supported in my dream of becoming a recording artist, and so absolutely cared for by a man. Not only did I trust and genuinely love Charlie, I would have bet my life on his love, loyalty, and faithfulness until the day one of us died. In fact, I worried that if anyone would be susceptible to the gripping temptation of infidelity, it would be me. I was in a male-dominated industry where flirting, sexual innuendos, sexual encounters, and full blow sexual affairs were commonplace and even accepted as a norm. I prayed I'd never be fooled again by a music industry where talent is as attractive as aesthetics and where musical connections are often mistaken for love connections. In fact, I promised myself that, if I married a good man like Charlie, I would sooner quit music altogether than cheat on him. Being a faithful wife to Charlie meant things had to change. No humoring flirtatious comments from men in studio sessions. No dressing in trendy, revealing outfits. No working all night in studios, only to come home for two hours of rushed sleep. And while I didn't have all of the answers about how to be a faithful wife and obedient Mormon in New York City's cutthroat music industry, I intended to make it happen.

# CHAPTER 32
# Cold Turkey

WHEN DAYDREAMING ABOUT GETTING MARRIED before becoming a Mormon, I imagined a proper wedding to include church pews filled with overdressed family and friends who spent as much money and time attending as the bride and groom; toddler flower girls who reliably stall during their walk up the aisle, preoccupied with red rose petals falling unevenly out of their dimpled fists, spotting the white velvet carpet underfoot with crimson kisses until a loving mom nudges them forward towards an archiepiscopal throne; a soaring ceiling with impossible hand-painted angels clothed in heavenly grace, peering down upon worldly sinners; rich colored stained glass windows splashing the silhouette of saints in sunbeams that escape through clear glass nooks, illuminating invisible particles that dance in the dark; oversized organ pipes that pierce reverent silence with a wedding march; a magnificent bride in a breathtaking gown passed down from generations never seen or heard; a stoic groom in Army blues, delicately guiding his bride through congratulatory bubbles and a saber arch salute by fellow soldiers; and a trio of trumpets that carry the new couple to a waiting carriage towards their happily ever after. However, I soon learned that marriage in a temple of The Church of Jesus Christ of Latter-day Saints is far from a day of showboating.

Because one must be a member of the church to enter a temple, none of our family was able to attend the wedding we worked two years to become qualified for; but a handful of chosen church members attended. The circular "sealing room" was entirely white, starting from the ground with spotless white carpet, an oval-shaped white marble alter topped by a hand-crocheted white lace overlay in the center of the room and white, upholstered chairs placed around the perimeter of walls that were papered fancily with a textured off-white textile. Once kneeling directly apart from each other on opposite sides of the alter, Charlie and I each had a view of a large, ornate mirror behind one another, which made our respective reflections duplicate for infinity. Around us sitting in all-white chairs, were our guests clothed in their Sunday's best, save white slippers that replaced their shoes to preserve the perfect carpet. Charlie was dressed traditionally in an all-white suit and I, instead of wearing the show-stopping gown I bought from the internet, borrowed from the temple a loose-fitting white dress that was covered in dainty lace details and looked more like a nightgown Grandma Cooper might wear to bed than a wedding dress.

In the small white room, an elderly officiator (a complete stranger) gave a beautiful speech about the sanctity of marriage, the beauty and divinity of eternal families, and the bountiful rewards promised to those who endure until the end. By being sealed, we were not only making a promise of faithfulness to each other, we were making a promise of faithfulness to God. If we cherished and honored our sacred covenants until the end, we could expect to not only enjoy a beautiful life on earth but also in heaven forever. Notwithstanding these promises, life could still present serious challenges. But if we stayed true to our faith together, we could expect to overcome anything, even death.

As I locked eyes with Charlie over the alter, tears streamed down his face. Never had I felt such peace, such assuredness, or such pure love emanate from someone towards me. The officiator concluded his remarks and sacred sealing ordinance, invited us to exchange rings if we so chose (an option that is traditional in the ways of the world but not required for the ordinance), and alas, greet our new spouse with a kiss.

As we got up to leave the sealing room, my Home Teacher, Joel, was last in line to greet us. He congratulated us both, first shaking Charlie's hand, then giving me two hugs—one from him and "one from your dad," which felt like an unexpected sucker-punch in the stomach despite its sincere and thoughtful intention.

Unlike my grand imaginations of an ideal wedding, after our sealing I went to the women's locker room and changed by myself into my giant wedding gown. I didn't realize there was a bridal suite to change in until after I was already dressed. I met Charlie and friends outside and we all took pictures as a group in front of the temple before jumping in cars and heading home. In the strangest way, our temple wedding "after party" felt as casual as my courthouse one. However, Charlie and I preferred it that way because the only thing we really wanted to do was go home and have sex. Unfortunately, just as that prospect seemed near, the small group of friends we drove with suggested going out for dinner on the way home. So Charlie and I sat patiently through dinner, shooting ornery facial expressions at each other that screamed "Don't these people understand that we have business to tend to!?" until at last, after a long dinner and a four-hour drive, we were dumped at our new apartment and finally commenced our life together as man and wife.

A week after our wedding day, we held a more traditional, wedding-like, ring exchange and reception for our family—Full Force included—at a reception hall in Queens before flying straight from our reception to our honeymoon at Disney World in Orlando, Florida. On the plane ride home, I had time to reflect about the utter sanctity of my spiritual bond with Charlie, about how different, special, and empowering it was to make a firm marital covenant before God, and about how safe I felt within the bounds of an eternal marriage. And I felt true peace for the first time I could remember.

Once home, work and music awaited me. Paul Anthony called me to tell me one of my songs was placed with Usher's new artist. Fury called me to tell me I was getting signed after all—I just had to attend one more meeting and the deal would be done. And work expected my arrival at nine o'clock in the morning just like any other average day. I called Gerry to celebrate since he was the producer on the Usher track and I asked for logistics on the recording session, which he gave with a warning that I might not be allowed to come.

"What are you talking about? I wrote and arranged the song. Of course I'm coming!"

"You'll have to ask Kelly."

"Kelly? You mean the girl who does nothing on the team? The girl who has absolutely nothing to do with placing our track. That Kelly?" I fumed.

"I'll see what I can do, J."

As soon as I hung up I felt awful. Just a day before I was at peace, completely serene and one with my spirit and my God. And with just one phone call, I was practically channeling my teenaged thug within. This wasn't the feeling I wanted anymore. Charlie and I wanted to have a family together. We wanted to grow old and successful together. But how could I maintain the peace I felt if I was going to have to constantly deal with the wickedness and trickery of the music business?

I didn't have time to dwell on drama. That week I was scheduled for an appointment with my gynecologist. I was extremely worried about intense lower abdomen pain and excessively heavy bleeding I was experiencing every month. I feared every worst case scenario.

Fury called to touch base and give me the date of the meeting with the record label that would seal my fate and *finally* put me on the map as, not just a songwriter, but a singer.

"Wednesday at two o'clock," he announced.

"Wait, I have a critical doctor's appointment at that exact time," I replied, thinking we could reschedule.

"Cancel it. This is more important," he snapped.

"I mean, my health is important. If I'm not alive, the label doesn't have an artist," I reasoned.

"Don't you do this to me, J. This is it. This is what I gambled on you for. We are doing this deal. Cancel your appointment," he insisted.

I dug my heels in.

"I can't do that. It was nearly impossible to get this appointment. We have to reschedule."

"They're not going to reschedule, J. Do you understand me? Do you know how many people would literally *kill* for the opportunity you have? Literally take a gun and murder someone for it."

"I'm sorry, Fury, but it's important I see a doctor. I have some things going on. Surely they'll understand?"

"I wouldn't count on it," he hung up.

Strike two. On my first day back, that made two out of two calls relating to my music career that caused me a world of distress. Was this how it was always going to be? Was I always going to be kicked out of my own sessions with the stars I was handing my talent over to? Was I always going to have to choose between taking care of myself and taking care of other people's money? Was I going to continue to compete as a woman in an industry full of sex-driven men and expect to garner respect, much less attempt to be a faithful wife? Was I going to be able to have a family and wipe baby butts and be a soccer mom? Was this recording artist persona even who I was anymore? The answer seemed clear: I had to either choose to be a star or choose to be an everyday average person who takes care of herself, her husband, and if God so blessed, her children.

When I decided to quit the music industry, I didn't put much thought into it. I didn't tally up the twenty-something years I had worked since my very first audition as a child. I didn't remember how many performances my mom sewed costumes for, drove me to, or did my hair and makeup for. I didn't recount how devastating it was to be kicked out of The Pros on my tenth birthday or the discipline required to, completely on my own, practice a single song for an entire year and outperform most of the kids in town to get into the Stars of Tomorrow show (the biggest opportunity in a tiny town). I didn't consider the guts it took to, not just leave home at seventeen and finish high school while supporting myself, but choose the biggest city and hardest place to make it to move to. I didn't reflect upon the people who heavily criticized and ridiculed me, all of whom I finally proved wrong. I didn't think about the burned bridges I left behind, purposely never looking or intending to go back. I didn't contemplate the struggle, the hustle, the sleepless nights, the stretching dollars and insulin, the losses, or the soul-selling. I didn't acknowledge the teams and people around me who personally invested to help elevate my career. And most of all, I completely failed to recognize that I made it. This piece of nothing Coloradoan, with the determination of a fly stuck in honey, made it.

Sure, I hadn't reached the tip-top yet. I had a list of song placements still waiting to be released and all but guarantee the fame and fortune I had always sought out to validate myself as everything I thought the naysayers believed I was not. However, I was exactly where one needs to be—in the company of music industry heavy-hitters—to realize even my wildest dreams. But I didn't think about that.

What I thought about was how annoyed I was at not being allowed into my own session with a superstar who needed me more than I needed him. I thought about how, at the level I was at, I couldn't keep an important doctor's appointment—an appointment that could have diagnosed something life-threatening based on my symptoms—because everyone's money was more important than my health. And while I was sitting there being mad, I was also terrified. I was afraid that I would carry on without sleep every night at sessions where I was the only woman alongside stars who don't respect the boundaries of a wedding ring. I feared that even though I was baptized in a good, stringent church, I would still fall victim to my own ego (or insecurity), stupid decisions, and possibly destroy my marriage by stepping out. I worried about increasingly not being able to go to church on Sunday without someone attempting to get me to listen to a demo tape or meet a singer they wanted me to help make famous. Above all, I was terrified that continuing my music industry hustle would mean destroying my fresh start and clean slate with God.

I sent an email to my publishing company to break the news that I was leaving the music industry forever, cold turkey. Then I called Fury. Then I called Full Force. I truly expected to receive desperate pleas to stay from each and every one of them but I heard absolutely nothing. Not a return email. Not a single strand of push-back from anyone. One would have thought I was just calling to tell them I would be back from the grocery store in five minutes because their collective response was, "OK." And after those phone calls, "JJ" died and disappeared.

# CHAPTER 33
# Call to War

QUITTING MUSIC WAS LIKE QUITTING DRUGS. I had major withdrawals. No more getting my ego rubbed by people impressed by my talent. No more artistic outlet for my busy brain. No more setting bars and reaching new heights. Just an entirely canceled dream.

I couldn't listen to the radio after I quit. My inclination was to automatically nitpick songs and artists, critiquing everything from vocal delivery and timing to theme originality and relativity. I would rant to Charlie about how a song could have been better, what the artist's team did wrong, or what classic beat or harmony was poorly sampled. When Charlie suggested I get back in the game if I was going to be such a critic, I resolved to stop listening to music altogether. But even without listening to the radio, news from the street still caught up with me when "Sugar Daddy" (the song I wrote with Cuban Link) hit the airwaves with my voice still on it. According to my sources in the Lower East Side, Cuban Link sent a few thugs with guns to the studio on Clinton Street and threatened the lives of everyone there if they didn't hand over the song data files. From there, he used the song without giving me credit. While anyone else might have sued for royalties, I chose to do absolutely nothing about it, valuing my life and anonymity over money. Besides, I heard the studio owner was so traumatized, he never left a house again without a gun strapped to himself and ended up getting arrested and serving a bid for illegal arms possession. I refrained from speaking about the song again with old contacts, thankful that I had gotten out of the business, knowing that the "old me" would have chased my credits down—do or die.

With the added knowledge that music had the potential to put lives on lines, I honestly thought Charlie would be elated that I gave up music for him—for us and our future—but he was the opposite. He somewhat alluded that much of my appeal as a wife was my success as a musician. But the one goal he had that was even bigger than marrying a woman he could show off, was his desire to become a father.

From day one of dating, Charlie understood that I might not be able to carry a child to term because, after the loss of my last baby, the surgery to remove the placenta seemed to have rendered me sterile. I concluded this because, before the surgery, I got pregnant easily; and after, never again. I half-wondered if the surgeon erroneously tied my tubes but never pursued testing to figure it out because a far better option was placed in our laps.

Several months prior to our marriage, a couple in our church approached us saying the baby they were fostering was going up for adoption. They wondered, given we were set to marry in the temple and presumably start a family right away like most Mormons do, if we would consider adopting her. They weren't planning on adopting a child themselves but wanted to make sure the baby was placed in a good home. They didn't have to say any more. We said yes unequivocally. And why would anyone not say yes to the enormous blessing of being parents to a child, much less a perfect six-month-old baby girl who emanated cheer with her shining, brown eyes, flirtatious toothless smile, adorable dimples, precious dark curly hair, and the most beautiful permanent suntan. In fact, she could have easily passed for Charlie's biological child.

We imagined we would need to be screened in order to adopt and we were correct. Since baby Gigi was in foster care, we were required to become licensed foster and adoptive parents through New Jersey state. (When you adopt in New Jersey, you must foster a child for six months before you can proceed and finalize an adoption.) We wasted no time completing several months of applications, classes, background checks, interviews, and home inspections to become licensed. During the interim, we visited baby Gigi weekly, and sometimes many times a week, to bond. According to Gigi's caseworker, a hearing would occur in six months, changing her plan from foster care to adoption, at which time our friends (who, being Gigi's original foster parents had first choice to adopt her) could designate us as her adoptive home. Gigi's foster parents loved her more than life itself, which made Charlie and me weary that they would not proceed with our collective plan, but we carried on because they insisted they were just fosterers.

When I wasn't fussing over becoming a new mom in the most unexpected way and helping Charlie land a job chauffeuring a local real estate broker around, the new downtime I had after work following quitting music was maddening. My internal engine roared, compelling me with a sense of urgency to do something extraordinary with my life. Something productive. Something meaningful.

It didn't take long for me to figure out how to transform my songwriting gift: become a high school English teacher. As a high school English teacher, I envisioned using my street vernacular, rapping skills, and songwriting prowess to teach students the craft it took me a couple of decades to get anywhere with. The only problem was, one can't teach high school English without a college degree. I wouldn't be able to just hustle my way into a teaching position like I hustled my way into writing songs. Realizing my new dream would require four years of fulltime college.

Most of the area universities offered a rigorous four-year English program that included four months of student teaching as a capstone. But that wouldn't work for a diabetic who had to work fulltime to stay alive—to stay insured. Moreover, the fact I never took an SAT or ACT (and graduated high school with one of the lowest cumulative grade point averages one can get) was problematic. I quickly figured out that my high school performance in and of itself ruled out a four-year college.

However, if I started at a junior college, I could transfer to a university after two years if my grades were high enough. Alas, my plan materialized. I arrived at Hudson County Community College, took the mandatory entrance exams that I scored just well enough on to be placed directly into College Algebra and English 101 (instead of pre-college classes that are offered for lower scorers) and my new role as a fulltime employee and part-time college student began.

Notwithstanding the massive redirection of my life, things stabilized for a few weeks until I got the call.

"I got called to Iraq," Charlie said matter-of-factly.

"No." I refused to believe him.

"Yes. I leave this month to California for training," he replied.

"But what about us? What about Gigi?"

"Jennifer, I don't have a choice. Unless you want me to go to prison."

"I mean, that might be a better option. At least we can see you and you won't die."

"I'm not doing that. I'm serving," Charlie was resolute.

Charlie's call to George W. Bush's brand new war in Iraq called "Operation Iraqi Freedom" might as well have been the same call I received when my dad died. I was shaken. Just as I had restructured my whole life around being home every night with my new husband and growing family, my husband of only a few months would not only go away for over a year and a half, he would be sent to an active warzone where he might not ever come back. Charlie was strong and accepting of his fate. But I was devastated.

After getting over the initial shock of Charlie's call to war, I sucked up my selfish hang-ups and got to work planning on how to keep everything together at home while Charlie served our country in Iraq. First, I confirmed with our friends that we would still adopt Gigi, even if Charlie couldn't be there when we became an official family. Next, I forced myself to make good on my tuition payment and go to school two nights per week after work.

After that, we set up Charlie's military pay so that it would direct deposit into our joint account, where we agreed I would push it over into savings while I managed household bills with my own paycheck so that we could save up to buy a house. Charlie's active military pay was at least twice as much as he made driving Mr. Sacks, his real estate boss, around. If we played our cards right— if I continued to work fulltime and pay all of our bills—we could use Charlie's military pay to buy a house when he returned from Iraq. The plan was a no-brainer since I knew I would always have to work fulltime until the day I died if I wanted health insurance for my preexisting condition.

Charlie's departure for several months of training in California was our trial run for saying goodbye when it came time for him to leave for war. We said our goodbyes without tears or pause, comforted by the fact that he would come back home before heading to Iraq.

I attacked life as a "married single" the same way I attacked my career in the music industry: with hyper-focus. I continued to report to the CFO's office at the advertising agency every weekday. Two days per week I attended college after work until ten o'clock in the evening. On free nights and Saturdays, I visited Gigi at her foster parent's house. And on Sundays I attended church.

After receiving an A+ on my first ever college essay, I was referred by my professor to the school newspaper, *The Orator*, and easily earned a (voluntary) position as a staff writer before getting unanimously voted in as co-editor. And despite what felt like an already heavy load, the Bishop called me into his office one Sunday and said he felt impressed to offer me a calling. The Jersey City Second Ward of my church needed a Young Woman's president and I fit the bill. Arriving at my own conclusion that one should not turn down callings from the Lord, I accepted, thereby adding to my plate a weekly nighttime activity and Sunday school program with a group of teenaged girls I picked up and drove to church from various hoods in Jersey City. What first felt like dark solitude when Charlie left was replaced with a jam-packed schedule that entirely ruled out any form of a conventional social life.

When Charlie completed training and came home for a couple of weeks before his final departure to Iraq, I put everything on hold with the exception of a single class of Algebra, which I was afraid to miss save I lose all command of the basic skillset I had acquired. Charlie and I spent our time together as if it would be the last, soaking up each other's company before the tough task ahead. And when the day came to escort Charlie to the 69th Regiment Armory on Lexington Ave in New York City, where he would depart straightaway with his unit to Iraq, we said our goodbyes with damp eyes and broken hearts.

After that goodbye, I was lucky to hear from Charlie once or twice per month and stopped anything, including darting out of class or work meetings, to take his calls, which were easily identifiable due to the large string of numbers that showed up on my cell phone caller ID. And as infrequent as his calls were, his connection was worse. Our best chance at a decent phone call was over a secured military line or a phone he borrowed from a New York *Daily News* crew who was accompanying his infantry's tour. We learned quickly to say "I love you" first and catch up last. As a result, letter-writing and email became our main form of communication.

The first letter I received from Charlie detailed his chilling account of arriving in Iraq. His unit was first shipped to Qatar, a tactical ally of the United States, before being broken up into groups to fly in military cargo planes into "Route Irish" in Baghdad, the literal eye of the stormy warzone in Iraq. The flight diverted from the commercial plane experiences the soldiers had encountered up unto that point, replacing commercial forward-facing coach seats with military jump seats that lined the interior walls of the plane. The plane's loud, rattling engine noise was juxtaposed with completely silent soldiers, each entranced in their own defense mechanisms—closing their eyes, praying, dropping tears, or staring stoically straight forward. Unlike commercial flights where a pilot calmly verbalizes the various in-flight happenings to keep passengers calm, Charlie and his fellow soldiers were only able to deduce what was going on by the sounds and movement of the aircraft. After nearly two hours of flying, the plane's engines suddenly roared and gravity forced the soldiers to the sides of their seats as the plane dropped to a sudden and prolonged nose-dive that made even the toughest soldiers beg their Creator for mercy. During what seemed like a certain death-drop, the plane zigzagged in the air while holding its steep dive until sharply leveling and striking a short runway.

"I'll write more when I can. Not much time. Lots of gun fire. Lots of bombs. Pray for me," Charlie wrote before ending his letter with a short salutation of his undying love.

My skin was covered in goose bumps and sweat had accumulated on my forehead. Had I not had the proof of Charlie's letter as his survival, I might have had a heart attack. I couldn't imagine the terror, the doom, or the magnitude of his position. I thought my life back home, worrying over and awaiting the return of a beloved soldier, was hard. But reading Charlie's letter reminded me of how clueless I was about the sacrifice of our soldiers, the privilege of peace, and the freedom of an unthreatened existence.

People at church approached me with beaming smiles every Sunday and asked, "How's Charlie doing?" as if he was on a business trip. How could I summarize the things he had shared with me in exchanges that were meant to serve as a quick hello between acquaintances? I learned over time to just say, "He's fine" instead of elaborating on his exact predicament, the latter which only drew a string of questions that were emotionally exhausting to answer over and over again. And just when Charlie and I collectively found solace in our impending adoption of Gigi, which intensified Charlie's resolve to come back home alive, her foster parents changed their mind the day before the court hearing to appoint us as her adopters and instead adopted her themselves. Using our sacred few minutes of phone time the next time Charlie called, I broke the news as softly as I could before losing the connection and crying.

My response to losing Gigi was to completely cut off her foster (and eventually, adoptive) parents. I felt betrayed. I felt disappointed that the baby we invested so much time bonding with would no longer be a part of our life. I felt devastated that Charlie didn't have the daughter he expected to come home to. And I felt angry. At the same time, after I had time to think and when I was completely honest with myself, I knew that Gigi was fully bonded to her parents and that it was in her best interests to stay with the family she already knew as her own. But the last time I spoke to her new father, who was largely absent because he was obsessively attached to his computer working on a family history program he hoped would revolutionize the genealogy industry, I challenged him.

"Now that you're Gigi's dad, I expect you to get off of your computer and give your all to that baby girl because that's what Charlie would have done."

Gigi's dad humbly agreed and we parted ways for good.

# CHAPTER 34

# Iraq

E ACH TIME CHARLIE CALLED ME, HE GAVE ME A quick overview of recent events. One week, an Iraqi missile reached his base, hitting the makeshift building that served as the base's gym and killing a female soldier. Other, far more serious and painful weeks, Charlie's good friends were killed, mission after mission, by roadside IEDs—improvised explosive devices—that locals placed strategically and set off as U.S. Army Hummers crossed their paths. Charlie's MOS (military occupation specialty) had evolved into a combat photographer role after he used his sleepless nights to produce an inspirational film that went viral among fellow soldiers before reaching the commander and being played for the entire 69th Infantry 1st Battalion in a meeting. After that, Charlie was provided with high-tech military cameras and video cameras, which he used to record missions—patrols, raids, and special operations—holding a camera in one hand and his weapon in the other. And with Charlie's new MOS came a new way to cope. Each time a fellow soldier and good friend was killed— Sgt. Bradley J. Bergeron, SFC Kurt J. Comeaux, Sgt. Armond L. Frickey, Sgt. Huey P. Fassbender, SSG Christopher J. Babin, SPC Kenneth Vonronn, Sgt. Warren A. Murphy, SSG Christian Philip Engeldrum, SPC Wilfredo Fernando Urbina, SSC Henry E. Irizarry, and many others whose memorial programs didn't make it back to the archive I kept on my husband's behalf—Charlie made it his personal mission to work tirelessly, organizing every aspect of each memorial service held on base, to give each soldier a proper and honorable sendoff to a heaven and God that Charlie slowly stopped believing in.

At one point, New York City started buzzing with the news that soldiers from Charlie's unit opened fire on a car that failed to stop for a patrol on Route Irish, the most dangerous road in Iraq, located just a mile away from Baghdad airport. The gunfire resulted in the death of an Italian Secret Service officer who had just helped rescue Giuliana Sgrena, a female Italian reporter who was being held hostage in Iraq. The car carrying Sgrena and the three Secret Service officers who had just successfully negotiated her release was headed to Baghdad airport for a flight home after a hugely successful mission. However, as the car approached the convoy and appeared to ignore an order to stop, a soldier panicked and opened fire. And the Italian Secret Service officer, Nicola Calipari, who had just rescued the reporter, used his body to successfully shield her at the cost of his own life. Because news from Iraq was constantly splashed across newspapers and TV screens at the time, I tried to avoid media at all costs, so I wasn't aware of the huge story. But then Charlie called.

"Babe. What are they saying on the news right now?" he asked, almost in a panic.

"I don't know. I don't look at the news, sweetie. Why?" I asked.

"Never mind. I get to come home for two weeks," he announced so plainly that I almost didn't have the opportunity to shed tears of joy. He gave me the date that was just weeks away and I promised I'd be there waiting to pick him up.

The day Charlie came home, I was supposed to drive four hours to a base to pick him up and I did just that but ran into a major obstacle. There was a huge accident on a highway near Newark that trapped me in an area that offered no form of escape. It was winter time and freezing outside and I noticed a bus stop where six people danced around with hot steam escaping their nostrils as they searched for a bus behind me in the most panicked way. After fifteen minutes of waiting at a complete stop, I felt awful for them, realizing that we might be there for hours and wondering if they were sufficiently dressed to last. Then I realized I had an entire empty car and trunk and a very warm heater. I unlocked my doors, popped my trunk, and told them to pile in. They looked at me confused for a moment, somewhat shocked that I was inviting them in, so I motioned again and said it in Spanish this time because I heard a couple of them speaking in the language. One by one, they followed my instructions to place their bags in my truck and pack tightly in my back and front seats. All but one of them fit, and the last man standing assured us that he would be OK outside (not that he had a choice).

My car full of strangers thanked me profusely during the hour it took to drive what would have otherwise only taken five minutes. I dropped them off at Newark Penn Station, only a little out of my way, and continued on to Charlie. After six instead of four hours driving, I made it to my husband and we embraced as if he was my father who had just come back to life. I was so grateful to see him in one piece and I felt inclined to celebrate and laugh and love but a couple of things were different. First, he didn't smell like he did before, always squeaky clean with several dabs of cologne. His hair, skin, and uniform all smelled like Play-Doh to me. Second, he wasn't his happy-go-lucky, funny self. And while I instantly noticed these differences, I didn't say anything. Instead, I praised God that he was home alive.

We stayed in a hotel room instead of driving to Charlie's parents' house (our next stop) in the middle of the night. I thought sex would dominate our night. Absence makes the heart grow fonder and war makes the heart explode with gratitude for every breath a soldier is blessed to still take. But intimacy was not foremost on Charlie's mind. He needed to talk. We sat on the hotel bed and Charlie poured out months and months of experiences that I could barely wrap my head around. He turned on his laptop and showed me photos. First, he showed me photos of himself holding tiny, smiling Iraqi children and told me about how his unit carried bags of candy to shower upon the local children each time there was an opportunity for a safe encounter. Then, he showed me a sort of Iraqi subway sandwich shop, where rotisserie goat was served on bread to locals and U.S. soldiers alike. Next, he showed me backed up sewage that pooled in the middle of an Iraq elementary school and explained how insufficiently developed Iraq was. At one point it almost felt like he was showing me photos of a vacation to a less-developed country but then his screen flipped to an unexpected, horrific, photo. He stared straight ahead without flinching but I gasped. There appeared a photo of an Iraqi woman, around eight or nine months pregnant, dressed in an all-black *saree* dress, laying on the side of the road dead.

"Oh my gosh, is she OK? Did you help her?" I was in denial about what I was seeing.

"She's dead. We run into dead bodies like this all of the time. It's war, Jenn," he said firmly. "I've taken thousands of photos. My job is to document our tour."

I told Charlie I didn't think I could handle seeing anything more. He closed his laptop but he continued to talk.

"Remember how I asked about the news story?" he said. "One of our guys messed up. He got scared and he shot down that car with the Italian reporter in it. And I had to go and take pictures of the man who died," he still didn't flinch.

"Oh my gosh, I'm so sorry Charlie. I can't imagine. Are you OK?" I didn't know what to say.

"His brain matter was splattered all over the car. His wallet had a picture of his wife and kids in it." He continued.

"Why did they make you do that? Don't they have a person for that?"

"I'M the person for that," he reminded me.

"Don't go back, Charlie. Please, just stay home. Jail is better," I begged.

"Just stop," he demanded.

"I'm sorry," I apologized.

We didn't have time to talk further because Charlie received a random call from Iraq.

"They're making me come back right now. I have to leave right now," he told me after he hung up.

"No! You just got here! They can't do that! You're guaranteed two week's leave. They can't do that!" I yelled.

"They can and they just did," he said frankly as he started to pack up his belongings.

Just as I was about to break down in tears, Charlie's cell phone rang again. I listened intently to Charlie's side of the conversation but was still unable to figure out what was going on until he hung up and confided in me.

"They changed their mind. They're going to let me stay but I have to erase my computer right here and now," he said. I didn't ask any questions as he formatted his hard drive and answered another call from Iraq a few minutes later to confirm that the job was done.

Charlie eventually fell asleep but I stayed awake, disturbed by everything that I observed since he stepped back on American soil, and more than anything, the empty shell of a man that he seemed to have become. Hours later, the sun finally rose and Charlie and I quickly showered and drove to a diner for breakfast before heading to Pennsylvania to his parents' house, where his mom had organized a party. Charlie arrived home to hugs and tears and balloons and a cake to belatedly celebrate the birthday he spent in a tank in Iraq. My mother-in-law and I sincerely loved each other but under those extraordinary circumstances, we each vied for Charlie's time and attention in a virtual tug-o-war. At the home where he spent some of the best parts of his life as a teenager, Charlie was slightly more himself. He smiled, teased his parents, and delighted in his mom's heavenly cooking. In Charlie's honor, Charlie's mom filled two tables with all of her specialties: *arroz con gandules*, lasagna, *pernil*, *pollo*, potato salad, white rice, *frijoles*, a fresh salad with Thousand Island dressing, and a New York cheesecake recipe she made up on her own and that bested any other cheesecake anyone had ever tasted. Nothing on earth quite compares to home or a mother's pure love.

After several days at Charlie's parents' house, we headed home and tried to pretend like everything was normal before Charlie shipped back to Iraq, which was arguably harder than the first time he left because death had proven to be an incredibly cruel reality for everyone at war and staying alive was often out of one's control. Sending Charlie back to Iraq to try his luck after he had already come home safely for a visit was excruciating. But we had no choice and forced our second goodbye.

When I returned to work after the vacation time I took for Charlie's leave, I learned that Grey Global Group (what Grey Advertising evolved to) announced a merger with WPP, and the fate of all the executives was up in the air. For the most part I felt confident that my boss' job, and therefore my job, would be safe. But commuting over two hours a day while keeping up with a fulltime job, part-time college, college newspaper, and church work, along with my continued intent on becoming a mother one day, made me contemplate a job search for a position on the same side of the river I lived in: New Jersey. And what might have been a cumbersome job search for some, was for me as easy as spotting a comparable job at an investment management firm in Jersey City, applying, and receiving a job offer before I arrived home after my interview. After nearly eight years at the ad agency and all that had transpired during that time, removing my job—the only constant in my life—was scary. But then I reminded myself that I had survived with flying colors far more frightening things.

I hit the ground running at my new job and put my very best foot forward, quickly learning my new position and assisting a pit bull of an investment manager, who sent me home with stomach aches every night. Around three months after starting the job, I went to Human Resources and gave two-week's notice that I was quitting.

"Do you already have another job?" the HR rep asked.

"No," I replied honestly.

"Do me a favor. Why don't you stay onboard until you can find something else. I'd hate to see you leave without another job lined up."

"OK, I will. Thank you," I conceded.

Charlie happened to call that day and when I told him I was quitting he became livid.

"I'm over here dealing with a lot. Don't do this to me. I'm coming home in less than two months and we have plans. You have to keep your job," he demanded.

"OK, I will," I quickly conceded because I didn't want to be the cause of any of my husband's problems. I went back to work the next day with a new strategy: handle the job like a soldier. I imagined that soldiers don't over-analyze orders from their superiors. They don't obsess about how they want to do things versus how their boss wants things done. They are team players who don't worry about people's moods or words or gossip or pressure so long as the job gets done. I told myself, if Charlie can be stuck in a warzone taking tall and life-threatening orders, I can work with a boss who demands mastery of my petty personal nemesis (tiny details), which I would be wise to master anyway even if such aptitude was earned through a trial by fire. The next time I received a visit from my Home Teachers from church, I asked them to give me a blessing with the hope of gaining greater spiritual strength to carry on. And I did, in fact, carry on.

Once I employed my "soldier strategy" my job became far more rewarding. The boss was happy, I was happy, and everything was running smoothly. Life had taken on a new, rigorous norm of "work, school, church, repeat" every week. So when Paul Anthony of Full Force called, I was caught completely off guard.

"The beautiful JJ. How are you my dear?" he purred.

"Wow! Hi! How are you!?" I replied dumbfounded, secretly hoping that Paul was calling because Full Force desperately needed my talent back.

"I'm glorious, sweetheart," he clapped back with his signature sass.

"To what do I owe the treat of your call?" I was dying to know.

"Well, my dear, I have some money for you. I need to know where to send the check," he revealed.

"Money?" I was again dumbfounded.

"Yes, money. You remember that little song we wrote for that Japanese artist? It turns out it was a big hit, baby. We just received our cut for records sales, a remix, a commercial, and for the song being used as a theme song for a popular TV series out there. Where do I send the check?" he asked, getting down to business.

I provided Paul with my home address, let him know it was wonderful to hear from him, apologized for leaving the music industry the way I did, thanking him for going out of his way to stay honest and pay me my fair share of royalties despite it, and wishing him and the rest of my Full Force family well. Within a few days, I received a check from Full Force's accountant for several thousand dollars and, after paying tithes and tucking away twenty percent for taxes, I deposited the balance in Charlie's and my savings account that we still planned to use to buy a home.

Hearing from my old music team was a tempting tease. I had adapted to my new, feverishly fast-paced and simultaneously boring life, and reminisced fondly on the days when I was completely consumed by music. Hindsight is 20/20 and memories always seem to make the bad times seem worse and the good times seem better. I reflected with complete clarity what I did wrong and right in the music business and felt a touch of adrenaline when I recollected the things I considered to be grossly unjust. But for the most part I looked back at my music career in awe, somewhat mourning that I spent nearly two decades investing in artistry that never truly saw the light of day.

My nostalgia about the music industry was short-lived because Charlie's return from Iraq became the thing that dominated all of my thoughts. After over a year and a half between training and a year tour in Iraq, the husband I had only had a chance to live with for around three months, was finally coming home. And when he did, we would start back at square one.

# CHAPTER 35

# Square One

WHEN CHARLIE CAME HOME FROM IRAQ FOR good, he suffered from PTSD, anxiety, night terrors, and a self-centered wife who was completely oblivious to it all. But that didn't stop him from hitting the ground running. His first order of business was to take a large chunk of the cash we saved and buy himself a Jaguar.

"We saved that money to buy a house," I reprimanded like a parent, upset that our hard work and responsibility was going to be squandered away on a frivolous car purchase.

"I need a nice car when I start selling houses. You have to dress for the job you want in life," he said.

"Unless dressing for the job you want requires you to forego buying the house you went to war for," I snapped back.

"Can you please just trust me?" Charlie asked.

"It's not that I don't trust you. It's that spending a huge lump of our cash on a car is a bad idea. Let's buy a house first and then talk cars," I demanded.

Charlie let the discussion go until we had lunch with some of the crew from NBC who came to Iraq and filmed a raid alongside him. They, along with reporters from the *Daily News*, promised that when everyone got home safely they would all buy houses from Charlie to help jump-start his real estate career. Despite Charlie and me dressing up for the lunch, the NBC crew wore shorts and t-shirts, and were quite casual and easygoing. After lunch when we all stood in a circle in the parking garage below the restaurant, a random woman walked up to Charlie and handed him her keys.

"Uh, ma'am? I don't work here," Charlie said politely.

"Oh, you look like you do," she barked.

It took all of my will power to refrain from telling the lady off. There was a circle of three white men, me (a white woman), and Charlie (a Puerto Rican), and she decided from a snap-judgment that Charlie was the garage worker. She treated the soldier who had just fought for her freedom in Iraq like a subordinate—like a nothing.

"That's why I want a nice car," Charlie said, not having to explain to me that no matter how nice he dressed, he would always be subject to people who equate being Spanish with being a blue collar worker.

"Get the jaguar," I said resolutely. "As soon as we get home, take the money out and get it."

By the time we got home I realized there was a smarter way to buy a fancy car: get a car loan. On Charlie's behalf, I contacted our military bank and helped Charlie apply but was immediately rejected. Charlie didn't have bad credit. He didn't have *any* credit. And if he couldn't get approved for a car loan, how in the world would we get approved for a house loan? The debacle gave me an idea. I told the banker on the line that, theoretically, Charlie and I could pay for the car entirely in cash. That said, I asked how much money down it would take for the bank to approve Charlie's loan. I threw out a number: seven-thousand? The banker on the other line entered the amount into his system and replied, "Actually, yes! With seven-thousand down he's definitely approved." Now, not only did we still have enough cash to put down on a house, Charlie had a credit record that I would ensure started off perfectly because I set up his payments to come straight out of my personal checking account.

Within two days a shiny black Jaguar was delivered to Charlie, which lifted his spirits to heights I hadn't seen since before Iraq. And while Charlie zoomed around Jersey City making the moves necessary to elevate his career, I started my last semester of community college and planted a seed:

"We lost a lot of time when you were in Iraq. Do you still want to have a baby?" I asked.

"Of course!" Charlie said.

"Can we start now?" I asked.

"Go right ahead," Charlie said.

With that, I called the foster care placement office and volunteered Charlie and myself as a "foster/adopt" home—a home that fosters children with the distinct intention to adopt. I asked the office to keep our information handy in the event they needed to place a baby who needed an adoptive home. Four months later, we received a call for a newborn baby whose mother was serving a long jail sentence for a third strike and rather petty shoplifting crime. The baby would, without question, go up for adoption.

When Robbie James was dropped off by a caseworker, I could hardly believe they were entrusting us—less-experienced foster parents—with a newborn. It didn't occur to me that all new parents are just as green. Charlie and I took turns holding the baby and basking in his peaceful sleep with reverent awe. A young married couple, our friends and fellow church members next door who already had a baby of their own, stopped by to give us a crash course on feeding. At the time, the wife, Megan, was staying home while her husband was barely making ends meet with an off-the-books job. I presented her with a mutually beneficial offer to serve as a nanny for our baby. Having only been at my job for ten months, I knew I couldn't take maternity leave. We agreed on a monthly fee that kept everyone comfortable and Charlie and my dream of becoming parents finally came true.

Life with a baby was an absolute joy. I was used to sleepless nights—they didn't bother me. I was almost done with college and muscled through my final classes with flying colors. When Megan and family abruptly decided to move, I found a daycare a mile away from my job that I jogged to and from everyday in my business suit during lunch to visit my sweet perfect baby. And with every month came the special surprise of new things our tiny angel could do. One month: hold his head up briefly. Two months: smile. Three months: babble. Fourth months: laugh.

Five months: greet us with coos and arm reaches as soon as he saw us in the morning. Six months: utterly steal our hearts.

Charlie snapped a photo of me in my cap, gown, and honors cords holding Robbie after accepting my Associate's degree. After two and a half years of mostly fulltime college at night after my fulltime day job, I graduated *summa cum laude* from Hudson County Community College and earned a full-ride scholarship to Rutgers University in Newark. Unfortunately, I couldn't accept the scholarship because the college didn't have evening or online classes for a Bachelor's in English. Either way, the thrill of earning an Associate's degree and arriving halfway towards my goal of a Bachelor's degree was soon overshadowed by a devastating call from Randy's caseworker.

We came to know Mofu Kalaba as a disorganized, unfeeling, and rather unprofessional woman, who visited our house randomly unannounced each month. She spoke ambiguously, never answering the direct questions we had about our baby's case. When can we file for adoption? Is there anything we should know? What does she need from us? She always just shrugged and mumbled something practically incoherent before leaving each time. Charlie and I decided she was absolutely worthless but harmless. That is, until the call.

"Uh, Jennifer. Yes. This is Mofu Kalaba," she needed no introduction. "Jennifer, we will be coming to pick the baby up on Wednesday—in three days."

"Pick the baby up for what?" I hissed.

"Pick the baby up to return him to his mother," she said as if it was common knowledge.

"What are you talking about!? Our baby isn't going back to his mother. She's in jail! Do you have the wrong person?" I yelled unapologetically.

"No, no. We had a court hearing today and the mother qualified for a program in jail but she has to have a child with her. Robbie is the only child, out of five, who she still has rights to."

"This can't be happening. I'll call you back."

My eyes flooded with tears as I told Charlie the news and fumbled with my phone to call Robbie's law guardian (a lawyer assigned to Robbie to represent his best interests in court proceedings).

"Ellen! They can't take our baby!" I yelled as soon as I got her on the line.

"Well, we all determined he should go back to his mom," she said casually.

"Wait a minute! Why would you do that without even talking to us!?"

"You're not a party in the case."

"Do you know that this baby has NEVER had a visit with his mother!? Do you know that he smiles and giggles and babbles when he sees us every morning and that he has never even cried in our care, not even once!? Do you really think it's a good idea to rip him out of our stable home in three days and put him IN A DISGUSTING JAIL CELL with a MOTHER HE HAS NEVER MET without the slightest form of transition!?" I lost all composure and the lawyer hung up on me.

I called back the caseworker to no avail and then panicked for the three days that followed. I stayed up the entire first night to write a twenty-five-page manual on every minuscule detail about how Robbie was used to being cared for, going as far as to photograph and include in the manual things like how he likes to be held. On the second day, I went to the store and bought a three-month supply of the diapers he was used to, wipes he was used to, bottom cream he was used to, baby soap and lotion he was used to, formula he was used to, food he was used to, along with extra pacifiers he was used to and a wardrobe that would fit him for another three months. I washed all of his belongings except for his favorite blanket, which I thought would be best if it still smelled like home. And then I carefully packed all of those things in a super-sized suitcase and prepared for the worst.

On day three, the caseworker finally got around to returning my call to let me know she would arrive in ten minutes, asking if we could meet her on the curb so she didn't have to walk up three flights of stairs to our apartment. Charlie carried Robbie's luggage down to the front door but didn't have the heart to stay and say goodbye. Once the caseworker arrived, I tucked my precious baby in his car seat, being careful to nestle his favorite blanket exactly where he liked it, and placed a pacifier in his mouth for comfort during his ride to the dark abyss that haunted my imagination. I carefully carried him to the state caravan, where the caseworker waited by the open sliding door, and I insisted on buckling in his car seat myself to ensure he was safe before kissing his forehead and saying my last goodbye.

I tried to hold in my pain but I yelped and burst into tears as I pushed past the caseworker who patted my arm and said, "I know it's hard." I walked up the three flights of stairs and ran to Charlie who was lying face-down on our bed and collapsed on top of him as we both started crying out loud. I had been through losing two pregnancies and a failed adoption. I had been through losing my grandfather. I had been through losing my father. I had been through supporting a soldier in Iraq who I wasn't positive would come back home alive. But the uttermost gut-wrenching loss in my life was that of my innocent baby boy; an unspotted lamb used as a pawn in a sin-ridden world.

I dutifully reported for work the next morning, where I had moved up to support the chief investment officer, a grandpa-like philanthropist who must have had a soft spot for assistants with foster babies because, during the previous week when the temperature rose past one-hundred, he refused to hear that I was going to sprint in my work clothes to the daycare and back to spend fifteen minutes with my baby. Instead, my boss insisted on driving me to the daycare in his air-conditioned car, waiting outside, and driving me back to work. So when I arrived to work looking less than together and describing as professionally as a crying secretary can that I lost my baby the day before, he deeply empathized and offered any assistance he could give.

For many weeks on end I called the caseworker and the law guardian to inquire about how Robbie was doing, if we could visit him, or if he needed anything but only one of my calls was picked up. And the caseworker used that single conversation to tell me the baby was "fine," I could never see him again (unless, of course, he wound up in foster care again), and to stop calling.

By the time Robbie left, I was already enrolled at New Jersey City University, pursuing a Bachelor's degree in English Literature. But after the ordeal of losing Robbie, I added a minor: Pre-law. And after I added the minor, I studied New Jersey Family Law, learning that, while foster parents aren't parties to their foster children's cases, they nonetheless have the right to attend and speak at every hearing (which may have not prevented Robbie's departure but would have at least prepared us and him for reunification). And after I read and read, I attempted to write a legislative bill requiring bare-minimum transition requirements for children moving between foster homes. But once it was clear that I was becoming obsessed to the point of ruining my own existence, I resigned to our irreversible loss.

Charlie quickly passed his real estate exam and began, not only selling homes, but finding us a condo to buy. As I perused the ads myself, I spotted a condo for sale in the building across the street from my old railroad apartment in Jersey City. I used to admire the building every day when I walked to the bus and always wondered what kind of rent it would take to live in the place. Now, the largest, two-bedroom condo in the building was up for sale at a price that was within the budget Charlie and I set. I called Charlie, who immediately went to check out the condo with his partner. Normally, if Charlie made a suggestion, I insisted on investigating things myself. But this time, I put my full trust in him.

"It's perfect. We better make an offer now or we'll lose it," Charlie warned.

"Do it," I approved blindly.

Buying and moving into our new apartment breathed new life into our relationship. Again, we were back to square one, experiencing a brand new start. This time, I had wised up enough to takes things slow. We both delighted in renovating our apartment and turning it into the exact replica of the blueprints in our heads. We made time for each other and often visited Charlie's parents in the Poconos, where we ate his mom's delicious food and hung out with his parents as if they were our best friends. We went to church every Sunday and observed all of the things I thought made us good Mormons: not shopping or doing college homework on Sundays, reading our scriptures daily, paying our tithes, and fulfilling our callings. And when Thanksgiving and Christmas came around, I praised God that Charlie was home safe, that we were still standing, and that I still had hope in my heart that I would become a mom one day. In fact, as I took a walk around my in-laws' neighborhood in the Poconos the day after Christmas, I had a comforting thought. *What if my forever baby is born today?* The idea that a blessing was right around the corner warmed my heart. And in the New Year, once we were quite stable, we completed home studies with two private adoption agencies to cast a wider net and increase our odds of becoming parents.

Five months later, by the time May rolled around and my college semester was nearing an end, I was itching to be a mom to the point I gave up and asked Charlie for a dog after I finished finals. Our building allowed pets and at least a dog would be a sure thing. Charlie agreed and for the first time, in a very long time, I looked forward to something without fearing a heartbreaking disaster.

# CHAPTER 36
# Baby Girl

BY THE TIME THE FRIDAY WHEN I FINISHED MY finals came around, I had completely forgotten about the dog deal with Charlie. I was wrapping up at work around four o'clock in the afternoon and the caller ID on my desk phone flashed a New Jersey state number. My heart skipped a beat and I answered the call.

A woman introduced herself, saying she got my number from her husband who conducted the annual inspection of our house. While we were certain we could never survive fostering again, we kept our license up-to-date in case Robbie went back into the system. During that inspection, the inspector, Hal, questioned why we didn't have a child placed with us and we summarized the story of Robbie. Hal advised that if we wanted an adoptable baby, we should speak to his wife, Tisha, who worked in a unit in Newark that almost always dealt with babies who ended up needing forever homes. We agreed to allow Hal to give his wife our number, so long as she only called us if there was a situation in which adoption was all but certain.

Tisha introduced herself to me as Hal's wife and got straight to business. She needed a foster home for a four-month-old little girl who was removed from her home suddenly and "severely crying all day." She mentioned the crying because she wanted to be completely transparent with me. I thanked Tisha for her call but explained that my husband and I were, frankly, traumatized by our foster care experience and simply didn't have the heart to do it again. I wished her well in finding a home for the baby and said goodbye.

As I removed the phone receiver from my ear and slowly went to place it back on the phone base, I had a distinct impression.

"I can't help you if you don't help yourself," the feeling said.

I immediately recognized this still small voice and quiet counsel as personal revelation. On my notepad at work, I had jotted down Tisha's phone number and I immediately picked up the phone and called her right back.

"Hi. It's Jennifer Gallegos. Do you still need a home for the baby?" I asked as if, in the few seconds since we last spoke she somehow landed a home. "I changed my mind. We can foster the baby," I said, hoping with every part of my being that I didn't divert destiny.

"Yes, I do. Thank you. The baby's caseworker will be in touch and bring her in a few hours after her well-child check is completed in the hospital. By the way, she's *real* pretty."

"I'm sure she's angelic," I paused. "May I have the caseworker's name and cell phone number?" I asked, armed with experience with what had before proved to be a disorganized system.

Tisha obliged, we hung up, and I rapidly dialed Charlie to tell him about the offer and my prompting. I asked him if we could foster as if I hadn't already said yes and he took a minute of silence before speaking again.

"It's up to you," he gambled on me.

"Then it's a yes. Thank you, Love. We're prepared this time."

Having an obsessive-compulsive personality type, I already had a nursery set up and an impressive inventory of baby items in our second bedroom. Our private agencies somewhat required this of us because newborns placed from private agencies were prone to arriving in their forever homes with next to no notice. But I went overboard. I had three types of formula, three types of pacifiers, baby clothes in both genders and varying sizes, the best brand of diapers in several sizes, baby wipes, the best rash ointment, baby sheets and blankets, a baby swing, an aquarium crib soother, a car seat, and not to mention a beautiful crib and dresser set. I had the best cared for, nonexistent baby in Jersey City. I didn't have to buy a thing to welcome a baby but went to the nearby Target anyway to be certain.

Mario Natis, the caseworker in charge of the baby, called my cell phone to announce his arrival and I ran to the street to meet him. Without hesitation, he handed over a screaming baby wrapped sloppily in a white hospital sheet. It was just before eight o'clock at night on May eleventh. The sun still dipped between crevices of rooftops and the air was too cold to celebrate spring. My impulse was to lay the baby down and wrap her properly but instead I stopped briefly on the sidewalk that led to our building to pull back the sheet and get a glimpse of the "pretty" face that Tisha advertised. There, I found the most angelic baby girl, brown eyes damp with tears, porcelain cheeks rose-colored from crying, delicate brown curly hair with natural blonde highlights, and a stringy body that hinted neglect. The baby stopped crying for a split second to connect eyes with me before exerting her last bit of energy to scream to the world that she was in pain.

Charlie wasn't home yet so, when Mario and I reached the apartment, I handed the baby back to him and jumped to action.

"She must need a bottle," I guessed.

I tried feeding the baby to no avail. Not even her pacifier was helping. As I struggled to sooth our precious package, Charlie arrived home and made a beeline for a glimpse of our new addition.

"She's beautiful," he said.

"I love her already," I replied.

"Me too," he admitted without any hint of reservation.

Charlie introduced himself to Mario before asking the baby's name, which I had completely overlooked doing.

"Let me look at the paperwork. Ok, here we go. Her name is Angelina," Mario replied.

"I once had a girlfriend named Angelina," Charlie replied as I shot him a look of distaste.

I handed Charlie the baby as I went to get the swing that had a built-in light show above, which I hoped would soothe our new baby girl. As soon as we placed Angelina in the swing we saw a different baby. She stopped crying and became hypnotized by the colored lights above, opening her mouth in awe until drifting off into peaceful rest after the hardest day.

By Saturday morning, Angelina was crying again and I wasted no time taking her straight to the Emergency Room. After having baby Robbie, who didn't cry once in six months, I concluded that something had to be very wrong and I was right. She was severely constipated. The doctor in the ER asked about Angelina's feeding history and I revealed that I didn't know other than the fact I had tried to feed her formula the night before. The doctor recommended switching her to soy formula, which I bought alongside her other prescriptions from the ER visit. By nighttime when Charlie finished his busiest day at work, Angelina was finally calm.

Once we were through the first hoop of helping Angelina feel OK, I looked in the pink baby bag that arrived with her the day before. The bag still had a tag attached to it that listed a charity organization that presumably gives out bags with basic baby supplies for free. Inside the bag I found a few travel-sized baby products, a stained denim dress with Dora the Explorer on it, sized for a two-year-old toddler, a heavily used pacifier that is unique in that it can only be bought from a bodega for a dollar, and an empty plastic bottle of pear juice. I gasped, praying that my precious, four-month-old angel had not been sustained on a diet of three-dollar pear juice.

Child Protective Services came to pick up Angelina three days later on a Monday to take her for her first visit with her biological mother and father, but they did not show. And week after week, they remained missing.

Before Angelina arrived, Charlie and I had booked a trip to Colorado to attend a family wedding. I remembered from Gigi's parents traveling all around the world, that it was possible to take a foster baby out of state so long as you got permission. Mario was a straight-shooting, letter-of-the-law caseworker who had no problem issuing formal permission for us to travel, which we were grateful for because we would have canceled our trip if we weren't allowed to take Angelina.

We arrived in Colorado and Grandma Cooper had pulled out my oldest uncle's fifty-year-old crib for Angelina to sleep in during our stay overnight before we ventured to a hotel in the mountains for the wedding. My sister arrived in Denver on a morning flight and, upon arriving at Grandma Cooper's, came straight to my room to see the baby. As soon as Cindy saw the baby, Angelina kicked and cooed in delight, stealing Cindy's heart.

"Is she going to have to go back?" Cindy asked, seeming reluctant to hear the answer.

"That's the plan. But her mom hasn't shown up for a visit yet," I was honest.

"Good," Cindy smiled at me in a way that made it clear she was rooting for us.

When we arrived home from Colorado, Mario let me know that he made a surprise visit to Angelina's biological parents' apartment in Newark, where Angelina's biological mother yelled at her boyfriend because he was entirely disinterested in participating in the meeting. Mario said he had two hunches about the man: first, he opined that the reason the man wouldn't participate was because he was high; and second, Mario felt that there was no way on earth that such a dark-skinned man could produce such a porcelain white baby. Still, the man's name was in the father category on the birth certificate so New Jersey had to treat him has such.

Mario handed Angelina's biological mother photos I had previously sent along for the visits she missed. My strategy was to build a relationship early so that, in the event Angelina was reunified, there would be a chance we could see our sweet baby again. Angelina's biological mother cried when she saw Angelina dressed in the type of pink frilly dress my mom used to dress me in, cradled in a plush pink blanket and wearing a soft headband, crowning our baby with a patch of purposeful daisies. She promised Mario that day that she wouldn't miss another visit.

But she ultimately disappeared and the state never heard from her, or her boyfriend, again.

After losing my baby boy, Robbie, I refused to leave anything to chance. I kept Charlie and myself abreast of every court hearing concerning Angelina. I exercised my option to fax the judge a statement before each hearing. And Charlie and I went the extra mile of attending all hearings, where I reliably took my time making planned, comprehensive statements.

At the first hearing, one month after Angelina's placement, I pleaded: "Your honor, I don't know if Angelina's biological parents are present today, but if they are here, they should be aware of some things. First, please let the record reflect that my husband and I will absolutely without any reservations adopt Angelina. In fact, we are pushing for it. Second, since being placed in our care, Angelina has continued to suffer from neonatal withdrawal. She was also diagnosed with a heart murmur—atrial septal defect, fossa ovalis with right to left shunting—and a milk allergy. While she is projected to lead a full and normal life, she still meets medically fragile criteria as outlined by the state and requires care around the clock by certified caregivers. As such, my husband and I have obtained infant CPR certification and completed recommended courses, in addition to rearranging our work schedules, to facilitate constant care. Lastly, please let the record reflect that Angelina's biological parents have not shown up to a visit yet. And now the extremely critical part: if Angelina's biological parents are working towards reunification, you better personally make sure they are fully capable of caring for a child at all, much less a child who requires such specialized care. Thank you."

After the hearing on the elevator down, a police officer looked at me and said, "Doctor?"

I looked confused before realizing he must have heard me recite Angelina's medical status.

"Nope. I'm just a mom," I replied.

"Same difference, right?" he joked.

"Yeah, right." I laughed.

At the second hearing, three months after Angelina arrived, I faxed the judge the day before and Charlie and I appeared to make our in-person statement.

"Your honor," I began. "Did you have the opportunity to read my faxed statement?"

"Yes. All twenty-four pages of it," he said sarcastically.

"Good," I was dead serious. "I won't verbalize everything again. However, I do want to reiterate critical facts. First, my husband and I wish to adopt Angelina. We are giving her everything we have and we always will. Second, let the record reflect that her biological parents have still failed to show up for any visits. Lastly, please remember that Angelina is a medically fragile child with specialized needs. Your honor, it is my understanding that the parental rights to Angelina's mother's previous children were involuntarily removed from her. As such, I motion that reasonable efforts to reunify not be made."

"Reasonable efforts" referenced a law in New Jersey that mandated, in circumstances where a parent's rights were involuntarily terminated (a lengthy, thorough, and downright arduous process that was in no way an easy endeavor to accomplish save a parent completely failing to comply with even the simplest conditions over a span of many years), the state had no obligation to attempt to reunify subsequent children. The law was meant to expedite permanency for children whose parents habitually failed to parent safely, or at all. I knew the law inside and out because I obsessively studied it after losing Robbie.

"Mrs. Gallegos, you're not within your rights to make any motions," the judge was firm.

"Then I request that the law guardian motions that reasonable efforts to reunify not be made."

"Thank you, Mrs. Gallegos. If that concludes your statement, you and your husband may leave the courtroom now."

Foster parents were only allowed in hearings during their statements. They weren't allowed to be present otherwise. Charlie and I waited outside when the hearing broke and the young, polite law guardian—a lawyer whose job it was to specifically advocate for Angelina—approached us.

"Good job in there," she complimented me. "The judge ruled no reasonable efforts for the mother." She smiled.

"You're kidding!?" I wanted to pinch myself.

"No, not kidding. There's some bad news, though. The same can't be ruled for the father. He doesn't have any history with the division."

And just like that, our hearts became heavy again.

At the third hearing, six months after placement, I faxed the judge the day ahead, our report, which had grown to thirty-six pages, and Charlie and I appeared with Angelina in tow to make our in-person statement. It was November and cold outside, so I dressed Angelina in a white fleece two-piece sweat suit, walking shoes since she started *running* at ten months, and a headband that drew attention to the impossibly perfect curls that bounced above her silky face and "Daddy's dimple," which we were sure she inherited from Charlie.

The judge spoke. "Good morning, Mr. and Mrs. Gallegos and good morning, Angelina! What a doll." The judge smiled at our angel. "I read your rather lengthy report and I'm pleased to hear that Angelina's left bottom molar has arrived," he joked at the ridiculous thoroughness of my faxed statement. "Do you have anything more to add?"

"Yes, your honor." I wasted no time. "I would like to remind the court that my husband and I are thoroughly bonded with and invested in Angelina. We're already a family and we will fight to the end for her. We know that keeping us together is in Angelina's best interests." I got emotional and my voice started to quiver, "We love her with all we have, your honor. She's our world. Please take decisive action today so we can move forward with adopting her."

Charlie and I left the courtroom and waited nervously outside. This time, when the hearing broke, a supervisor came to greet us.

"Hi, Mr. and Mrs. Gallegos. I'm Wilma Stockingham."

"Pleased to meet you," we each shook her hand.

"I just *had* to come to this hearing today because I heard about you and I heard about this," she showed us the report I brought many copies of, covered in a yellow jacket and tabbed within by court hearing dates, doctor diagnoses, general happenings, and our statements. "I've never seen anything like this. Would you be willing to come train for us?"

"Thank you but I already have my hands full," I declined politely with a smile and a wink, showing off my little girl.

"Mr. and Mrs. Gallegos, they're moving forward with terminating parental rights," she said in a way that didn't particularly celebrate the news.

"Wonderful!" I blurted.

"Now, we just need to contact the adoptive parents of Angelina's half-siblings to see if they want to adopt her," Wilma informed us.

"No way. She's bonded to us. She's stable. That's not in her best interests," I growled.

"I'm sorry, but we have to check," she replied.

"Then prepare for war," I said sharply, staring Wilma directly in the eyes until she looked away.

Months after that hearing our new caseworker, Zeni, a beautiful young African American woman with a flair for fashion, called me.

"Hi, Jennifer." she opened.

"Hi. Please tell me you don't have bad news," I said without internal editing.

"Actually, I have good news. We contacted the other adoptive parents to no avail."

"You're kidding?" I said before realizing I didn't want to test that question.

"No, I'm not kidding. We will proceed with the adoption now."

After I hung up, I quickly dialed Charlie and told him the news. After all we had been through, neither of us had the audacity to boast. We just sat reverently on the phone and said in our own way to each other, "We did it."

# CHAPTER 37
# Double or Nothing

I HAD BECOME USED TO MY WORK LIFE BEING STABLE, and my personal life being a bit of organized chaos. But once we were formally approved to adopt Angelina, roles reversed. My boss retired and I moved laterally to a different position in the firm, serving as one of two senior executive assistants to a team of portfolio managers in the "bull pen." And before I even switched desks, I heard rumors that the woman I was going to work very closely with was a handful.

The only time I had seen Gloria before was in passing. She worked on the opposite side of the building for the most cut-throat boss in the firm (who only she could handle) and was renowned for her tenure—twenty-seven years—at the firm. Some colleagues brushed her off like a new driver brushes off a 1968 Ford GT40, clueless about the value and power of such a classic. However, what the gossiping girls didn't realize about me is that I didn't really care one way or another. I had carried my soldier mentality forward to that very day and, whatever my firm needed from me, I would execute without taking anything personally. All I cared about was getting my job done each day without taking it home to my family, which goal I had been successful at so far.

On the first day sitting next to Gloria, I immediately rubbed her the wrong way. My desk was organized in a simple and pragmatic way that ensured that all the tools I needed to work at lightning speed were at my fingertips. Gloria's desk was loaded with knick-knacks, stacks of paper that only she understood the genius organization of, a giant blown-up Chiquita banana (that would have been confiscated from anyone other than her at our strict, corporate firm), old cut-out photocopies of comics with office-related jokes taped everywhere, a box of Nips cheese crackers, a CD in her hard drive that constantly rotated throughout each day what seemed like the same exact song, and a sign that read "I don't worry about job security because no one would want my job!" which she stuck on my side of the fancy, cherry wood cubical wall that divided our desks.

"Hey, Gloria!" I said. "I just have one request. Can you keep this little sign on your side?" I pulled the sign off of the wall and handed it to her. "I, for one, need my job."

I laughed thinking Gloria would understand I had nowhere near the clout she had. But she took the sign, narrowed her eyes, swung around and stuck it on the side of her desk that faced a stunning view of the brand new Freedom Tower, which commanded the skyline in Lower Manhattan.

The next day I was working feverishly to tend to my teams' constant demands when Gloria said, "Hey, Jennifer. Do you want to split these filing cabinets?"

I went to look but got flustered and said, "I'll have to figure that out later. I can't now."

My poor bedside manner resulted in a second strike with Gloria. One more misstep and I'd surely be out. I could tell that I rubbed Gloria the wrong way a couple times but I didn't realize she disliked me. Still, working so closely together, we were somewhat forced to constantly chat back and forth to tend to the day's business and, as we did so, inherently injected candid personal chitchat into our conversations. Before we knew it, we became fast friends.

After working together for a while my phone rang one night. It was Gloria.

"Hi, Jenn. It's me, Gloria."

"Hi, wow. Is everything OK?"

"Yeah. I just wanted to know if the baby is OK. You said she was sick today."

"Oh! Yes. She's doing much better. Thanks so much for calling. I really appreciate it."

"OK, no problem. I just wanted to check and see how she was doing."

Gloria had no way of knowing this but I hadn't had a call from a friend in what seemed like a million years. I almost didn't know how to act on the phone with her, speaking outside of the context of work. But the calls kept coming—to check if I made it home OK, to tell me about a sale at Shop Rite, to inquire how I did on a final at school, or just to say "Hi." Soon, Gloria became my best friend and I deeply cherished her as a person even before I started telling her so.

The finalization of Angelina's adoption approached and an adoption lawyer was assigned to us by the state. Being rather savvy with paperwork, I finished a huge stack of required adoption forms in one day. Given such proficiency, the adoption should have been a breeze. But our lawyer was the male equivalent of that caseworker who oversaw Robbie's placement: good for nothing. Gloria heard me complaining on the phone.

"You know, Jenn? I find that the best way to get results is to go there in person. If I were you I'd go right now."

It was eleven o'clock in the morning and a fifteen-minute train-ride to Journal Square where the lawyer's office was located.

"Go ahead," Gloria said. "Take an early lunch. I'll cover you."

Not only did showing up to that lawyer's office get the job done and Angelina's adoption finalized, but from then on, I showed up in person any time I needed to get something done.

Now that Gloria was my bestie, all the girls on our floor seemed to warm up to her. She brought in and fed all of us her homemade noodle pudding (one of the few things she knew how to cook) whether we wanted it or not; she taught us a bunch of "Jewish words" as she called them, including "*beshert,*" which means "meant to be" and which we both used often to describe our friendship; she brought life to every party; and when one of our bosses treated us to lunch twice a year, she drank two glasses of wine and made us hysterical with laughter with her entertaining stories and glossed-over stare into her computer screen afterwards. Gloria made work one of my favorite places to be. And once I earned her friendship, I wondered how I ever made it through life without her in it.

My mom and Cindy flew in for Angelina's adoption party, and Gloria took trains all the way into Jersey City from the suburbs instead of letting us pick her up. We celebrated Angelina's adoption in our church building with a homemade carnival that I obsessed over for months, including hand-making a huge floating balloon decoration that took all day to assemble and tested my sister's patience when I insisted on doing it by myself. In fact, I tended to always demand to do everything, oversee everything, and have a say in everything. During my mom's visit, she pulled me aside.

"Jenn, you're too hard on your husband," she said.

"Mom, it's just a stressful time," I replied, annoyed that I was a grown woman getting a talking-to.

"I realize that, but do you hear yourself? You can't treat your husband like that and expect him to stick around," she concluded before switching the topic.

I recognized that I was being my quintessential aggressive self but I felt that Charlie knew I loved him, that we were both burned out from several years of very intense ordeals and that, ultimately, we had an eternal marriage that was unbreakable.

The party was mostly a hit. A couple of church friends gave lovely (but way-too-long) talks about eternal families, after which time we all enjoyed a casual but tasty spread of sandwiches, soft pretzels and dip, chips, salads, soda, baked treats, and a cake with a photo of our little family of three on top.

Back at work, Gloria couldn't wait to point something out to me.

"Jenn, I have news for you. Your daughter is going to be just like her mother: BOSSY!" she laughed.

"I can always rely on you for the complete truth, Gloria," I teased her.

"But did you hear her in the hallway during the party? She said NO RUNNING and pointed her finger at all of the kids." Gloria laughed.

"Boss lady, boss baby," I replied and we both laughed until the real bosses slammed their doors to signal to us that we were being too loud.

After Angelina's adoption, Charlie and I were relieved from state regulations that prohibited us from getting a babysitter for Angelina for even a single night out. Therefore, we could finally go on a date after several years without one. But we were so used to switching turns taking care of Angelina and doing things by ourselves when the other person was watching the baby, we didn't take full advantage of our freedom. Instead of getting some balance back in our marriage, we focused on other things. For me, the focus was on the baby, work, school, my church calling, and odd, completely unnecessary projects. For example, painting a giant Disney Tinker Bell on Angelina's bedroom wall. I spread myself razor-thin as a matter of homeostasis. Being busy was my brain's norm. And Charlie had the same exact problem.

One thing Charlie and I both aspired for was making sure that Angelina had a sibling. We agreed to wait a year and then complete another home study for a straight adoption of a child who was already "free and clear" (meaning parental rights were already terminated). Foster care was out of the question because we refused to gamble Angelina's heart after breaking each of our own twice before. After our final home study was complete, we were warned it may take several years to be matched with a child for straight adoption but it only took one month.

Camden, New Jersey was statistically the poorest city in the United States at the time and going there to meet our new little nugget was like going to a third world country. Charlie, whose aunt and three cousins lived there, warned me that we would need to exercise our street smarts to stay safe. Since we were in the neighborhood, we first made a quick visit to Charlie's relatives but stayed only fifteen minutes when it looked like our car was about to be stolen. Charlie had upgraded to a brand-new Mercedes after his first huge real estate check while I paid all of the household bills with my income. From Charlie's family's house we drove a mile away to the foster home of our future son.

A Spanish woman invited us in and told us to sit down while she went to get our future son, a tiny toddler, who was crying loudly upstairs. When she reappeared, she was holding the most handsome little dumpling we could have ever imagined. Nasir had a full head of tight, curly brown hair, tiger like almond-shaped brown eyes with admirably long eyelashes, smooth, perfect skin, just enough "baby" left in him to snuggle and love but old enough to walk and do things for himself, save with a very limited, ten-word vocabulary. Nasir had a whole set of congenital anomalies including severe asthma, cleft palate, a lazy eye, and chronic ear infections that collectively resulted in global development delays. But none of those things scared Charlie and me. What scared us was, when Nasir's foster mom abruptly placed him on the floor, leaving him alone with Charlie, Angelina, and me without introduction, Nasir threw a world-class tantrum. (And who could blame him?)

On the ride home from that visit, Charlie admitted that he almost walked right out, thinking that perhaps Nasir always screamed the way he did during the tantrum we were greeted with. But as we continued to visit week after week for four months straight, Nasir proved to be a big mush who not only grew to recognize us, but eventually got extremely excited to see us each visit. Once we established ourselves as family—once he was visibly excited to see us arrive and visibly distraught to see us go—we brought him home for good.

Unlike when Angelina was placed with us and I had to keep working, I got to take six weeks of family leave with Nasir. John Corzine signed a law into effect that provided new mothers of all varieties with partial pay from the state for family leave. Before the law was passed, my workplace only provided paid leave for mothers who gave birth—not for adoptive moms. Because of this, I made it a point to also keep Angelina home during my leave for Nasir as a sort-of redo. During those six weeks, Nasir's vocabulary grew from ten words to one-hundred-and-forty. Whether Angelina, or Charlie and I were responsible for Nasir's new areas of growth, one thing was certain: every gain Nasir made was hard-earned.

Nasir had eight different specialists to tend to varying congenital anomalies: a primary pediatrician, pulmonologist, cardiologist, neurologist, urologist, ophthalmologist, ENT, and plastic surgeon. But other than giving Nasir daily nebulizer treatments, oral medications, and trying to avoid colds and ear infections, he wasn't a terribly difficult toddler to care for physically. Caring for him emotionally, however, was slightly harder. Despite our valiant effort to facilitate a long transition period between homes, we still weren't "mom and dad" (the foster parents who had raised him from birth). And if the sudden loss of that attachment didn't make his time adapting to us extra difficult, being a "terrible two" put the nail in the coffin. For Nasir and us to grow our love while simultaneously handling normal (and abnormal through no fault of his own) toddler outbursts was challenging. But Nasir was a champion whose sweet nature outweighed his toddler frustrations and made up for everything we lacked as parents.

A few months after Nasir arrived, I felt fairly consumed with kid stuff, which irony was not lost on me since all I wanted and prayed for, for years on end, was to have children with Charlie. I had cut my load down by pulling out of school for a few semesters. However, I still managed a fulltime job, a sizeable new church calling I felt I had to take, and two special needs children with seven or eight times the amount of appointments (and patience requirement) as non-special needs kids. Moreover, someone in church kept referring "brides on a budget" to me and I found myself inundated with an unpaid wedding-planning load that I failed to say no to. I justified my volunteerism as a creative therapeutic outlet. But in actuality, it was just a really huge and unnecessary burden.

From the time Angelina was around nine months old, Charlie got into the habit of going out with friends every weekend to balance the demands of fatherhood and work while I stayed home every weeknight and weekend with the babies. I didn't mind my one-on-one time with my children but ultimately realized I needed to follow Charlie's lead and create some me-time too. I saw on social media that most of my thirty-something friends were running 5Ks, 10Ks, and half-marathons and without too much contemplation, announced to Gloria at work one day, "I'm going to run a half-marathon." I downloaded a couch-potato-to-marathon training program and registered to run the Newport Liberty Half Marathon and raise money for type 1 diabetes. Normally, I was completely mum about my disease despite having lived with it for twenty-six years. At thirty-four years old, I finally came out of the closet.

Gloria, my new best friend in life and partner in crime at work, convinced me to post my fundraiser on the office intranet and tracked my pledges while I spent four months running during early mornings, lunch breaks, and for an hour or two on Saturdays. At some point I joined a running club and Gloria helped me compete in a contest where the first fifty members who logged onto a website at exactly two o'clock in the afternoon and entered their email address would win a fifty-dollar gift card. Gloria and I watched the clock like hawks and counted the seconds down before each successfully entering my email address within fifteen seconds of the contest's start time. And when I didn't immediately appear to win anything, Gloria insisted my running club was a scam and all but forced me to end my membership. Two weeks later, I received the fifty-dollar gift card I won in the mail. When I brought my winning letter into work to show Gloria, we cried with laughter.

Preparing for the race became my greatest escape. The running was cutting my body up and making me feel healthy and attractive. The support from so many people was making me feel loved. A getaway with Charlie, where we drove with the kids a few hours away, stayed overnight in a hotel, and used the gift card I won on a decent dinner before my first 10K the next day, made me feel like life was normalizing. And the comradery with Gloria was filling my soul.

The only problem was, my feelings and reality weren't in sync.

# CHAPTER 38
# Text Message

F OR OUR SEVENTH WEDDING ANNIVERSARY, Charlie bucked the system, arranged for his parents to come to our place to watch the kids, and surprised me with a dinner at an expensive Italian restaurant in Jersey City. I was up for spending time together but immediately complained that heavy Italian food wasn't going to help me shed the ten pounds I had gained writing thousands of pages of college essays and eating alongside toddlers. Charlie turned immediately cold and I walked my complaint back a bit to deescalate the situation. As we drove within a few blocks of the restaurant, Charlie handed me a small gift bag and told me to open it.

"What's this?" I asked.

"Just open it," he said.

I pulled out a bottle of perfume and thanked him halfheartedly in a tone that made obvious I wasn't terribly excited. In fact, I was well-known in my family for being the absolute *worst* gift receiver on the planet. I always thought about what the giver could have done instead with the money they spent and never about how thoughtful a person was to go out of their way to think of me. But since Charlie clearly pulled major strings just to take me to dinner, I forced myself to at least not be a complete jerk.

"There's more. Dig deeper," he said.

I pulled out white tissue paper to find a box underneath.

"Open it!" he encouraged.

In the box was a sizeable engagement ring that made the ring he proposed to me with seven years earlier look like a joke

"What is this?" I asked perplexed.

"I want to start over," he said.

"I don't understand. I like my old ring," I said while simultaneously attempting to process why we would start over a union that was finally going in our favor.

"Let's start fresh," he said.

He made me put on the new ring and we had a lovely but somewhat awkward dinner consisting of me trying to enjoy the moment but feeling confused by the idea that we needed to start anything over. We arrived back to our apartment to find his parents, who looked at me sideways as if I should have burst through the door and run to show them the new rock on my finger. Instead, I said "Hi" casually and said, "Oh, yes. It's very nice," when my mother-in-law grabbed my hand and knowingly moved her eyebrows up and down at me, proud of her son for the successful mission of surprising his wife with such a luxurious piece of jewelry. The problem was, I didn't get it. I didn't get that Charlie had saved up money on the side for a year to buy an expensive ring. I didn't get that everyone but me knew he was going to surprise me with the best dinner a person can buy in Jersey City and the biggest gift he had ever given. I didn't get that his parents made a three-hour trip to watch our kids, so Charlie and I could have less than two hours of normalcy. I didn't get any of it. The night that Charlie intended to be magical ended with me "saving" my new, unfamiliar ring in its fancy box and putting back on the old ring I adored.

True to my obsessive-compulsion, which everyone at my job seemed to develop if they stayed long enough, I ran every step of the two-hundred-and-thirty-mile training program and completed my half-marathon in a respectable time without walking, even manually checking my blood sugar while running. A couple of weeks after my race, I flew to Colorado to celebrate Grandma Cooper's eighty-fifth birthday with my entire family on my mom's side. Charlie declined to go, citing his asthma, which the elevation in Colorado exacerbated. While I was disappointed that Charlie would miss something that was so important to me,

I didn't think twice about carrying on and flying alone with two toddlers in tow.

When the kids and I returned home from Colorado, everything seemed grand. Charlie showered us with hugs and kisses, repeating over and over again how much he missed us all. For once, life finally felt really solid. The court hearing to finalize Nasir's adoption was just a month away. Given Charlie's new enthusiasm for our marriage, I could barely wait to finally hire a babysitter (which we were prohibited from doing prior to our adoption finalization) and recover the marital balance Charlie and I decidedly sacrificed to parent our two beautiful babies. I looked forward to finally sitting back and enjoying, without any arduous life obstacles, the life Charlie and I had imagined from day one.

During the week after I returned for Colorado, I went to retrieve an umbrella from the trunk of Charlie's car and found something odd. First, there was an old umbrella I had never seen that said "Bronx Zoo" on it. Second, there was a Target store bag bubbling over with sheets of scrapbooking stickers of hearts and little sayings like "I'll love you forever." Seeing the bag made me smile and I peeked further to find women's fuzzy pajama bottoms with hearts all over them. I've always been a straight-shooter so I went directly back inside to talk to Charlie.

"Where'd you get a Bronx Zoo umbrella from?"

"Oh, I borrowed it from a client when I was showing houses the other day."

"Oh, I see. Also, I accidentally saw the bag from Target," I admitted.

He looked like a deer caught in headlights. "What bag?" he seemed confused.

"The bag with the heart stickers and Women's pajama bottoms?" I questioned.

"Ah! You ruined your surprise!" he said. "I was going to make you a little something."

"That's sweet," I replied to his explanation that made perfect sense. "Just one question though. Why pajama bottoms?"

"Oh. Um. I don't know how to say this," he paused. "I don't mean to hurt your feelings, but garments are really unattractive. Can you wear pajamas over them from now on?" he asked.

I was blindsided. Endowed members of the church wear religious garments instead of traditional underwear. We both wore them. Although, he had suddenly stopped.

"Sure, OK." I was embarrassed and tried to end the conversation as quickly as possible to spare myself from further shame.

Two days later, Charlie called me randomly.

"Someone stole everything from my trunk. My computer, everything."

"How?"

"When I went to press my alarm, I pressed the trunk release instead. Everything is gone."

"Well, was there anything on the computer that is irreplaceable?"

"Not really. But it just sucks that that happened."

"Sorry, Love."

"It's OK."

I never received a scrapbook filled with adoration or those fuzzy heart-spotted pajama bottoms but I did make it a point to keep my garments covered in pajamas or a robe from there on out.

Things seemed fine except, for someone who professed to miss the kids and I like crazy, Charlie sure didn't show it. By the time the next Friday arrived, he announced he was going to spend the weekend in Philly with the rapper and team he hadn't seen since we started dating. Because I was used to being home alone with the kids on weekends, I didn't think much of it. And as trusting as I was of my eternal partner, I probably wouldn't have ever thought about it again had something not changed.

One of the things I loved most about Charlie was that he was a high communicator. He always checked in one way or another several times per day no matter where he was. But this time, there was radio silence.

I started to worry when I didn't hear from Charlie for a full day and went to call his parents (who he also called at least one time per day) but realized I hadn't had a chance to enter any contacts into my brand-new phone after dropping my old phone in the ocean. I could recollect the first six digits of my in-laws' home number but nothing more. I quickly realized I could pull up Charlie's and my joint phone bill online and, with the first digits I knew, quickly determine my in-laws' full number from Charlie's bill since he called them so much. But when I scrolled through his "current usage" page, only one phone number dominated the page. And as I scrolled down and discovered hundreds of hours of phone calls and thousands of texts to that one number, my heart hit hyper-speed and my stomach sunk.

He had to be cheating. There wasn't a clearer sign on earth than a sudden absence and a phone bill like what I was looking at. I finally found his parents' number and called them, trying with all I had not to burst into tears.

"Hi, Dad," I lovingly called his father.

"Have you heard from Charlie today?" I asked without pausing for pleasantries.

"No. Let me ask Maite." I could hear him yell to his wife in the background, asking the same question. "No, Jennifer. Neither of us have heard from him. Is everything OK?"

"Well, he said he was going away for the weekend with his friends but I haven't heard from him. I'm sure he's fine. Probably just having fun," I lied before gently saying goodbye.

I may have been a completely transformed, honest, faithful, and gospel-abiding Mormon, but in the words of my gradually acquired East Coast vernacular, "Mama didn't raise no fool." I ran the suspicious phone number through a background check for two dollars online and ascertained that the number belonged to

"D. Fernandez" in Bronx, NY. My adrenaline rushed into a tidal wave of fury. Suddenly, I connected the Bronx Zoo umbrella with the women's pajamas and the mushy stickers that were magically stolen out of Charlie's car. And I took the most drastic and forward measure I could think of: I typed the suspicious phone number into the "to" area of a new text message and wrote the most purposefully worded text in my entire life.

"Hi! This is Charlie's wife. Can you please have my husband call me immediately? Thanks so much! -Jennifer Gallegos"

I wrote that text fully intending on blowing Charlie's cover, making sure the person who received the text was as blind-sided as I was and all but begging for her (because I was sure it was a *her*) to come find me so I could beat her to a bloody pulp before I annihilated Charlie. Within thirty seconds my phone rang. It was Charlie.

"Hey, David got your text. What's up?" He said, sounding like he was in a rush.

"David who?" I demanded

"David Fernandez. Remember? The guy who was in that music video I did back in the day?"

"No, I don't remember. But whatever." I was dumbfounded. "Do you want to tell me why you and '*David*' have been calling each other for hundreds of hours and texting thousands of times for what appears to be six months now!?" I wasn't going to fall for his lies.

"Well, to be honest. He's just been there for me. He's been through a divorce, too, and he was just helping me out."

"'Divorce, too?' You've never been divorced. So, you're talking with other people about divorcing me? You didn't think you should talk to your *wife* about that!?"

"I mean, I wasn't talking about divorce. I've just been going through some things. That's why I wanted a fresh start. That's why I got you a new ring. Anyway, I gotta go. The guys are calling me," he said as if he didn't just drop a soul-shattering bomb.

"That doesn't make any sense, Charlie. You go have fun with your 'guys.' In the meantime, I'll be running a full background check on this phone number and you better pray it doesn't belong to a woman. Because if you're cheating, you'll never see your daughter again," I threatened with the only thing I knew would kill him as much as he was killing me.

I didn't sleep for the two nights that preceded Charlie's return on Sunday morning. The kids were playing and I was watching the New York City Marathon on the tiny TV in the nursery when Charlie walked in casually and the babies sprinted to cling to his legs and squeal with delight. I quickly distracting the kids with a movie and got straight to business, telling Charlie, "Let's go talk."

We entered our bedroom, each sat on the bed, and Charlie dropped his head and started crying while telling me he had something to tell me.

"You're cheating," I said plainly.

"No!"

Charlie's body started to quiver. Tears plunged from his eyelids to his lap as if jumping from a bridge. His nose began to drip and his breath shortened like a small child whose toy was just taken away, making it hard for him to form the words. Finally, after some seconds, he mustered up the courage to say, "I want a divorce."

"What are you talking about? You never even told me you were unhappy!" I started yelling.

"I've tried," he said.

"We've been through so much and we were *finally* getting to a good place where we could operate like a normal family and now you're bailing!?" I tried to reason. "You realize we are twelve days away from adopting our son, right? You waited until now to do this!?"

"I'm still adopting him," he insisted.

"Oh, great. So now he'll be adopted into a broken home. That's perfect," I stabbed. "Well, I'm keeping your last name," I declared.

Despite my utter state of shock, I was no less cognizant of the fact that our kids already had many odds stacked up against them. They were adopted, which comes with a lot of loss, a lot of questions, and a lot of red tape. We had already encountered discrimination and had to prove with our daughter's birth certificate that she was our child when she was hospitalized with a fever. The nurse said it was hospital policy for adoptive parents to have to prove their parenthood. They just took the word of biological parents. The point is, with so many things that made Angelina and Nasir "different," I didn't want them to also lose some semblance of a family unit. I wanted them to have two parents with something exactly like them, if only our last name.

Charlie and I went back and forth until it was clear to me that there was no changing his mind. He wanted a divorce, he was leaving the church, and as soon as he could, he was moving out. But first, he begged.

"Please don't freeze the bank account."

"Charlie, I love you and I trust you. You may have already stopped loving me but I still love you. I can't just turn my love off like a switch right now."

"Just, please don't freeze the account," he repeated.

"I'm not going to," I insisted.

Before Charlie left for the day, I pled with him to stay with the children for two hours so I could go speak to our Bishop. Once alone with our Bishop, I explained the whole ordeal and concluded I was to blame.

"Honestly, Bishop, it's my fault. We don't have sex enough. I'm always exhausted from work, school, church, and the adoption stuff. I'm not my best. I thought we could make it twelve more days until the adoption was finalized and we could start getting back to normal without the red tape, caseworker visits, and heavy restrictions."

"Do you think there might be another woman?" the Bishop asked as politely as he could.

"I thought that, too, but he said no," I replied.

The Bishop was as stunned as I was and offered some counsel that failed to counter my racing thoughts. When I got home, Charlie immediately left and didn't come home until the middle of the night. I had yet to sleep for the third night in a row and when Charlie easily fell asleep on the couch, I went over, draped my lifeless body over him, and cried. He woke up,

"Jenn, don't do this. You're making it so hard," he said.

"Please don't go," I begged, crying. "I'll change. I'll do whatever you want," I pleaded.

He told me that, perhaps in the future, we could explore working it out. But at that moment, he had to go. He couldn't stay there anymore.

Before leaving the condo for the last time as its permanent resident, Charlie advised me that he would continue to come each day in the morning to get the kids ready for school so I could still make it to work before the stock market opened and so the kids would still see him every day. Walking the ninety-pound blue-nosed pit bull that we rescued (but Charlie grew to despise) and caring for "the babies" alone at night would be my job.

I arrived to work on Monday morning only a skeleton of myself. First to arrive around seven-thirty, I worked quietly in the bullpen with a body and spirit that felt constantly electrocuted with the reminder that my worst nightmare was, in fact, a reality. When Gloria arrived at her desk, I swiftly whisked her away to an empty office and broke down crying.

"Charlie is leaving me!" I blurted out.

"Leaving where?" she asked.

"Leaving my marriage," I replied.

Gloria wasn't as shocked or blindsided as my Bishop was. Instead of speaking calmly about how my Father in heaven loves me, knows firsthand every pain I suffer—even every hair on my head—and will help me through, Gloria got straight to business.

"Freeze your bank accounts right now," she counseled.

"Charlie asked me not to. Why would I?" I was confused.

"Because you have two kids to raise and he will empty it and leave you with nothing," she replied knowingly. "When I got divorced, my ex took every last cent. I went from living in a dream home to moving into a tiny studio apartment in Brooklyn with disgusting, red-painted walls. I still hate the color red to this day," she digressed.

"But, Gloria. You don't understand. In my church, we are married eternally. NO ONE in my church gets divorced. It's unheard of," I tried to explain that marriage and family are the central part of the Mormon faith.

"Believe me, Jenn. Five years from now you're going to laugh about this," she assured me.

The idea of laughing at losing a man I gave up everything to be a faithful wife to made me cry. When another colleague, Liz, showed up at my desk for a random business need, the flood gates opened. Only, instead of getting straight-forward advice from a seasoned woman like Gloria who had been there, done that (and endured far more), Liz hugged me in a way that made me feel like someone understood my loss.

By Tuesday, it was clear that, if I didn't seek professional help, I could very possibly die. I hadn't slept or eaten for nearly four days—managing my blood sugar by setting my insulin pump on the basal rate (the bare minimum delivery of insulin to keep me alive) and forcing down water, or juice if my blood sugar went low. Through my church, I found a counselor of Mormon faith (who I felt would better understand the spiritual significance and entirety of my loss) and who quickly determined that I was in grave danger. The level of my depression and despair, she concluded, necessitated medication.

"But I don't even take Tylenol. I've literally only taken four or five Tylenol in my entire life," I informed her.

The counselor explained that, when depression was serious enough to put my life at risk (be it lack of eating coupled with type 1 diabetes or suicide, which her evaluation concluded was a risk), medication was appropriate.

"I highly recommend it, if only temporarily to get you through," she said.

The next day I took off work while the babies were at daycare and saw my doctor, who prescribed one long-term antidepressant and one fast-acting medication for panic attacks. Resigned to the fact that I was in the darkest place I had ever been in my life, I started taking the daily medication as prescribed and filled the fast-acting prescription, promising myself I would avoid taking the latter, a highly addictive tranquilizer, at all costs.

For the days that followed, Charlie popped in and out of the apartment at various times unannounced to see the babies or take a shower. His whereabouts the rest of the time were a complete mystery to me; although I had a hunch. I kept thinking to myself, "Husbands don't just get up and leave. Much less, with a toddler daughter and the finalization of the adoption of a toddler son just days away." I knew there had to be something more. I didn't want to entertain the idea that Charlie was cheating because it hurt so bad. Besides, he told me he was not. Still, I had to know one way or another definitively.

I easily located a private investigator in the Bronx, to whom I provided the suspicious phone number and basic information I had already gathered online. The investigator on the phone said her company would not only provide me with the full name and address of the owner of the phone line, but much more. For then, I explained that all I really wanted to know was if "David Fernandez" was really a "Debbie Fernandez" or something.

Nasir's adoption day came and my fading family of four dressed in our "Sunday's best" for a hearing that was far swifter and more straightforward than Angelina's. As we stood packed in an elevator on our way up to see the judge, I attempted to hold Charlie's hand, which dangled as if dead. I thought that such a touching and meaningful event, which we had dreamed about when we were hopelessly in love, might somehow change Charlie's mind about me. But it didn't seem to. Charlie smiled dutifully during courtroom photos with the judge and even accompanied us to Sears for a family photo I insisted on, excusing himself for long periods at a time to answer texts and talk on the phone. By that day, I was certain there was another woman. All the moves I remembered making as a cheater, all the idiosyncrasies that were plainly obvious even if I hadn't, were all glaring. I was no longer dealing with a man who just wanted out of a very hard-earned marriage. I was dealing with a man who was escaping reality with virtual reality love goggles.

I never thought I would be relieved to solve a mystery that, one way or another, probably would not save my marriage. But I was still thankful when the private investigator left me a message to say he had all the information I asked for, and much more.

# CHAPTER 39

# Two Toddlers and a Pit Bull

B EFORE I HAD A CHANCE TO CALL THE PRIVATE investigator for the big news, I had a planned meeting with my Bishop, who served as my unpaid spiritual counselor alongside my paid counselor. Other than Nasir's adoption, which went as smoothly as a wedding staged on a golf course during a hurricane, the only thing I had to report was that I was going to review the results of the private investigation that night.

The Bishop was quiet for a moment before saying, "Jennifer, as your Bishop and your friend, I highly advise you to not go forward with reviewing that information. No good can come from it."

"I mean, I already paid for it and I feel like I deserve answers," I said.

"That may be true. But my fear is, the answers may be more harmful than helpful," he reasoned. "I would cut your losses and spare yourself the additional turmoil."

"You're right," I conceded.

The private investigator was floored when I told her I had a change of heart and instructed her to keep my money and shred the results. And when I hung up the phone I knew it was the correct decision. I already knew Charlie was cheating. What additional evidence did I need?

Thanksgiving came and Charlie agreed to come over for half of the day before going to eat dinner with "friends," which I knew really meant "mistress." I accepted the half day without contest for the sake of the children. Charlie arrived around noon and, instead of visiting with the children, spent three hours cutting his hair, showering, and getting ready for his dinner that night. I held my peace, thinking how stupid he was to think I wasn't on to him. We indeed sat down for a Thanksgiving spread that I cooked but, right after our meal, Charlie announced he could only stay another hour. Livid, I excused myself from the table and checked my phone to see if there was somewhere the babies and I could go for a distraction. I found a movie and reemerged from my bedroom, telling the babies to say goodbye to their daddy as we had plans at two o'clock and had to leave right then and there. Even though I knew it probably wouldn't faze Charlie, I wanted him to get a taste of his own medicine. I wanted Charlie to feel as unimportant as he made our kids seem that day. But because I didn't want him to think I would do something crazy, I was decent enough to tell him that we were going to a movie. While I knew this would only give him more time with his mistress, I was relieved of the sight of him.

My empty stomach was turned inside-out and I could feel my heart pounding through my chest. I wanted to confront Charlie right then and there, but I didn't want to ruin my children's idea of Thanksgiving with what was sure to be an all-out brawl. I broke a "panic attack pill" in half and gulped it down with water before treating my babies to the latest Disney love story on the big screen, which turned out to be the most sickening way to exacerbate a broken heart.

A few days after Thanksgiving, when Charlie came for a visit, I sat the children down with a movie to watch and asked Charlie if we could speak behind closed doors for a moment. We sat on the bed in the same exact places we took when he told me he wanted a divorce.

"I know you're cheating," I directly confronted him. His mouth formed a slight smile and he started shaking his head from side to side as if he was amused and I was crazy. I came stronger. "Don't play me and don't play yourself, Charlie," I said. "I know you're cheating. I hired a private investigator. I know your girlfriend's name. I know where she lives. I have photos of you both," I purposely lied to force an admission. Charlie stopped shaking his head and looked me straight in the eyes, his smile replaced with a scowl.

"And why do you think that is?" he said sternly.

"Because you're a jerk?" I was done being nice. "Do you not remember how much I've sacrificed for you!? Do you not remember sleeping on a floor in the projects before I came along!? I gave up a whole career just to be faithful to you! And while all of your friends in Iraq were getting divorced or receiving video tapes in the mail of their wives cheating on them or going to the ATM to find empty bank accounts, WHO was holding you down!?" I was furious. "What about the deal we had, Charlie? I've been paying the majority of our bills for seven years with the promise that I could teach high school English and have summers off with the kids as soon as you got your real estate career off the ground. And now that you have, you're driving some hood rat around in the Benz you insisted on buying while I paid our mortgage and all of our bills!? And now you're going to leave me here alone to care for two toddlers and a pit bull while I continue to work full time!?"

"The children can come with me…"

"OVER MY DEAD BODY!" I spoke over him.

If there was anything my childhood taught me, it was that children need a mother's love. I'd be damned if my children had a random side-chick or any number of women paraded in and out of their lives like I did as a child. The buck would stop with me. I ended my conversation with Charlie, but not before reminding him about what he once said about me.

"You know how you always say I'm the type of person someone would want to have on their side?"

"Yeah."

"Believe that," I warned as if I was wildly powerful instead of a woman who was slowly wilting away.

While the initial confirmation of Charlie's cheating was heated, subsequent days were eerily calm. He came over for a visit on the weekend and sat on the couch wanting to tell me more about the woman he was in love with.

"She's not what you think. I think you'll be surprised," he said as if I was looking forward to meeting and getting to know the stranger he was talking about. "When she was a kid, she survived cancer," he further advertised.

*And what a noble life she led thereafter*, I grudgingly thought to myself.

"She has two children—eight and ten," he said.

"Wait a minute. You mean to tell me you're leaving our babies to go raise someone else's kids?" I snapped.

"They have a dad. Listen, let me tell you how I met her."

"No! You can keep that to yourself. I don't want to have to roll that information around in my head the rest of my life. Besides, all I need to know about her—what's her name?" I stopped to ask.

"Dina," he said.

"Ah, yes. Dina Fernandez, *not* David Fernandez. Well, everything I need to know about *Dina* is contained in the fact that she's sleeping with my husband. I know *exactly* what type of woman she is." I concluded.

The following weeks presented various "tests" of my good will. Charlie was having a hard time keeping up with getting the children ready in Jersey City every morning because he was going back and forth to the Bronx. Gloria told me to free him of the responsibility and do it myself. That would not only free him, but free me of depending on him. And when I called him to tell him that, rather than fighting with me, he was grateful for the break from driving across the George Washington Bridge in thick traffic every morning. However, because he wouldn't get to see the children in the mornings, he asked for visitation at night.

"Of course. Come by or take the kids whenever you want, as much as you want. They need to see you. However, I have one condition: they can't meet your mistress" I enforced.

"Why not?" he asked.

"First, you're not married to her. And if we've agreed to continue raising the children in a Christian faith that prescribes marriage before living together, then we should lead by example," I started. "Second, no mistress is meeting my babies. Who's to say she'll last?" I challenged.

"Well, we want to get married and have our own children one day," he said in a way that made him seem like a clueless teenager.

"Good for you. I wish you the best of luck with that. You're still not bringing my babies around her." I dug my heels in.

"I mean, they're going to meet her eventually anyway," he said.

"That's *if* you work out," I reminded him. "Besides, I haven't seen any divorce papers yet," I pointed out.

"About that," he spoke in a way that automatically alerted he needed something from me. "How much did it cost you to handle your own divorce last time?"

"A decade ago? Around eight hundred dollars, uncontested, without kids," I replied, not letting on that I was floored by his question.

"Can you handle our divorce so we can save money on a lawyer?" he asked.

"No."

"Why not?" he insisted.

"Because I'm not divorcing you. I made a promise before God that I would be faithful until the end and I fully intend on keeping that promise. You want the divorce—you do it."

The couple of months that followed required the grit and survivor spirit I was practically born with. And whatever I lacked, my long-term anti-depression medication had started supplementing by then. I woke early to get showered and dressed before packing lunches and getting the babies out of bed and dressed for the day. Then, I bundled everyone up in snow gear and navigated in the dead of winter below-freezing temperatures, snow, and ice, to walk our pit bull—Silva—who was so strong, I previously broke my finger in half just trying to walk him when he was still a puppy. After finishing our dog walk, the babies and

I would inch down an icy hill to daycare before I made my way to an elevator on a cliff that dropped me down to Hoboken. From there, my lightning-fast twelve-minute light rail ride to work delivered me to the doorstep of my job. My return home was a nearly identical but reversed version of the morning, with dog walks remaining my biggest challenge.

Now that Silva was full-grown, controlling him with a tiny toddler on each arm was next to impossible, if not irresponsible and dangerous. As if I hadn't already lost enough, I knew I had no choice but to find a new family for my beloved dog.

"Put an ad on the office intranet," Gloria suggested.

"For a pit bull? There's no way anyone in corporate American is going to adopt a pit bull."

"You never know!" Gloria countered. "Try it and see!"

By the time Gloria made this suggestion, I should have realized that she was always right. An executive from our firm quickly volunteered to adopt my beautiful Silva. However, when Silva proved too large for my colleague's wife and small children to manage, they nonetheless fostered him in their suburban dream home for many weeks until I found Silva his loving and fiercely committed forever home.

Life without Silva may have made my morning routine safer and smoother, but it didn't spare me of my own single-mother mishaps. For example, I locked myself out of my condo building's loading dock after taking the trash out at two o'clock in the morning one day. Without a cell phone, I had the option of running somewhere in my pajamas for help or figuring out how to get back into my apartment by myself. Honestly, I hated asking for help in broad daylight, much less in the middle of the night. So I promptly decided to climb in my house slippers the chain-linked gate that kept undesirables out of our parking lot to get to the sidewalk outside. From there, I entered the code numbers to the building's main door. I prayed that someone didn't close the second security door all of the way (for an easy way in and problem solved) but it was locked. I went outside and eyeballed the brick wall that led up to a huge window that I always left unlocked because I was certain no one could get up to it. And despite thinking it impossible, I had the audacity to try. I used a ledge built into the brick to climb up and reach the window before failing to budge it open because my fingers kept slipping.

I returned to the foyer of the building, daydreaming about how Spiderman effortlessly sticks to buildings and wishing I had such powers, scanning the room for anything I thought might help me break in. I spotted some rubber bands laying on the floor and remembered how I once wrapped rubber bands around my fingers to sort papers at work. Determined, I weaved my five fingers in and out of several rubber bands on each hand and climbed back up to the window. With a few, desperate pushes upward, I was able to get the window up enough to jam my fingers through the opening at the bottom and open it all the way up. After hurling myself through the opening and praying neighbors didn't call the police, I never left my windows open again and always left a spare key in a magnetic box under my mailbox.

While I continued to prove day after day that I could make it on my own, I still hated being alone. And even though I wasn't sure I could ever love Charlie again in the same way, I held on to hope that he would change his mind.

# CHAPTER 40
# Wild Child

Each day at work, I revealed to Gloria in whispers a new development about Charlie. He conspired with church friends to stay rent-free with his mistress and kids in a condo; he canceled visitation indefinitely until I agreed to let the babies meet the mistress; he called asking me to copy his mistress on emails (instead of calling or texting him) regarding the children because she was worried I was still having sex with him; and he tattooed his mistress' life-sized portrait on his chest. With constantly incredulous things to wrap my head around, I skipped past the shock and sadness stages of the mourning process and moved rather easily to anger. And Gloria turned out to be, not only my life coach, but my lifesaver.

I saw the therapist once a week during my lunch break. But each time I came back to work after meetings and Gloria asked what the therapist said, my resounding answer was, "She said my friend Gloria is exactly right."

"Jenn, my bill is in the mail," Gloria lovingly joked. And Gloria was right. It was a waste of time going to a therapist who always said Gloria gave me spot-on advice, including: "put your kids first," "never talk bad about Charlie in front of the kids," "don't make the kids feel guilty for loving you both," "always be a lady," "be thankful Charlie is still in the picture," "bite your tongue until it bleeds," "it takes two to tango—don't blame everything on the other woman," and my personal favorite in her thick Brooklyn accent after she got tired of hearing the broken record I had become about what a jerk Charlie was, "Life sucks, Jenn. Get over it!"

Despite having lost all love for Charlie the moment I truly realized he was cheating, I felt obligated to my children to do everything in my power to work it out. On several different occasions, I gritted my teeth and asked as sincerely as possible for Charlie to reconsider, which he humored until one night when we had an hour-long conversation over the phone. Charlie admitted he still loved me and that the hardest part about what he had done was hurting me. He slowly explained that since Iraq, he had never been the same. He stopped believing in God. He was depressed. He thought that having Angelina would change everything. And when it didn't, he at some point became suicidal.

"She saved my life," he said of his mistress. "She's my world," he said somberly in a way that simply couldn't be contested.

After that call, I held a private burial of my marriage. No amount of words would suffice to attempt to explain to everyone—my family, my church, my friends, or even my God—what Charlie's quiet admissions proved. This wasn't a fling. This wasn't a mistake. This was a decision that was long-past made. If need be, I could look my children in the eyes when they became adults and tell them I did my best. More importantly, I could honestly tell them that, if death was their father's alternative, I was thankful he chose life instead—with or without me.

When I expressed to both my therapist and my Bishop that I was going to proceed with filing for a divorce, they each said they couldn't counsel me to divorce due to our religion (which only allows such people to counsel against it), but that they understood.

Uncontested divorces in New Jersey only require that the plaintiff attends the final hearing. Accordingly, I arrived alone at the same Jersey City courthouse I adopted my two children with Charlie at. By that time, I had lost (from stress and not eating) the weight I gained after marriage. I wore to the hearing a beautiful powder-blue midi dress, khaki-colored trench coat, skin-toned stockings and heels, and my hair pulled back into a polished up-do. I didn't have a fancy speech prepared for the judge. In fact, I fudged some of the paperwork, forgetting to date two pages. I simply stood there somber, confirming as prompted the provisions in the divorce decree. After the gavel dropped, I walked out of the old courthouse and down the steep concrete steps a free woman.

Up until that point, Charlie was not supposed to introduce his girlfriend to my children until I met her. And I refused to meet her while I was still married to him. So, within days of the divorce, Charlie was so anxious to move on with his life, he set up our first meeting at Chuck E. Cheese's.

Gloria and I might as well have been planning for war underneath the West Wing of the White House. We painstakingly reviewed every possible scenario that could occur during my meeting with the mystery woman. What if she rushed in and caught me with a sucker punch and a catfight ensued? What if she was a celebrity—like JLo or Beyoncé—and completely robbed me of the few shreds of self-esteem I had left following the gutting of my wifehood? What if my kids cried? What if Charlie lied to my face in front of her? What if Chuck E. Cheese himself came to our table and took off his costume head to reveal a green alien who sprayed us with morphing saliva that automatically transported us to an alternative universe? You name it, Gloria and I had it covered. We had the defense tactics of professional Jiu-Jitsu fighters, picking apart war to come up with a winning strategy.

As I drove with my two toddlers to Chuck E. Cheese's, I gave myself a silent pep talk. Gloria had already instilled in me the most important thing to remember: I wasn't there for me; I was there for my kids. Gloria and I agreed that I should welcome the mystery woman as if I was meeting a family member for the first time because, in actuality, my kids *were* meeting a new family member (however temporary) and they would be watching me. Gloria and I also agreed that I should kill everyone with kindness (even to my own detriment) and speak with the poise I routinely demonstrated at work. Finally, when Gloria reminded me to "always be a lady," I reminded myself to do whatever it took to not have a physical altercation with the woman. Doing so would, with one hundred percent certainty, get me locked up in jail and my children would be sent to their father (and consequently, their father's girlfriend). As long as I could execute the plan Gloria and I masterminded, I could leave the meeting with my family of three intact.

The kids and I waited in the entrance of Chuck E. Cheese's when we saw Charlie's car pull in to park. My nerves rattled like a diamondback as I saw figures approaching the front door. Charlie came in first, followed by two children, and then a lady who I glanced at and deduced was a random family member since I was used to Puerto Rican families traveling as a large unit. I immediately said "Hello" to and hugged the children in the split seconds before the mystery woman—the guest of honor—arrived. But much to my surprise, she was already standing right in front of me.

"Jennifer, this is Dina," Charlie surprised me by introducing the woman who in no way resembled the exotic, home-wrecking vixen I had imagined.

"Hi! So good to meet you!" I lied through my teeth, smiling, hugging, and kissing on the cheek the woman responsible for destroying me, as my starry-eyed children watched.

"It takes two to tango, Jennifer. She's not the only one responsible," Gloria's voice played in my head.

I went to introduce my babies but, as I suspected, Charlie had been letting them see his mistress behind my back. I hid my contempt and continued into the building, where we grabbed a table and followed the kids around to play arcade games for a while before our pizza came and we congregated to eat.

"Mommy! She has the same nails as you do!" my princess proudly pointed out, delighting in the thing I had in common with our new family member.

"How about that?" I said, smiling but actually livid inside after seeing an engagement ring on her finger that was the size of the Titanic and kicking myself for giving Charlie several thousand dollars as a sort of peace offering when I thought he could use some help.

We ate as if there wasn't a gigantic elephant in the room and released the children to play so we could sneak in a ten-minute talk.

"I know this must be as awkward for you as it is for me," I said exactly how Gloria had rehearsed me to. "The bottom line is, I want our kids to enjoy happy parents and happy homes. So I look forward to making this work. Dina, as long as you treat my children as well as your own children—no, better than your own—you won't have any problems with me. Charlie and I worked very hard to become parents..." my eyes teared up a bit in a moment of unplanned vulnerability as I locked eyes with Charlie. "And I know that we both want nothing but happiness for them in life."

"Well, you're lucky. At least you have help. I raised mine on my own," Dina said, completely oblivious to my stellar self-control.

*Lucky? This woman stole my husband and now she has the audacity to sit in front of me when I'm acting like a lady and tell me I'm lucky? Beat her ass, Jenn! Jump over this table right now and bust her in her face!* "Yeah, wow," I replied out loud. I was at a loss for words but resisted my inner thug, trying desperately to empathize with a former single mother who came in and reversed the roles, making me a single mother instead.

After our meeting when Charlie said goodbye to the children and left with his new family, Angelina began to cry—no, scream—for her daddy. Charlie came back and gave her a hug, lying that he "had to go to work" and I played along with him and soothed my baby girl enough to get on the road home. The babies in the back of the car could not see the tears running down my face in the front. I was relieved and hurt at the exact same time.

*You can do this, Jenn. You have to. Your babies need you*, I reminded myself.

A month after our divorce, Charlie made his mistress his wife the same day I was supposed to attend my dear friend's wedding. Charlie's parents had agreed to come watch the children for me but ended up having to split their time between an impromptu courthouse marriage in the day and watching their grandbabies at night. Charlie stopped by my condo to drop something off and when I answered the door, he nearly had to pick his jaw up from off of the floor.

After the ordeal I had been through, I invested a sizeable wad of cash to make sure that I felt confident when I went on my first night out in over seven years. The weight I lost revealed a flat stomach and strong muscles I had toned during running season. My newly-svelte body was spray-tanned and semi-permanent leg makeup inconspicuously covered up the scar on my shin that I normally hid with pants. My dark brown hair was blown straight with wispy bad-girl bangs that fluttered over my natural blue eyes. A little black dress fit me like a glove and accentuated my small waist and plump *derrière*. I even went as far as to have my teeth professionally whitened. I wasn't the girl Charlie married. I was better. And he was perceivably stunned.

As I left for the evening and walked to my minivan (which I replaced the next month with a loaded black sedan I always wanted), Charlie sat in his car outside. I felt his eyes follow me to my van and watch me drive away and I wondered if I outshined his new bride or created a smidgen of regret in his heart that day. Either way, I was done with living my life in anguish, obsessing over someone else's worst mistake and punishing myself for my role in it. I decided that, going forward, my children were the only people I would allow myself to obsess over ever again.

I arrived at the wedding to raving compliments (minus a few glares from various Mormon wives) from well-wishers who could tell I was on a celebration tour. I took the bull by the horns, located the DJ who I met online and who asked me to be his date (despite the fact he was working the wedding the entire night) and introduced myself. Not only was he impressed by my carefully crafted look, but many single men in the house were, too. The Cuban drummer tried to get my number. A few male partygoers smiled and whispered to each other while making flirtatious eye contact with me. And I caught the attention of a twenty-four-year-old man from church, who I coincidentally drove to his first prom, taught how to drive, and dropped off and picked up from his two year church mission years before. The kid I once knew grew up to be a tall, dark, and extremely handsome man. He tapped me on the shoulder at the bar to "holler" at me before realizing who he was attempting to hit on. If there was ever a time when I truly felt like a strong, attractive woman, that night was it. And since my DJ date was occupied the whole night, I hit the dance floor alone and ended up dancing the night away with the man from church who could have danced with any lady he wanted. But that night, he chose to dance with me.

The next Monday at work, after telling Gloria about the unexpected encounter with Charlie, the wedding reception, and some newfound attention from various men, Gloria started calling me "wild child," insisting that the world better watch out.

# CHAPTER 41
# Six Feet Under

WHEN MERELY BREATHING BECOMES YOUR benchmark, success is as simple as surviving. Nine years have passed since my life seemed irretrievably over. And while the event of divorcing and becoming a single mother is just a sliver of my story, it taught me the most about myself. But instead of mourning a marriage, I've accepted my loss and moved on. I only look back to respectfully bow, like a warrior bows to defeat, humbled by my weaknesses and empowered by the strengths earned in battle.

The natural reflex when you're hurt is to run, hide, and never look back. But when you share kids with your foe, you are forced to make a decision: you must either put yourself, or your children, first. The right decision is easy to determine because it always requires the greatest virtue. As a co-parent with Charlie, I had to overlook my adult grievances. I had to bite my tongue and fake smiles. I had to choose only the biggest battles to address in the smallest, most subtle ways. I had to be considerate and communicative. I had to love my enemy. I had to put on a happy face and say, "Of course I do!" when my four-year-old daughter asked innocently, "Do you love Dina?" when she was unsure if loving her stepmother was OK. I had to have a sense of humor. I had to have a backbone. I had to be my children's rock and example of consistently amicable and cohesive parenting with someone I previously couldn't figure out how to stay married to. I had to be the best version of myself I've ever seen. And Charlie did, too. But in doing all of these things, we earned an unexpected reward on top of happy, loved, and well-adjusted children: we each got a close friend back.

Today, when my children are dropped off or picked up, you'll find parents kicking tires on the porch like my grandparents did with good neighbors. You'll find brief calls and texts, not just to check on the children, but to say "Hello," share an accomplishment, or chat about the latest news. You'll find expressions of appreciation on Mother's Day and Father's Day, or just because. You'll find supportive spouses who are not intimidated by the process of amicable co-parenting. You'll find respect and understanding. And you'll find peace.

I have spent a large portion of my life trying to become someone. When I moved from Fort Collins, Colorado to New York City, I imagined fame, fortune, and a carefully crafted façade to be the hallmarks of success. I looked at the lives of others and formulated in my mind what constituted true happiness and a life well-lived. Sometimes, I admired the green grass on the other side so much, I forgot to water my own. Other times, I achieved things I swore would satisfy my long search for happiness, only to find myself anything but. I have rubbed elbows with superstars and I have been a few cents shy of a subway token on payday. And after shaping a life I was certain would never fail, only to fail in the worst way, I now know the truth: the success I am is not, and may never be, tangible. There will be no shiny brass awards to gather dust on shelves. There will be no permanent place amongst the world's Who's Who. There will be no star on Hollywood. There may not even be a fancy headstone. But there will be love. And when my days are complete and my children—my legacy—gather to remember me, they may not be able to name a song I wrote or a famous person I once knew. But they will laugh with my father's chuckle and smile with my mother's eyes and each in their own special way, will sing.

I'm no longer a fighter. Now I prefer dancing instead, where everyone is still standing after the song ends. And dancing alone in life for a while taught me in the most difficult way the value of a good partner.

Do you remember my dancing buddy at the wedding? The man who made my first night out after my divorce one of the most liberating nights of my life? I married him. Remember that Bachelor's in English degree that got cut short? It took a total of twelve years of nighttime college courses alongside fulltime work and motherhood, but I finished it. Remember those two precious babies I was blessed with? They're now happy, healthy adolescents. And remember that teenaged girl who ran away to New York City to become someone? She did it.

"Hello, my friend," Gloria's voice boomed through my car speakers during our daily call on my car ride home after work at the same job I have held at an investment management firm for fourteen years.

"Hi."

"What's wrong? Your voice sounds funny."

"Ugh. Tough day at work. Sometimes I wonder how people would talk to me if they realized exactly who they are speaking to. You know what I mean? If they realized how much someone like me has been through and that I'm not the idiot they suppose me to be. Eh. I don't care if one person doesn't like me," I concluded.

"I have news for you, Jenn. More than one person doesn't like you," Gloria blurted out.

We both laughed until tears blurred the bumper-to-bumper traffic ahead of me and I was forced to wipe my eyes and focus on driving.

"But, Jenn. You know where the perfect people are, right?" Gloria asked seriously.

I paused, attempting to guess before a loving Brooklyn accent solved the riddle for me:

"Six feet under."

# Acknowledgements

I would like to express deep gratitude and thanks to the following people:

My best friend, Gloria, without whose support, wise counsel, relentless cheerleading, pep talks, brainstorming sessions, first reads, and daily phone calls, this book (and the woman I have become) would not exist. "Nailed it!"

My mom, sister, and belated dad—my rocks—who have deeply loved and rooted for me since they named me Jennifer. If you weren't already my beloved family I would choose you as friends.

My dear and loyal husband, Ernest, who prefers I go broke chasing dreams than get rich wasting talent. You have my whole heart. >>_<<

My two children—my world and my greatest gifts. Nothing makes me prouder than the individuals you are becoming. You constantly touch my heart with your kindness, helping hands, friendliness, honesty, and desire to make good decisions and live modest lives—virtues and wisdom far beyond your years. You inspire me. Thank you for your interest in our family history, your maturity in exploring hard topics, and your constant encouragement. May our booming belly laughs, silly songs, dinky dances, utter joy, and pure love live in your hearts always. And may our frank talks, strength found in struggles, and fighting spirits earned in trials by fire empower you forevermore.

My children's father, "Charlie." My children have the world's best dad and extended family, including a loving stepmother and stepsiblings. Charlie, I'm so proud of all you have accomplished in life and I am blessed for our lasting friendship.

My aunts, Mary and Cheryl, who go out of their way to always make everyone feel special, who have taught me through their examples the value of letter-writing, kind words, and thoughtful check-ins, and who read everything I write. I cherish you.

My little cousin, Nick, for your infectious and unwavering positive energy, grit, work ethic, integrity, big dreams, and big support. We got this!

My extended family on both sides. Thank you for loving me unconditionally.

The Leethams, a wonderful family and dear friends whom I credit with salvaging the broken parts of my childhood. (I still can't believe the grandchildren get to touch the garden!)

Gay Slade and Karen Lesser, gifted women who nurtured the music inside of me for nearly a decade (from the time I was a six-year-old singing "Maybe" at an Our Gang Singers audition).

Stefi, Stina, Jenny, and Jess—my ride-or-dies. I wouldn't have survived adolescence (or have had as much fun) without you.

Arcenius, for your investment and faith in a teenage girl's talent and for your straightforward business and even keel. Everything I needed to know about recording, I learned at Noise in the Attic.

Full Force, six of the most genuine, family-focused, fair, humble, hardworking, fun, faithful, and wildly talented people I've ever had the pleasure of working with. Thank you for gambling on me and taking me to the top.

JayUno, my biggest fan. I'm so glad we're still friends after all of these years!

Anita Diggs, for your time, thoughtful critique, and expert commentary on the first draft of my manuscript.

My coworkers, who have heard bits and pieces of my story at the water cooler for years on end and who have supported my journey in writing it all down.

My friends (and foes) who have influenced my path. Thank you for making me a stronger, wiser, and better person. (Work still in-progress.)

And to you, fellow warrior, for your time and for reading. Everyone has a story. You should write yours down, too!

3 years old - family portrait

6 years old - Our Gang Singers

6 years old – learning how to waterski with Dad's help

8 years old – photo in front of our house and
the aspen tree Dad planted

8 years old – driving our go-kart just before being
diagnosed with type 1 diabetes

10 years old - The Colorado Academy of the Arts

15 years old - quartet

19 years old - headshot

# Biography

Hit songwriter Jennifer Y. Johnson-Garcia has been a professional writer for over 23 years, with credits in radio, television, and print including editing *The Orator* newspaper at Hudson County Community College for a year. Jennifer holds a BA in English from Thomas Edison State University, where she graduated with a perfect cumulative 4.0 GPA. She is a wife, mother, business professional, animal lover, singer, and jack of many trades.

To learn more, visit: jyjohnsongarcia.com

# Thank you for reading GUBSOTAT!

Please take a moment right now to review the book on
Goodreads and Amazon

CPSIA information can be obtained
at www.ICGtesting.com
Printed in the USA
FFHW010902101019
55428731-61222FF

9 781733 956000